For Formal Organization

For Formal Organization

The Past in the Present and Future of Organization Theory

Paul du Gay and Signe Vikkelsø

OXFORD
UNIVERSITY PRESS

OXFORD

UNIVERSITY PRESS

Great Clarendon Street, Oxford, OX2 6DP,
United Kingdom

Oxford University Press is a department of the University of Oxford.
It furthers the University's objective of excellence in research, scholarship,
and education by publishing worldwide. Oxford is a registered trade mark of
Oxford University Press in the UK and in certain other countries

First Edition published in 2017
Impression: 1

Published in the United States of America by Oxford University Press
198 Madison Avenue, New York, NY 10016, United States of America

British Library Cataloguing in Publication Data
Data available

Library of Congress Control Number: 2016937257

ISBN 978–0–19–870512–3

Printed in Great Britain by
Clays Ltd, St Ives plc

Acknowledgements

This book has taken quite a while to write and even now the argument it expresses still seems somewhat provisional. Probably, it always will. The text derives from a research project—'What Makes Organization? Resuscitating Organization Theory/Revitalizing Organizational Life (WMO?)'—funded by the Velux Foundation in Denmark and hosted by the Department of Organization (IOA) at Copenhagen Business School. The idea for that project developed initially from our shared love for the look, smell, and content of ancient organization and management texts. It grew to encompass a sense of the importance of the stance or outlook towards organization that those texts expressed, and how poor by comparison much of what passed for organizational analysis in the present appeared to be. This book is really all about that stance or outlook and why we still regard it as important right here, right now.

As with any project of this sort, we have accumulated a number of debts along the way.

First and foremost, we wish to thank the Velux Foundation, and in particular Henrik Tronier, for their belief in, and financial and moral support for, this project. We also owe a debt to the WMO? team at IOA—Karen Boll, Susanne Ekman, and Thomas Lopdrup-Hjorth.

We would also like to thank the staff of the Churchill Archives Centre at the University of Cambridge, where the Papers of Lord Wilfred Brown are deposited, for their quiet, precise, and always judicious assistance.

At various points during the life of the WMO? project we were lucky enough to have been joined at IOA for varying lengths of time by a remarkable group of interlocutors: Chris Grey, Ian Hunter, Ellen O'Connor, and Charles Perrow. Their work has motivated this book in ways they are probably unaware of and in some cases might find quite odd. Needless to say, neither they nor any other persons mentioned here are to blame for any failings this book may have.

We are grateful to the many people who have discussed the project with us and offered much needed feedback. We would especially like to thank: Paul Adler, Frans Bevort, Haldor Byrkjeflot, Catherine Casler, Tim Dartington, Mitchell Dean, Bente Elkjær, Christian Frankel, Rasmus Ploug Jenle, Kristian Kreiner, Magnus Larsson, Renate Meyer, Mette Mogensen, Glenn Morgan,

Niels-Christian Nickelsen, Sean Nixon, Anne Roelsgaard Obling, José Ossandón, Trine Pallesen, Kirstine Zinck Pedersen, Andrew Pettigrew, Dean Pierides, Ursula Plesner, Michael Pryke, David Saunders, Marianne Stang Våland, Jesper Strandgaard, Marilyn Strathern, and Grahame Thompson.

We would also like to acknowledge a debt to David Musson and Clare Kennedy at Oxford University Press. As ever, David has been a wise counsellor and staunch ally, for which we are very grateful.

Portions of the book draw upon previously published papers. Some of the arguments aired in Chapter 1 first appeared in Du Gay and Vikkelsø (2014) and in du Gay (2015). Chapter 3 incorporates arguments first developed in Du Gay and Vikkelsø (2012). Chapter 4 develops arguments made in Du Gay and Vikkelsø (2013). Chapter 5 borrows arguments from Vikkelsø (2015).

Paul du Gay and Signe Vikkelsø, Copenhagen, March 2016

Contents

Contents

List of Figures

Introduction

Debates about the ('higher') purpose and usefulness of organization theory (OT) have periodically shadowed the field since its inception. In recent years, disquiet has mounted once again. The latter has arisen in relation to, for instance, what has been variously described as the overly theoretical and often a- or anti-organizational state of OT, and its abstraction and lack of practical purchase in the light of pressing economic, social, and political concerns that are often profoundly organizational in nature (see inter alia: Davis, 2010, 2015; Suddaby et al., 2011; Alvesson, 2013; Alvesson and Sandberg, 2013; Lounsbury and Beckman, 2014, 2015). As one critic puts it:

> There are real, tangible, pressing problems to be solved, and OMT (Organization and Management Theory) researchers have the tools to address them. Arguably, no other field is so perfectly placed to make sense of our current situation as OMT, given that it sits at the crossroads of so many diverse disciplines (sociology, psychology, political science, anthropology, economics and all the business school disciplines). It is therefore frustrating when we devote so much of our attention to things that might be considered frivolous, or at least not so pressing. The emergency room is not the right place for elective plastic surgery. We should be able to give confident advice to policymakers, activists, and businesspeople, grounded in research... (Davis, 2015: 314)

At the same time as OT itself has been undergoing a process of intense self-examination and self-criticism, the world it ostensibly examines, describes, and seeks, in whatever ramified sense, to intervene in—the world of actually existing organization and organizations—has itself been subject to considerable substantive and normative problematization, disruption, and self-examination/doubt. Aside from the organizational scandals and breakdowns at Enron, Arthur Andersen, WorldCom, and so on at the beginning of the present millennium, and, more recently, those attaching to and indeed constitutive of the global financial crisis (GFC), most of the pressing matters of concern dominating public debate in a range of areas—the refugee crisis confronting Europe as we write, rising levels of inequality, the 'disruptive' effects of new technologies on the nature and structure of work and employ-ment (as with 'Uberization', for instance)—both raise, and involve at their core, fundamental practical and normative matters of formal organization. And yet it is precisely the idea of 'formal organization' that seems increasingly defunct both in the practical world of management and organization, where substantive developments are deemed to presage an epochal shift to an era of 'organizing without organizations' (Shirky, 2008) and the arrival of 'a post-organizational society' (Hamel, 2009), and concurrently in OT itself, where we witness the emergence of a wide variety of theoretical vocabularies—for instance, those associated with 'process', 'assemblages', 'institutional logics', 'agency', 'networks', and 'flows'—often widely at variance one with another and yet nonetheless united by a shared (negative) capability: that of 'disappear-ing' the field's core object: formal organization (King, Felin, and Whetten, 2010; du Gay and Vikkelsø, 2014; Lopdrup-Hjorth, 2015). Consequently, while the term 'organization' continues to be used, it is stripped of any substantive meaning; while the letter seems still to be honoured—talking organization—the spirit and significance of the matter have been lost entirely. Rather, 'organization' in OT is increasingly a simulacrum referring, for instance, to the processual, fragmented, and ongoing activity of 'organizing', or is simply becoming 'an epiphenomenon' (King, Felin, and Whetten, 2010: 290) that is constituted and explained by other, allegedly more 'foundational', phenomena, be they, for instance, contracts, capabilities, processes, fields, sense-making, networks, or practices, to name but some of the more popular manifestations (du Gay, 2015; Vikkelsø, 2015). This loss of belief in 'formal organization' can be found in every part of OT, broadly conceived, from critical management studies (CMS) (Tadajewski et al., 2011), through so-called state-of-the-art OT Handbooks (Tsoukas, 2003), up to and including popular and ostensibly more 'practically focused' management theory texts (Peters, 1992; Christensen, 2011). Increasingly, it would appear, formal organization as a concept is a problem and an anachronism.

Clearly, the disappearance of 'formal organization' as the core object of OT is seen by many as a liberating move and, in certain ways—ways we explore in this book—as engendering a shift of focus towards a more fundamental or realistic 'theoretical' appreciation and approximation of the 'truth' of the stuff of organizing. As one prominent Handbook in the field put it (with evident approval), 'Gone is the certainty, if it ever existed, about what organizations are; gone, too is the certainty about how they should be studied, the place of the researcher, the role of methodology, the nature of theory. Defining organization studies today is by no means an easy task' (Clegg, Hardy, and Nord, 1996: 3). On the other hand, many analysts of the 'post-organizational society' persuasion point to the historical contingency of formal organization, and to the contemporary dynamics—the uses of digital technology, the effects of globalization, the political and economic preference for markets and networks over hierarchies, and so forth—leading to its substantive occlusion, which in turn leads them to argue that holding onto norms, techniques, and devices of formal organization is anachronistic. Formal organization here is represented as fundamentally out of synch with the demands of the present and the presumed future—a 'zombie category' in Beck and Beck-Gernsheim's (2002) memorable phrase. In other words, whichever way matters are approached, formal organization is deemed to be past its sell-by date. So, why would anyone possibly be interested in 'rediscovering' and indeed defending such a passé notion? What possible benefit could such a project entail?

There is, of course, some small pleasure to be gained from a certain stubborn and studied perversity, and to seek to say something positive about formal organization in the present might indeed appear perverse in certain company. However, there are sound conceptual and practical reasons to reconnect with formal organization as a core category and object for anyone seeking to understand and intervene in organizational life, and we seek to articulate some of these in this book. The book constitutes an initial statement only, and the aim is to extend and deepen the explanatory reach and power of the argument, such as it is deemed to possess any, in more detailed studies of particular schools of thought in OT, both contemporaneous and historic, and specific developments in the worlds of organizing, again both historic and contemporary.

Formality as the 'Law' of Organization

> If our civilization breaks down, as it well may, it will be primarily a breakdown in the administrative area. If we can make a real contribution toward preventing such a breakdown, I believe this contribution will be in the administrative area.
>
> W. B. Donham, quoted in *From Higher Aims to Hired Hands*, 2010

> I found Supreme Headquarters a fascinating place ... It was full of interesting people, not least persuasive young men interested in selling short cuts to victory, of which they held the rights of way ... Few of them had anything really new to say and the few that had, usually forgot that a new idea should have something to recommend it besides just breaking up normal organization.
>
> Field Marshall Viscount Slim, *Defeat into Victory*, 2009

'Formality' has long been considered a fraud in the social sciences, perhaps most vehemently within sociology (Stinchcombe, 2001), so to see it once again receiving a critical hammering is perhaps not too surprising. As a number of scholars have argued (without endorsement), sociologists have frequently tended to position themselves on the side of 'substance' in opposition to 'formality' in any number of contexts—law, economy, government, and organization (Callon, 1998; Latour, 2005). Yet formality is central to the distinction 'between law and the rest of social life' (Stinchcombe, 2001: 2), and thus to law's raison d'être and effectivity (Weinrib, 1988), and, until comparatively recently, the term 'formal organization' designated a key difference between specific units, purposively constructed to attain explicitly formulated goals, and 'social organization' more generally (Barnard, 1968; Stinchcombe, 2001). As Blau and Scott (1963: 5) famously put it, such organizations 'have not spontaneously emerged in the course of social interaction' but have been deliberately designed to achieve certain goals and established with a number of explicit (formal) authority structures and roles: 'such organizations can be defined as formal organizations' (see also March and Simon 1958: 1–4; Barnard 1968: 4; Blau 1968: 297–8). This 'formal establishment for an explicit purpose', Blau and Scott continued, 'is the criterion that distinguishes our subject matter from the study of social organization in general' (Blau and Scott, 1963: 5). Only by means of such specification, Blau and Scott (1963) argued, could a particular object, one deemed a 'key phenomenon of our time' (Perrow, 1991: 725), be precisely categorized and thus analysed and intervened in; at the same time, only by such specification could a new 'semi-discipline', or 'field' as March (1965: xiv–xv) termed it, emerge—one we now know as OT—dedicated to the analysis of this object. A field, in other words, for which 'formal organization' was and is *the* 'core object' (du Gay, 2015; Lopdrup-Hjorth, 2015; Vikkelsø, 2015). Thus, the adjective 'formal' not only provided specificity to an object of study, it also assisted in providing a clear focus for the development of a field of study, OT.

What, then, happens when formality is supplanted? Is the specificity of both the core object and the field dedicated to its analysis eroded? What might the consequences of such a development be for those dedicated to undertaking organizational analysis, for instance, or, more significantly, for the fulfilment of the particular purposes to which formal organization is the crucial means? For Chester Barnard, the answer is quite clear: most of what one would find 'reliable, foreseeable, and stable' was accomplished by formal organization (Barnard, 1968: 4); if formal organization did not exist, organizationally speaking we would, according to Barnard, be in 'a state of nearly complete individualism and disorder' (ibid.: 120). The chief executive, Minister of State, and organization theorist Wilfred Brown, commonly referred to as 'the British Barnard', concurred: appeals to 'informality' as the bedrock of organizational creativity, innovation, freedom, and flexibility did not tally with his business experience (Brown, 1965b: 153). They were, rather, appeals to disorganize; to return to 'a natural condition' in the Hobbesian sense. As Brown (1965b: 153–4) put it, 'a deliberate policy of leaving organization unformulated is tantamount to the deliberate setting up of a situation of anarchy. I use the word "anarchy" in its original sense, i.e. "the want of government in a state".' Echoing Hobbes's (1996: 128) (in)famous statement, 'where no Law, no Injustice', Brown argued:

> It is not absence of law, which allows creative use of discretion, but an explicit area of freedom bounded by the law which reduces anarchy and allows the individual to make his contribution . . . A little reflection will surely enable each of us to see that we want a system of law, despite the fact that at times we find it irksome, first, because we desire to be protected from the effect of the unlimited decisions of our fellows and, secondly, because without limitations on our freedom of decision, we must carry unlimited responsibility.   (1965b: 153–4)

As a result, work, and thus 'organizing', would be conducted in 'a twilight of continuous uncertainty' (Brown, 1965a: 63):

> If the need for formal organization is denied and as a result there are no written or explicitly recognised prescribed bounds to the work roles, then, clearly, no one really knows what decisions he or anybody else is authorised to make.
>
> (Ibid.: 69)

For Brown, the almost permanent suspicion or overt denigration of formality and formalization among those ostensibly seeking to undertake organizational analysis 'distorts the whole frame of reference within which organization as a subject is considered'(Brown, 1965b: 158). In other words, the attempt to conduct such an analysis whilst dispensing with 'the formal' is profoundly un- or anti-organizational; it is also quite antithetical to the securing of certain 'values' that advocates of 'informal' and 'spontaneous' social organizing deemed particularly important, such as 'freedom':

> Formalization of organization delineates roles and role relationships; formalization of policies makes clear to people the area in which they have freedom to act. Without a clearly defined area of freedom there is no freedom. This, in fact, is a very old story . . . *there is no real freedom without law.*
>
> (Brown, 1965a: 69–70; original emphasis)

If 'formality' is something akin to the 'law' of organization, what happens when that law is ignored, occluded, upended, or in some way dispensed with either by those ostensibly analysing 'organization' or by those actually seeking to undertake organization? It is striking, we contend, that those seeking to dispense with 'formality' rarely provide detailed descriptions of the (daily) consequences of the organizing practices they in turn commend. Rather, rhetorical persuasion and meta-theoretical arguments predominate. As we have just seen, for Barnard and Brown a Hobbesian 'natural condition' is the logical result of dispensing with 'formality'. That doesn't mean that there would be no successful organizing activity or a complete absence of any ordering, but rather that what the latter are and how they contribute to the securing of an overall purpose can only be known after the event, as a historical fact; there will be no prior, logistical guarantees. The latter, after all, are the provenance of 'formality' (Stinchcombe, 2001). For Blau, dispensing with 'the formal' entails jettisoning the very criterion that 'distinguishes our subject matter from the study of social organization in general' (Blau and Scott, 1963: 5). The absence of that criterion makes it difficult for OT to present itself, both to its own members and indeed to the 'outside world', as qualified to undertake its core task: organizational analysis. It is this task that gives OT its distinctiveness (furnishing it with determinate content and purposeful differences from other enterprises):

> When we seek the intelligibility of something, we want to know what that something is. The search for 'whatness' presupposes that something is a this and not a that, that it has, in other words, a determinate content. That content is determinate because it sets the matter apart from other matters... (Weinrib, 1988: 958)

With the absence of 'the formal' those 'purposeful differences' disappear and we return to the undifferentiated, amorphous world of 'social organization', where anything, more or less, can appear grist to the analytic mill (King, Felin, and Whetten, 2010). As Lopdrup-Hjorth (2015: 454) puts it:

> [B]y shifting the emphasis of the concept 'organization' from a specific purposefully constructed entity...to the study of how 'social order', in the widest conceivable sense, is generated...it has been possible to open a whole new, and potentially limitless space, in which organization scholars now can study a whole range of phenomena. With this transformation, 'the (formal) organization' formerly at the centre of OT, and the object around which a common vocabulary was developed, is relocated to the periphery as merely one, rather contingent, instantiation in a big sea of organizing now deemed more worthy of investigation. By embarking upon such a conceptual shift, scholars within OT have not only conveniently arranged for themselves the possibility of studying almost anything, they have also, it seems, found a way of bypassing all the negative connotations hitherto clinging to the concept of 'organization'.

This strange inversion is identifiable in any number of theory programmes within the field of organization studies, broadly conceived. We find it manifested, though in very different ways of course, in process theory, new institutional theory, and agency theory, for instance. The latter either explicitly or implicitly attempt to offer a general theory of organizing activity, but if, and it is a truly big 'if', a theory of all organizing activity were to emerge, it wouldn't be a theory of 'formal organization', but rather a theory of 'X', where 'X' is too loose and general to do much detailed explanatory work (Rorty, 1988: 6).

Let's focus briefly on an example to help clarify the thrust of our argument. In his iconic paper on the legal structure of the firm, the practising corporate lawyer and legal academic Jean-Philippe Robé (2011) explored the implications of agency theory and its generalized and generalizing organizing theoretics for understanding the actual, that is, practical, legal structuring of one of its foundational categories—the firm. For Robé (2011), it is essential conceptually—as happens practically in law—to differentiate the category of 'firm' from that of 'corporation':

> The firm and the corporation are very often confused in the literature…The two words are often used as synonyms. They correspond, however, to totally different concepts: a corporation is a legal instrument, with a separate legal personality, which is used to legally structure the firm; the firm is an organized economic activity, corporations being used to legally structure most firms of some significance…The confusion between the two is at the origin of countless mistakes, some of which have very serious consequences.   (Robé, 2011: 3)

In the canonic work of the agency theorists Jensen and Meckling (1976: 310), organizations, such as 'firms (. . .), universities, hospitals (. . .), cities, states and the Federal government', are reduced to 'legal fictions which serve as a nexus for a set of contracting relationships among individuals'. According to them, it makes little or no sense to try to distinguish those things that are 'inside' the firm (or any other organization) from those things that are 'outside' it:

> There is in a very real sense only a multitude of complex relationships (i.e., contracts) between the legal fiction (the firm) and the owners of labor, material and capital inputs and the consumers of output. (. . .) The firm is (. . .) a legal fiction which serves as a focus for a complex process in which the conflicting objectives of individuals (. . .) are brought into equilibrium within a framework of contractual relations. In this sense the 'behavior' of the firm is like the behavior of a market, that is, the outcome of a complex equilibrium process.   (Ibid.)

Besides confusing 'firm' and 'corporation' in the manner described by Robé (2011), Jensen and Meckling's characterization effectively depicts formal organization as a fictional or pseudo-entity, behind which a complex set of more fundamental processes are at work. In providing such a description they did not merely present a perspective that seems to share a certain family resemblance to later proponents of a process theoretical perspective—that is, a world of surface phenomena (i.e. formal organizations) behind which an ontologically primary reality of processes rule sway. As Lopdrup-Hjorth (2015:454) has argued, they also presented a programme loaded with prescriptions. If organizations were merely 'fictions', and all that remained were individuals contracting with each other, then the ontological status and moral purposes hitherto accorded to organizations no longer made much sense. All that remained were essentially economic maximization problems, and the question of how to design appropriate governance mechanisms through which opportunistic individuals (managers, for instance) could be brought into alignment with the interests of shareholders, whose sole concern, allegedly, was maximizing profit (for a fuller statement of this argument see Lopdrup-Hjorth, 2015).

Jensen and Meckling's (1976) article has become one of the most famous and widely cited management articles of all time. Underneath their often impenetrable jargon and abstruse mathematics, however, lay a simple metaphysical argument developed most famously by Milton Friedman (1970) six years earlier:

> In a free-enterprise, private property system, a corporate executive is an employee of the owners of the business. He [sic] has direct responsibility to his employers. That responsibility is to conduct business in accordance with their desires, which generally will be to make as much money as possible while conforming to the basic rules of the society ... The manager is the agent of the individuals who own the corporation.   (Friedman, 1970, *New York Times Magazine*, SM17)

As Robé (2011: 60), among others, has argued, this analysis is vaguely appropriate to explaining what happens when the owner of a small coffee shop, for example, decides to retire and entrust the management of her or his business to a hired hand. The manager of the coffee shop is the employee of the owner of the business and has a relation of direct accountability and responsibility to her or him. In this sense the manager is an agent. If the owner is unhappy with the manager's performance, the owner can return to work and run the shop personally. Applied to formal organization, however, and explicitly to a large corporation with listed shares, this analysis is completely wide of the mark.

First, as Robé (2011: 60; see also Denning, 2013) points out, a corporate executive is not an employee of the shareholders. She is an employee of the corporation, which is a separate legal person. Second, the shareholders in no sense 'own the business'. They own shares issued by the corporation used to legally structure the organization. This is entirely different:

> The shareholders just can't step in and run the business, as owners could do. If a shareholder wants to run the business, she must go through the corporate procedures required to be appointed as officer; but even then ... she would not be allowed to act as an *owner*. She would have to abide by the constraints and duties provided for by corporate law, with the ancillary liabilities if she breaches them. To obtain the full autonomy of the owner, she would have to purchase all the shares and get rid of the corporation altogether (dissolve it). She would then own the assets and liabilities directly and she would be the counter-party to the contracts with the other resource providers. She would *then* be the indisputable owner of the business—with all the unpleasant ensuing consequences: unlimited liability, no partitioning of the personal and business assets, fragility of the business since the cluster of contracts connecting the property rights would be centered on an individual person potentially affected by all the incidents of life (sickness, divorce,

death, etc.). This would seriously affect the business, making its financing impossible if it is of some importance. No external financier would extend substantial financing to a business based on the fragility of human life.   (Robé, 2011: 60–1)

Here, Robé offers a detailed description of the consequences of organizing according to the principles laid out by Friedman, and therefore by Jensen and Meckling. They are not optimal.

Furthermore, Robé (2011: 61) continues, as an officer of the corporation, the executive has no responsibility or mandate to conduct the affairs of the organization in line with the shareholders' desires. As she is not their agent she is not under their direct supervision. She reports to a duly constituted Board of Directors. The latter too are not the agents of shareholders. Finally, there is no legal duty to maximize profits in the management of the corporation (ibid.: 60–1):

> 'In a free-enterprise, private property system' in which limited liability corporations have been introduced in the legal system to allow the structuring of firms requiring the use of significant amounts of capital, Friedman's description of the law is totally false. If the law were as he describes it, no large firm would have developed since the benefits of assets partitioning, limited liability, corporate group creation and the development of securities markets would never have occurred. Issues of governance would admittedly be much simpler and very much in line with his conclusions—but we would be living in a frugal economy in which enterprise governance (the governance of boutiques and cottage industries in relatively closed polities) would hardly exist as an issue. If one wants to keep the advantages of large concentrations of capital and of large firms, in a world of positive transaction costs, one has to address governance issues while taking into account the *reality* of the legal rules without which such large concentrations of capital would not have been possible in the first place.   (Ibid.: 62)

Robé's focus on the *reality* of the legal structuring of formal organization brings into stark relief the metaphysical presuppositions informing agency theory and their less than salutary effects when operationalized. As he (ibid.) indicates, in so far as Friedman's analysis 'is vaguely' connected to a reality, it is to that of 'the frugal economies of the eighteenth century' where no large firms existed, or to the world of mom and pop businesses. The consequences of adopting Friedman's strictures, then, take us back into the undifferentiated world of 'social organization' as Blau put it, where no formal organizations exist; similarly, echoing Barnard and Brown's predictions, Robé argues that, in dispensing with formal organization, Friedman's analysis also paves the way for a return to an organizational 'state of nature'—operationalized 'it has toxic consequences' (ibid.: 65):

> The dominant analysis is... there to assist forcing the concentration of management's efforts on the promotion of the interests of the sole shareholders who are

being wrongfully presented as 'principals', as owners. As we have seen, the whole purpose of modern corporate law was precisely to sever *any* property right connection between the shareholders and the assets used in the operation of the firm. It is only because agency theory disregards the reality and importance of the legal instruments used to structure large firms-as-they-are that a widespread ideology that 'shareholders own-the-firm-so-management-must-maximize-profits' could develop. (Ibid.: 62–3)

This approach, as Robé's argument is at pains to point out, is, among others things, resolutely anti-empirical. It does not confront legal and organizational reality, instead it develops an elaborate theoretical simulacra that represents itself as the 'real' state of affairs underlying that reality: a state of affairs that cannot be ignored and which trumps formal law and organization's surface 'fictions'. Friedman's (and Jensen and Meckling's) simulacra share something with the analytic philosophies that preoccupy Bas van Fraassen (2002) in his book *The Empirical Stance*. In this, van Fraassen (2002: 3) asks how so much contemporary philosophy could have reverted to the 'moribund *vieux jeux* of metaphysics?' In exploring this question, van Fraassen provides some conceptual and methodological tools that could prove useful in enabling us to undertake a similar exercise in organization studies. Via Robé's analysis, we have already begun to suggest the ways in which agency theory represents just such a metaphysical reversion in the field of organizational analysis as it is broadly understood. As we hinted at earlier, though, agency theory provides by no means the only instance of such a regress within OT. The currently popular 'process theory' and the ever-expanding new institutional theory, for example, also share a similar proclivity, though they do so in differing ways, as we will indicate later in the book. We begin, though, by introducing aspects of the argument developed by van Fraassen (2002) and by fellow travellers, such as Pierre Hadot (1995, 2009) and Ian Hunter (2006, 2009a, 2009b), in cognate disciplines, as a prelude to accounting for the (re)emergence of metaphysical speculation as a core feature of much contemporary work in organization studies.

From 'Theory' to 'Stance'

> The rats were devouring the house, but instead of examining the cat's teeth and the cat's claws, they only concerned themselves to find out if it was a holy cat, a pious cat, a moral cat.
>
> Mark Twain, *Personal Recollections of Joan of Arc, by the Sieur Louis de Conte* (1896)

In his critique of contemporary analytic metaphysics and objectifying epistemologies, the philosopher of science, Bas van Fraassen (2002: 61), has argued that 'all the great philosophical movements' are, in effect, 'stances', and that becoming an 'empiricist' or a 'materialist' (a Stoic or an Epicurean, a post-structuralist or a critical theorist) is thus 'similar or analogous to a conversion to a cause, a religion, an ideology'. This is a bold statement and one easily susceptible to misunderstanding, so let us proceed with care. After all, what exactly is a 'stance' if it is not simply another word for 'ideology', on the one hand, or a matter of 'purely subjective, merely subjective value judgement, and thus unamenable to rational debate' and so forth, on the other? (Van Fraassen, 2002: 61–2). For van Fraassen (2002: 47–8):

> A philosophical position can consist in something other than a belief in what the world is like. We can, for example, take the empiricist's attitude toward science rather than his or her beliefs about it as the crucial characteristic. Then we are led to the following suggestion... A philosophical position can consist in a stance (attitude, commitment, approach, a cluster of such—possibly including some propositional attitudes such as beliefs as well). Such a stance can of course be expressed, and may involve or presuppose some beliefs as well, but cannot simply be equated with having beliefs or making assertions about what there is.

Van Fraassen (2002: 61) indicates that the reaction to this idea of 'philosophy as stance' within philosophical circles has mainly focused on the idea's presumed negative implications for what philosophy can be, and how philosophical differences could be resolved. He writes, with not a little irony, '[J]ust how long did it take to settle those disputes over the reality of universals, the nature of knowledge, sceptical doubts, objective necessity in nature, and so on? How easy was it to reach agreement on those issues?' He continues, although the prospect of seeing philosophies as stances will 'not be to everyone's liking... let us not colour the project with guilt by association'. After all, if we approach opposed philosophies, not as rival theories of truth, but as rival 'stances', we can see them as specific activities, and can thus subject them to empirical examination, projecting and representing the minute detailed descriptions of the consequences of taking up their attitude, commitments, and approach, and, not least, of exploring what they do to those 'called' to or by them, and how they do it. For van Fraassen (2002: 62), no stance is innocent or above the fray, and his work is focused, in particular, on the ongoing battle between what he terms the 'empirical stance' and the 'metaphysical stance' in various fields of contemporary philosophy.

For van Fraassen (2002: 62), then, while 'stances do involve beliefs and are indeed inconceivable in separation from beliefs and opinions', they are not reducible to them. Rather, the important point is that a 'stance will involve a great deal more, will not be identifiable through the beliefs involved, and can persist through changes in belief'. He illustrates this point by comparing and contrasting two distinct and rival stances that are often, wrongly in his view, represented as different *theses*: materialism and empiricism.

Van Fraassen begins by indicating that, when seen as stances, both materialism and empiricism express a positive attitude towards science, but not the same attitude. Characteristic of materialism, van Fraassen (2002: 3) argues, is a deference towards the *content* of science. The latter takes two distinct forms. First, a belief that 'the scientific description of the world is true, in its entirety, or near enough' (ibid.: 63). Second, 'a strong inclination towards completeness claims for the content of certain sciences' (ibid.: 63):

> 'This is true, and nothing else is true' would express such a claim. Because of the difficulties surrounding such claims, and the dim appreciation that the claim is less important than the deference it betokens, we usually hear something else, something like 'what else *is* there?' But that too is only a challenge masquerading as a factual question. (Ibid.)

More precisely, it is a *metaphysical* challenge posing as a factual question.

For the empirical stance, on the other hand, the positive attitude towards science is not directed to the content of the sciences but rather to their methods, to their forms and practices of enquiry. In this sense, science is a paradigmatic form of rational enquiry, and to take it up as such, as an attitude, is precisely a key feature of the empirical stance. *But*, and this is crucial, that does not entail adopting a deferential attitude to the content of any science per se. From this key difference then, van Fraassen (2002: 63) concludes that, while taking up the materialist stance entails adopting the attitude that science is what teaches us what to believe, taking up the empirical stance entails adopting a very different attitude or comportment, one in which science is more nearly what teaches us how to give up our beliefs: 'All our factual beliefs are to be given over as hostages to fortune, to the fortunes of future empirical evidence, and given up when they fail, without succumbing to despair, cynicism, or debilitating relativism' (ibid.).

Van Fraassen's approach to philosophical positions as stances rather than as theories shares a family resemblance to the programme of work undertaken by Pierre Hadot in the adjacent field of the history of philosophy. Hadot's programme can also be seen as, in part, a reaction to the metaphysical reversion associated with much contemporary philosophical work, and it is remarkable how his own understanding of philosophy as primarily a 'way of life' clearly echoes van Fraassen's approach to philosophy as a 'stance'.

Hadot was first and foremost a historian of ancient Greco-Roman philosophy, and his work has had a profound effect on how ancient philosophy as an activity is to be conceived of and understood.

His approach to ancient Greek philosophy as *a way of life*, and not as an activity involving the construction of a thesis or a theoretical system, is elaborated in a series of texts beginning (in terms of their availability in English, that is) with *Philosophy as a Way of Life* (1995), and proceeding through *The Inner Citadel* (2001), his pioneering study of the meditations of Marcus Aurelius, *What is Ancient Philosophy?* (2002), and culminating in the posthumously published, *The Present Alone is Our Happiness* (2009). For Hadot (2002: 1), a crucial distinction needed to be made between the history of philosophical ways of life and the history of philosophies, 'if what we understand by philosophies are theoretical discourses and philosopher's systems'. Unpacking this distinction involved Hadot in two moves: on the one hand, informing the reader of a set of empirical arguments that decisively showed that, for the Greeks, philosophy was not the construction of an abstract theoretical 'system', but rather a choice of life or 'stance'; and, on the other, allowing the reader of the ancient works, and of Hadot's own texts, to turn towards philosophy thus understood (Hadot, 2009: xi). For Hadot, ancient philosophy should be viewed in terms of the way of life or stance—attitude, commitment, approach, method, comportment, a cluster of such—it elaborated, one which was aimed at bringing about a transformation of the individual adopting it. Ancient Greek philosophies did not attempt, 'to provide a systematic theory of reality, but to teach their disciples a method with which to orient themselves both in thought and life' (ibid.: 90):

> When Plato writes his dialogues, when Aristotle gives his courses and publishes his course notes, when Epictetus writes his letters ... in all these cases, indeed, the philosopher expounds a doctrine. However, he exposes it in a certain way—a way that aims to form more than to inform.   (Ibid.: 88)

For Hadot—in a clear echo of van Fraassen's basic point—the task of ancient philosophy is not primarily one of communicating 'an encyclopaedic knowledge in the form of a system of propositions and of concepts that would reflect, more or less well, the system of the world' (quoted in Davidson, 1995: 22). As he put it:

> What is ultimately the most useful ... ? Is it discourse on language or on being and non-being? Isn't it rather, to learn how to live ... ?
> (Hadot, quoted in Davidson, 2009: x)

Definitions were nothing by themselves, independently of the road travelled to reach them. The philosophers of antiquity were not interested in 'ready-made knowledge', but with imparting that comportment, training, and education that would allow their disciples 'to orient themselves in thought, in the life of the city, or in the world'. At their heart, oral or written, ancient philosophies are 'ways of life intended to make those subject to them practice a method, rather than a doctrinal exposition' (Hadot, quoted in Davidson, 1995: 21). Rather than aiming at the acquisition of an abstract knowledge per se, the stance was aimed at realizing a transformation of one's vision of the world, one's conduct in it, and a metamorphosis of one's persona. Philosophical ways of life or stances were practical, required training, education, and effort, and were lived; they involved a shift in one's comportment—one's way of being:

> We must discern that the philosopher's underlying intention, which was not to develop a discourse which had its end in itself but to act upon souls. In fact, each assertion must be understood from the perspective of the effect it was intended to produce in the soul of the auditor or reader. Whether the goals was to convert, to console, to cure, to exhort the audience, the point was always and above all not to communicate to them some ready made knowledge, but to form them. In other words, the goal was to learn a type of know-how; to develop a habitus, or new capacity to judge and to criticize; and to transform—that is to change people's way of living and of seeing the world.   (Hadot, 2002: 274)

As Hadot (1995) argues, philosophers of antiquity were philosophers because of their existential attitude or stance. The latter was the foundation of their philosophy and required those seeking to adopt it to undergo a conversion— again the term deployed by van Fraassen (2002: 61), as we have previously indicated—to change the conduct of their life. As van Fraassen (2002: 61) put it: 'all the great philosophical movements have been of this sort, at heart, even if different in purport'. Both van Fraassen and Hadot deploy their key terms— 'stance' and 'way of life'—to suggest a different approach to philosophy as an activity, one where metaphysics and ontology are entirely absent, and where, instead, there is a calling back to experience and volition, a rebellion against high theory as an end in itself—a rejection of the theory format of what knowledge and opinion are—and a focus on situation, role, context, and conduct. As Davidson (2009: xii) indicates, in contrast to the *analytic* metaphysics that both van Fraassen and Hadot eschew precisely because it takes us further away from rather than closer to the matter at hand, the notions of stance and way of life have a practical focus and intent that allows them to 'be applied and extended to unexpected domains', including, as we will argue later in this section to organizational analysis.

Like van Fraassen and Hadot, the historian of ideas Ian Hunter also has the reversion to metaphysics in his sights, although, unlike them, his main focus is not analytic metaphysics but the various philosophical problematizations of positive knowledge huddled under the headings of postmodernism and post-structuralism. In a series of illuminating articles, Hunter (2006, 2007, 2008, 2009b) seeks to explore the shared intellectual comportment and attitude that has come to characterize a range of distinctive positions within the humanities and social sciences, again, both mainstream and 'critical'. Focusing particular attention on the history of the proliferation of high theory in the post-1960s humanities and social sciences, Hunter (2006: 80) indicates that what has come to be known as the 'moment of theory' began when a certain kind of philosophical interrogation surfaced inside a wide variety of disciplines—linguistics, literary criticism, sociology, organization studies, political economy, the 'psy' disciplines, and jurisprudence—'where it assumed the form of an array of associated but rivalrous theoretical vernaculars' (ibid.). In other words, the 'moment of theory' cannot be readily identified with a common object or even a shared language. If this is the case, though, what, then, is it about these manifold forms of theory (which includes, inter alia, structuralism, post-structuralism, deconstruction, 'process' ontology, and so forth) that has prompted both exponents and detractors to acquiesce in a single name—'theory'—for them? According to Hunter, the answer to this question resides in the shared intellectual comportment or attitude they exhibit, albeit to differing degrees:

> This attitude is sceptical towards empirical experience (in a more or less Kantian way) [...] which it regards as foreclosing a higher level ('transcendental) experience—and hence cultivates openness to break-through phenomena of various kinds. (Ibid.: 81)

In the course of pursuing this programme, Hunter (2006, 2009a, 2009b), has developed the idea of 'philosophical self-fashioning' as a methodological concept to open up the question of what kind of activity post-structuralism and associated movements in 'the moment of theory' is, and what sort of intellectual persona is cultivated when adopting this attitude:

> By re-describing philosophising as a particular kind of activity...this approach allows us to treat poststructuralist theorising itself as a concrete historical reality rather than an intellectual symptom of one...It should be clear that in offering this characterisation of poststructuralist theorising we are not attempting to falsify it. As a concrete historical activity such theorising is no more capable of being false than is chess, yoga, or the Eucharist, and, by that same token, no more capable of being true. What we are doing, rather, is seeking to transform the register in which post-structuralism is understood: from that of a theory that might be true or false to that of an irrefragable activity, whose character is open to historical description and whose contextual circumstances are open to historical investigation that might indeed be true or false. Of course, this shift results in a dramatic change of outlook, as it means that an intellectual discipline dedicated to disclosing the pristine indeterminacy beneath empirical reality is itself treated as an empirical reality of a particular kind, hence as an object for an empirically-oriented intellectual history. (Hunter, 2009b: 9–10)

In following this programme, Hunter (2009a: 270) therefore resolutely turns his face against an assumption framing many of these 'moments of theory';

namely that philosophical concepts are indeed cognitive by dint of their capacity to reveal the truth of reason or being—or the truth of the latter's inaccessibility—and, as such, are therefore capable of acceding to knowledge in all departments of existence: law, politics, and organization, for instance. Without attempting to settle the matter, Hunter (2009a: 270–1) explores empirically key concepts in the postmodern canon—'the transcendental reduction', difference, and being—in terms of the acts of self-transformation that operationalize them, with a view to seeing whether they do indeed function as a means to a generally accessible cognition. With regard to the former, for instance, he argues that:

> Husserl's *ēpochē* or 'transcendental reduction' can be properly re-described as a particular kind of 'spiritual exercise', one in which the philosopher is required to suspend his commitment to all existing knowledges and natural experiences in order to clear a space for the manifestation of the 'transcendental phenomenon', or Being...As such, the transcendental reduction appears as an act of self-transformation aimed at establishing a certain spiritual superiority in relation to 'natural selves'. This means that it is restricted to the circle of those undertaking the exercise, with no apparent general connection to 'external' objects or phenomena that one could call cognitive.

Like van Fraassen, Hunter's stance is resolutely empirical, based as it is in 'plain' contextual intellectual history. Hunter thus seeks to provide an empirical historical characterization of post-structuralist theorizing that locates it in a historical context without—as so much philosophical history does—engaging in the hermeneutic reduction that treats it as the intellectual symptom of a hidden historical reality (a theory of theory, as opposed to a history of theory).[1] In deploying the contextualist empirical historical method and approaching post-structuralist theory in terms of the acts of self-transformation and self-cultivation they require, Hunter (2009a) also explicitly links his own project to Pierre Hadot's studies of classical philosophies as 'ways of life'.

So, what then follows from approaching OT through the frame provided by van Fraassen, Hadot, and Hunter, and why might such a shift of perspective be useful to 're-covering formal organization'? Well, if we treat organization theories as expressive of a particular stance, our attention is then directed to the attitude or comportment towards formal organization that is entailed by the adoption of that stance as the crucial characteristic to be explored. This enables us to describe in detail whether and how the adoption of a particular stance takes one closer to or further away from formal organization as a

---

[1] See, for instance, the discussion of the 'new historicism' as a theory programme, and the differences between 'plain' history and philosophical history and the stance towards empirical matters they adopt in Fish (1994).

distinctive practical object, and thus to articulate the *organizational* conse-quences that flow from adopting the stance.

As we indicated earlier in this Introduction, the attitude, comportment, or stance characterizing 'the moment of theory' is sceptical towards empirical experience because it regards the latter as foreclosing a higher-level ('transcen-dental') experience. It is not difficult to detect the presence of such an attitude or comportment in a range of organization theories—including process ontol-ogy and various CMS, for instance. The consequences of adopting this stance include a scepticism towards formal organization as precisely something which forecloses access to a higher-level breakthrough experience and which therefore needs to be transcended. Chia (1999: 211) embodies this comport-ment when he writes (with endorsement, obviously) of the implications of taking a 'processualist' approach to organizational change:

> Relaxing of the artificially-imposed structures of relations, the loosening up of organization. Such a relaxing strategy will allow the intrinsic change forces, always kept in check by the restrictive bonds of organization to express themselves naturally and creatively.

Similarly, as we saw in Robé's argument concerning the legal structure of the firm earlier in this Introduction, the attitude or comportment characteristic of agency theory is also sceptical towards empirical experience. In his article, Robé argues that agency theories do not confront the empirical (legal) reality of formal organization, developing instead an elaborate theoretical simulacra that represents itself as the reality underlying the surface fictions of formal law and organization. Friedman's (and Jensen and Meckling's) simulacra have a strong family resemblance to the metaphysical analytic philosophies that are the focus of van Fraassen's (2002) book, not least in their ambitious project of an ontology able to go beyond answers to formal organizational questions that have already been dealt with practically by empirical corporate law, for instance.

In a nutshell, what unites these two very different theory programmes is the shared stance, attitude, and comportment they adopt towards organizational reality. This stance is *metaphysical* in the sense elaborated by van Fraassen, Hadot, and Hunter; it involves the subversion, transcendence, or occlusion of the category of formal organization by the development of an often highly elaborate, ornate, and intricate set of simulacra that pass under the same basic name (organization). Cultivating such a stance, regardless of the theoretical vernacular in which it is clothed, involves 'disappearing' formal organization by interpreting it into something else; this 'something else' then serving as the basis by which organization is to be understood and assessed. This transcend-ence, occlusion, or disappearance of formal organization and its simultaneous replacement by theoretical simulacra (such as 'the nexus of contracts', but equally, 'rationalized myths', 'capabilities', 'assemblages', 'becomings', 'discursive formations', 'action nets'—the list, as ever, is very long) characterizes the metaphysical stance as it manifests itself in the field of contemporary organizational analysis. In so doing, it seems to honour the letter—talking organization—while losing the spirit and significance of the subject entirely. In what follows, then, one of our tasks is to try and show this up for what it is, and to bring to light the ways in which its strenuous labours address matters of considerably less significance than its advocates believe. Another is to attempt to show how an alternative attitude or method, one we term 'the classical stance', precisely approaches matters of 'formal organization' in what one of its practitioners described as 'a conscious and responsible manner' (Parker Follett, 1982: 21). This designation, 'the classical stance', contains clear echoes of the well-known categorization 'classic organization theory', but is not reducible to or synonymous with it. It would indeed be nostalgic, anachronistic, and unworldly to suggest that somehow revivifying 'classical organization theory' (which in and of itself cannot in any meaningful sense be represented as a coherent, unidirectional body of thought) would help provide an answer to any number of contemporary matters of organizational concern. Rather, our use of the term 'classical' is meant to signify key aspects of the stance (approach, comportment) adopted by classic OT that we wish to highlight and commend in this book. In other words, it is not the *content* of classic OT per se we wish to emphasize, but rather the *approach* and *comportment* it exemplifies that we are most interested in affirming. Thus, we deploy the term 'classical' to refer to a geographically dispersed, institutionally disconnected, and historically discontinuous 'stance', characterized, inter alia, by a pragmatic call to experience, an antithetical attitude to 'high' or transcendental theorizing, an admiration for scientific forms of enquiry (in the Weberian sense of the 'disciplined pursuit of knowledge', and, as such, not reducible to the laboratory sciences, nor to the content of the sciences per se), a dissatisfaction and devaluation of explanation by postulate, and, not least, a practical focus on organizational effectiveness, for instance, born of a close connection to 'the work itself', or, as we shall have cause to term it, 'the situation at hand'. Our referencing 'classic organization theory' is therefore aimed primarily at highlighting a particular attitude, comportment, or stance, and indeed an associated 'persona' who bears it. In so doing, we are able to highlight this particular approach to formal organization as an object of analysis, one with a distinctively practical focus and ethos—what we term *a practical science of organizing*—that differs considerably, as we have seen, from many contemporary (metaphysical) approaches in organization studies. In viewing classic OT as a stance, and not, first and foremost, as a cluster of theories, a historical period, or a canon of 'pioneers', the range of work that can be deemed 'classical' within the field of OT expands considerably.

Alongside the 'usual suspects'—figures as F. W. Taylor, Henri Fayol, Mary Parker Follett, and Chester Barnard—we might reasonably include, among many others, the early work of members of the Tavistock Institute of Human Relations and its affiliates, figures such as Eric Trist, Eric Miller, Elliott Jaques, and Wilfred Brown, for instance. Seeing classic OT as a stance also enables us to upend the reflex accusation of anachronism and contemporary irrelevance directed at it from the present. As Charles Perrow (1979: 58–9) succinctly put it, despite all the opprobrium heaped upon the work of practitioners of the classical stance, 'all the resources of organisational research and theory today have not managed to substitute better principles (or proverbs) for those ridiculed'. The latter, and the stance involved in developing them, 'have worked, and are still working, for they addressed themselves to very real problems of management, problems more pressing than those advanced by social science'. In other words, the classical stance in OT can be applied to contemporary matters of organizational concern without any need to 'update' it. Second, and relatedly, we suggest that, rather than simply advocating or offering a systematic 'theory' or set of principles of organization, practitioners of the classical stance are also fundamentally concerned with enunciating a practical concern with organization and management as a 'vocation' (Weber, 1989, 1994), 'habitus' (Mauss, 1979), or 'a way of life' (Hadot, 2011). While Barnard, Parker Follett, and Wilfred Brown, for instance, are clearly preoccupied with matters of form and system, they are not at all interested in developing a conceptual edifice as an end in itself. Metaphysics and ontology are almost completely absent. They are not seeking simply to 'inform', but equally to persuade, transform, or produce a 'formative effect' for a specific audience— most notably those, including themselves, for whom practising organization is 'a way of life'. In so doing, they equally share a fundamental recognition that principles underdetermine conduct. This helps explain their mutual concern with 'casuistry' (not a term they use, but something they constantly practice).

In making this case, though, a critical question frequently emerges: What distinguishes this stance from the ostensibly practical or consultancy thrust of the work of so-called 'management gurus' such as Tom Peters, Michael Porter, Michael Hammer, or Clay Christensen, for example? While there is no doubt that output of these and other popular management writers is lapped up by many practising managers and executives and can often be shown to have a practical effect, the stance such writers adopt to organization is quite different from that characterizing the 'classical stance' in OT. Indeed, as we will have cause to note a number of times throughout this book, the attitude and comportment adopted by these and other writers more frequently approximates to the 'metaphysical stance'. Despite his reputation as a something of a 'realist', it is not for nothing, we suggest, that Porter's persona has been described as that of a business metaphysician (Denning, 2013).

The Argument and Structure of the Book

As indicated earlier in this Introduction, a key proposition of this book is that OT has dispensed or lost touch with the 'classical stance', has increasingly adopted a 'metaphysical stance', and, in so doing, has increasingly assisted in the disappearance of its own core object—'formal organization'. The book is then an attempt not only to show what is at stake in the battle between the classical and metaphysical stances in OT, but also to indicate as clearly as possible why cultivating and practising the former is preferable to adopting the latter. Our central contention is that there is much to be gained for OT in reconceiving itself as a practical science of organizing in the manner of its classical antecedents, and in reviving and readopting the classical stance. In so doing, cultivating a renewed interest in its own 'canon' of concepts and tools might also prove useful. More so, indeed, than in continuing to look to a host of other disciplines and interdisciplinary fields, either for theoretical highs, critical capacity building, or that contemporary holy grail, 'relevance and impact'. Not least because many of these—sociology and social theory, science and technology studies, cultural studies—are themselves heavily imbued with the metaphysical stance.

Certainly, there are many practical organizational problems for OT to address. Contemporary public debates about the conduct of economic and organizational life attest to this. Over the last three decades, organizations have been associated with a growing uncertainty regarding their basic purposes and core tasks. One example concerns the rise of 'soft management' with its use of learning metaphors and storytelling to motivate staff, and work-related stress epidemics and change fatigue, which increasingly call into question the ability of modern organizations to balance the rhetoric of change and learning with a due regard to the limits of staff commitment and the basic requirements of tasks (Illouz, 2007). The financial crisis made this even more acute, and gave rise to an intense reconsideration of the contemporary norms and practices of managing and organizing (*Financial Times*, 2009; Phelps, 2009). Many taken-for-granted assumptions about the efficacy and effectiveness of contemporary management theory and practice were put into question. The ethos and techniques advocated and taught in business schools did not escape unscathed from this period of critical reflection either (*The Economist*, 2009). Interestingly, the voice of OT was notably absent from this intense public debate, posing some important questions: If OT has nothing to say about controversies affecting its core object—formal organization—then why might this be the case, and what can be done to resuscitate it, and therefore revive its explanatory reach and practical relevance?

It was not always thus, so how has the current impasse arisen, and what can be done to overcome it? As we have suggested, one of the central hypotheses of the book is that OT's silence on matters of concern relating to its core object is in part a product of the way in which its predominant modes of theorizing have developed in the recent past. In large part, we find that the academic field of OT has fragmented into separate domains of micro, meso, and macro foci on organizations, and corresponding programmes of 'organizational behaviour', 'strategy, identity and culture', and 'power and institutional fields', with fewer and fewer attempts to think across levels or evaluate the practical difference and usefulness of concepts such as 'learning organizations', 'strategy-as-practice', and 'institutional entrepreneurship'. This book therefore constitutes an intervention into contemporary debates about OT, its purpose, object, and practical relevance. As indicated, the overall ambition of the book is to resuscitate the 'classical stance' in OT; to indicate what OT, as a practical science of organizing, can and should be doing in the present. It thus questions the defocusing of the organization and its inner workings that has been a result of intense problematizations and critical interrogations undertaken within OT over the last few decades. This defocusing has taken many guises: within-organization theories drawing on the discipline of economics, such as agency theory, for instance, which have reduced the organization to a nexus of contracts (e.g. Fama and Jensen, 1983); and within-organization theories drawing on economic sociology, the environments within which organizations arise, compete, and wither away, have come to be a major area of interest studied by organizational ecology (e.g. Hannan and Freeman, 1993). Finally, within more critically and philosophically inclined studies, organizations have been depicted as sources of repression and incarceration (e.g. Burrell, 1997), just as the very act and function of managing has been rendered illegitimate, no matter which practical ends it is designed to serve (e.g. Parker, 2002).

The rationale of the book is that OT at its outset was preoccupied with *organization*: its specific workings, tasks, formal conditions, and management (e.g. Taylor, [1911] 1998; Barnard, [1938] 1968; Roethlisberger and Dickson, 1939; Simon, 1947; March and Simon, 1958; Lawrence and Lorsch, 1967; Follett and Graham, 1995). In contrast to this, in recent times, a range of frequently metaphysical problematizations have shifted the areas of concern towards, inter alia, liquidification (processes, flows, innovation, bottom-up spontaneous organizing, etc.), externalization (networks, user involvement, co-creation), and a host of, frequently epochal, 'social' constructions ('risk society', discourse, power, identity), all of which have the effect of 'decentring' organization in favour of its 'outside'. At the same time, theoretical interest has gathered around ever more esoteric topics, arcane theories, and an almost promiscuous celebration of 'difference'—often underpinned by a moral and political agenda aiming to insert, produce, or pave the way for resistance to 'positive' organizational and managerial knowledge (Lopdrup-Hjorth, 2013, 2015).

On the one hand, these developments have been a huge scholarly success, since several kinds of disciplines and perspectives have been brought to bear on the study of organization. On the other hand, however, questions and doubts have arisen regarding the general implications these developments have had for OT. For instance, the question of whether organization scholars today have anything to say that has relevance outside of small groups of specialized, like-minded academic peers has been raised (Alvesson, 2013). This unease and self-doubt has, more specifically, also become manifest by questioning whether the preceding decades' theoretical preoccupation with discourse, power, and subjectivity, and the like provides a fertile point of departure for addressing contemporary key economic and organizational questions that became, as we suggested earlier in this Introduction, ever more pressing, in light of the financial and sovereign debt crises (Prichard and Mir, 2010).

Accordingly, it becomes necessary to question whether and to what extent contemporary OT has run out of steam? Does it have anything of relevance to say? How, more specifically, has the current impasse come about? And what can be done to revitalize OT as a practical and theoretical endeavour? The increasing abstraction and fragmentation of OT has had the effect of distancing OT from its core object, not least by dissipating its practical analytic focus. This book therefore seeks to contribute to the goal of reviving OT through a reappreciation of the heritage of OT as a practical science: 'the classical stance' referred to earlier in this Introduction. This historical focus is double-edged. For not only does the project seek to revive OT through reconnecting it with its own past practice, it also seeks to indicate how the historic products of that orientation may still have some traction for contemporary organizational problems. After all, recent management discourse, particularly its more populist variants, has made much of the irrelevance of past theory and practice to present and future challenges (Caulkin, 2008). This disdain for history was made most explicit, perhaps, in the norms animating the business process re-engineering movement, which advocated a 'clean sheet' approach to managing and organizing, and where past practice was simply deemed an anachronism (Hammer and Champy, 1993). Indeed, a pervasive assumption that past practice is simply a deadweight on the future is seen as having contributed to some of the major problems associated with contemporary practices of managing and organizing. This idea of mining the past of OT and the devices it has elaborated in order to deal with current and future challenges is no mere proposition. It can be witnessed in action, in the present, if one cares to look; a point we will return to throughout the book.

We begin by outlining in detail what we mean by the classical and metaphysical stances in OT, why the former has gradually lost out to the latter as the dominant mode of doing OT, and why this is significant. In Chapter 1,

'The Idea of a "Classical Stance" in Organization Theory', we introduce the idea of a 'classical stance' and provide examples of this attitude or comportment 'in action'. We note, in so doing, for instance, that the early writers on organizations and management were typically practising managers, executives, or consultants themselves, or closely associated with the practicalities of organization. In this sense, OT took off as a practical science of organizing, developing a number of tools (conceptual, technical, ethical, and so forth) that were largely shaped in relationship to the core object of study—formal organization. For various reasons, these tools are now treated as predominantly historic artefacts with little to no traction or raison d'être in the present. In line with this, the history of OT is often portrayed as a narrative of theoretical progress, whereby the important but relatively unsophisticated, narrowly focused, and instrumental bootstrapping efforts of the early pioneers have been followed, progressively, by ever more sophisticated understandings of organization and organizing. In Chapter 1, we dispute this assessment and the dismissal of classical OT that it entails, pointing instead to the latter's enduring significance and relevance to the present when viewed as a *stance*. In Chapter 2, '"Outside Organization": The Idea of a "Metaphysical Stance" in Organization Studies, we address the rise of a 'metaphysical stance' in OT, and the concomitant argument that the object of OT, formal organization, is both conceptually and empirically untenable. Clearly, as we argued earlier in this Introduction, stances can encompass a wide range of theoretical vernaculars, so we should not expect the metaphysical stance in organization studies to be identifiable through a shared language, set of beliefs, or normative commitments, for example. At first sight, it seems hard to pinpoint any such shared deportment or attitude within the field of organization studies, broadly defined. And yet, as we will argue, such a shared comportment or attitude can be discerned if one is predisposed to look for the clues as to its existence. One such clue, we suggest, lies in the idea, implicit in much contemporary scholarship in organization studies, that one can get a better purchase on the intelligibility of matters organizational by looking beyond 'organization'; that what was once deemed to lie 'outside organization', as its margins, contingent context, or backdrop, for example, is now deemed central or constitutive to an understanding of what 'organizational life' is all about. It is this focus on the 'outside' or 'extrinsic vantage point' that provides us with some important clues for the presence of a shared intellectual deportment, attitude, or stance within organization studies which is beginning to surface, one we describe as 'metaphysical' in orientation. Having outlined the key characteristics of this shared attitude and established its provenance within contemporary organization studies, we then proceed to examine the implications of such a 'metaphysical stance' for the enterprise of analysing, and, indeed, performing, organization, comparing and contrasting this with the 'rival' classical stance introduced in Chapter 1. In Chapter 3, 'Metaphysical Speculation in Organizational Theorizing: On the Lost Specification of "Change"', we address one of the most pervasive symptoms of the metaphysical stance: the continuous reference to 'change' as an indisputable ontological premise. The notion of 'change' has become ubiquitous in contemporary organizational discourse. On the one hand, change is represented as an organizational imperative that increasingly appears to trump all other concerns. On the other, change is addressed as an abstract, generic entity that can be theorized, categorized, evaluated, and acted upon without further specification. The chapter investigates the way 'change' is addressed and evaluated in four central academic traditions within the field of OT—the organizational development (OD) tradition, the emergent change tradition, the strategic change tradition, and the critical management tradition—and argue that all four traditions view 'change' as a fact beyond dispute, but differ only in relation to the way 'change' should be evaluated and managed. We argue that none of the four schools of thought take measures to empirically specify the notion of change, but rather can be seen to advance their arguments from the terrain of a metaphysical stance. We also argue that their combination of absolutism and abstraction has some unfortunate consequences for the precise assessment and practical management of particular organizational changes. Based on rereadings of two classic, but partially forgotten, contributions within OT—the work of Wilfred R. Bion on group assumptions, and the work of Wilfred Brown and Elliott Jaques on 'requisite organisation'—we suggest that contemporary discussion of organizational change could benefit considerably from regaining a lost specificity; an empirical grounding in the detailed description of content, purpose, and elements of change as a prerequisite for any normative appraisal or critique. In other words, it should adopt the classical stance to formal organization.

In Chapter 4, 'Metaphysical Speculation in Organizational Theorizing: On the Expressivism of "Exploration"', we depart from James March's (1991) famous paper, wherein he argued that establishing a requisite and ongoing balance between what he termed 'exploration' and 'exploitation' is a key facet of organizational survival and flourishing. For March, neither capacity can be ignored, or indeed privileged, in and of itself on general or a priori grounds, as both are necessary and their combination in practice is crucial. In the chapter we suggest that, within much contemporary organizational theorizing that has adopted a metaphysical stance, there is a pronounced tendency to ignore his basic premise and to treat 'exploration' as something approximating to an 'expressivist' ideal, by which we mean that the capacities, dispositions, and 'values' routinely huddled together under this heading—innovation, disruption, dissonance, entrepreneurship, and so forth—have been allotted a *moral* primacy over and above, and indeed, in basic opposition to, those capacities and dispositions March labelled 'exploitation'. This tendency to moralize organizations through the prism of 'exploration' resides not simply in popular and populist management thinking—that work which most readily approximates to a 'commentariat' brew, where a pre-commitment to certain norms (liberty, flexibility, improvisation, and so forth) leads to a denunciation of bureaucratic forms of organizing—but it also has its counterpart in critical denunciations of that theorizing, and of the organizational forms it seeks to privilege, namely, 'post-bureaucracies'. However, this denunciation does not depart from a disinterested assessment of the capacity of such post-bureaucratic forms to effectively combine exploration and exploitation in the manner suggested by March, but rather from an assessment of the failure of such forms to embody the ideals of exploration fully enough. The moral ideals themselves are not problematized, nor is the primacy accorded to them questioned. Instead, post-bureaucracies are accused of surreptitiously enhancing 'exploitation' and thus of not giving full expression to the norms of 'exploration' as they were claimed so to do. In what follows, we investigate this contemporary tendency to privilege 'exploration' over 'exploitation', and examine some of the consequences of this shift of emphasis, not least the resurfacing of a sort of 'one best way of organizing' that it inaugurates. Chapter 5, 'Task and Purpose as (Continuing) Core Concerns', focuses on the gradual occlusion of two key concepts in the canon of formal organizational analysis: 'purpose' and 'task'. For practitioners of the 'classical stance' in OT, in order to understand the virtues and problems of a particular organization, and to assess the form and necessity of managerial action, it was considered absolutely crucial to address the organization's basic purpose or core task. Without a clear understanding of its task, an organization was deemed to lose its ability to realistically assess the strengths and weakness of its inner arrangements and the threats and opportunities posed by 'the environment' in which it existed. Reflecting a wider trend in the social sciences, the field of organization studies has increasingly adopted a metaphysical stance to guide and frame its analyses of life and dynamics in organizations. Where classic organizational analyses would describe organizations in terms of core objects such as 'purpose', 'task', and 'coordination', contemporary organization studies emphasize, much like other social science disciplines, broader topics such as 'network', 'identity', and 'change'. The chapter argues that this altered focus and vocabulary is accompanied by a diminished ability to specify and intervene in the practical reality of organizations. It further argues that a discipline's core objects are not anachronisms to be discarded, but crucial devices for specifying reality in ways that have proven to be practically relevant in the past and still are. In Chapter 6, 'Authority and Authorization', we seek to rehabilitate the concept of 'authority' within organization studies, indicating, in much the same way as we did in relation to 'task', the centrality of the concept to organizational analysis as a practical science. After all, within organizations of all descriptions, authority and authorizing relationships continue to be of the utmost practical importance. Indeed, it is difficult to think of a system of effective coordination where authority is absent. This exercise in recovery is necessary in no small part, we argue, because the contemporary disavowal of the importance of authority both as a key concept within organization studies and, more significantly, as a constitutive element of formal organization per se, has some clear and present dangers. We shall have cause to specify these throughout the chapter, when we discuss particular cases where organizing without authority is attempted or encouraged, or where clear lines of authority are absent or such lines are tangled or blurred. In specifying the importance of authority along both intellectual and practical axes, we will stress once again the significance of *formality*. For many scholars of organization formality is a dirty word or a fraud. For us, though, as for the practitioners of the 'classical stance' we refer to, formality and formalization is central to understanding and performing organization. If that centrality is denied, and, as a result, there are no written or otherwise explicitly recognized or prescribed limits to work roles in organizations (i.e. no duly constituted *authority*), for instance, then clearly no one will really know what decisions they are authorized to make. Such a condition is unlikely to approximate to a sunny upland of enhanced freedom, creativity, innovation, and performance, but rather to a stressful and anarchic 'state of nature' (Brown, 1965a; Stinchcombe, 2001). More significantly, perhaps, the purposes for which the organization is instituted are unlikely to be met. Formal organization, in a very real sense, will not exist without duly constituted, and thus clearly defined, authority. In the concluding chapter, 'Comportment and Character in Formal Organization and Its Analysis', we provide a summary and overview of the arguments that have been made in the foregoing chapters, and indicate why we regard revitalizing the 'classical stance' as an important and significant endeavour within the field of OT and, indeed, in the world of formal organization.

1

The Idea of a 'Classical Stance' in Organization Theory

Introduction

In a number of general accounts of the history of management and organization theory (OT), it is customary to arrange the many, diverse contributions into a singular (almost teleological) narrative, charting the unfolding of an increasingly complex and sophisticated analysis of organization and organizing—what Bryson (1986) termed, in another context, the 'essential copy' (Wren, 2005; Robbins et al., 2006; Greenberg and Baron, 2008).[1] Departing, more often than not, from the mutually independent work of Frederick Winslow Taylor and Max Weber and their respective interests in the effective management of labour, on the one hand, and the ethos of bureaucratic office holding, on the other, the first port of call in the historical tour is what is termed 'classic management theory' (Perrow, 1979) or 'classic organization theory' (Shafritz and Ott, 2001). In this tradition, a disparate group of figures, including, for instance, Henri Fayol and Lyndall Urwick, but also Mary Parker Follett and Chester Barnard (as 'hinges' between the so-called 'scientific management era' and the 'social person era') (Wren, 2005: 321), are represented as seeking to formulate and systematize a repertoire of basic or 'universal' principles to be applied to and in organizations. One common feature of their very

---

[1] The presence of the ideal of the 'essential copy' within organization studies, as elsewhere in the human sciences, is evidenced by the dynamic of theoretical achievement—the triumphalist progression towards increasing theoretical sophistication and verisimilitude. This takes many forms within the field and is not restricted to any particular 'systemic' theoretical vernacular (Marxian, Luhmannian, Habermasian, or Giddensian, for instance). The manner in which the currently popular and influential neo-institutional theory (NIT) attempts to 'cover all bases', as it were, by bringing unto itself 'discourse', 'materiality', 'affect', and so on and so forth to bolster its explanatory reach, is, we suggest, precisely indicative of its fidelity to the ideal of 'the essential copy'. Each advance of NIT—whether through taking a discursive or material 'turn', for instance—consists of a presumed removal of an obstacle between it and the essential copy: the perfect theoretical capturing or rendering of organizational reality.

different work is frequently highlighted: that their point of departure is from 'within' organization, rather than from one of the classic academic disciplines, as they all, in one way or another, had direct, practical experience of management and organization from their positions as business executives, directors, or consultants (O'Connor, 2012). More often than not, their practical focus is considered a weakness when seen through a critical academic lens, for example, as it seems to indicate a restricted vision imposed by the dictates of an inherently 'managerialist' perspective.[2] Indeed, the so-called classical theorists are often portrayed as a group of practitioners with scientific aspirations who took an important step towards understanding aspects of organization, but one characterized by a narrow, instrumental outlook and a certain naivety in their eagerness to formulate so-called universal principles. These limitations are linked primarily to their focus on organizational effectiveness, which is deemed to inhibit their capacity to exercise sufficient 'distance', and/or to pay due attention to the broader social, cultural, economic, and political landscape within which organizations exist and organizing and managing is undertaken:

> Like Michels and Weber, most of them took a limited view of organizations as being merely administrative hierarchies with well-defined tasks to perform, and they thought they were creating rigorous, scientific theories [...]. But unlike Michels and Weber they used the plain language of managers, they rarely attempted to compare organizations from different areas, and they focused their thinking on how to make organizations more effective.   (Starbuck, 2003: 167)

The focus upon effectiveness is frequently viewed as indicative of a simplistic understanding of organizations as formal and rational entities that reflected the inherently managerial preoccupation of the writers in question:

> It seems clear that the rational-model approach uses a closed-system strategy. It seems also clear that the developers of the several schools using the rational model have been primarily students of performance or efficiency, and only incidentally students of organizations [...] The rational model of an organization results in everything being functional—making a positive, indeed an optimum, contribution to the overall result.   (Thompson, 1967: 6)

In line with such characterizations, the history of OT portrayed in many texts turns out to be a narrative of theoretical progress, whereby the relatively

---

[2] Similar criticisms were also directed at the work of members of the Tavistock Institute of Human Relations (Child, 1969; Silverman, 1970; Fox, 1971). In his review of Miller and Rice's (1967) *Systems of Organization* in *The Sociological Review*, for example, Duncan (1968: 262) writes of the authors' 'isolation from academic sociology and the restrictive vision imposed by previous consultancy assignments', and concludes that: '[I]t is important to distinguish between sociological problems and the problems with which managers are preoccupied. Excessive involvement with the latter inhibits clarification of the former.'

unsophisticated, narrowly focused (and narrowly instrumental), bootstrapping efforts of the early pioneers have been followed, progressively, by ever more sophisticated understandings of organization and organizing.

In this chapter, indeed throughout this book, we dispute the basic tenets of this characterization of classical OT, and, in so doing, attempt to reconstruct understanding of this received term. At the heart of our argument lie the following propositions: that OT, viewed as a *practical science of organizing*, has at its disposal a number of tools (conceptual, technical, ethical, and so forth) that it has largely shaped itself in relationship to its own core object—formal organization; that for various reasons, these tools are now treated as predominantly historic artefacts with little to no traction or raison d'être in the present; that this assessment is primarily based on a set of programmatic commitments which have had the effect of dissolving or disappearing organization studies' core object—formal organization—and of depriving the discipline of access to some significant and useful 'organizational reality devices'[3] that could indeed have traction in the present; and that a suitably contextualized re-engagement with, and reappropriation of, the resources of 'classical organization theory' may well serve to enhance the relevance and reach of contemporary organization studies both intellectually and practically. In this chapter, we seek to advance this argument by elaborating upon the idea of the 'classical stance' in OT outlined in the Introduction to this book. In particular, through an engagement with the work of a number of acknowledged 'classical organizational theorists' we seek to indicate that the classical stance in OT can be seen to entail, inter alia, a pragmatist call to undertake experience, an antithetical attitude to 'high' or transcendental theorizing, an admiration for practical scientific forms of enquiry that are relevant to and useful for the conduct of organization—furnishing *a practico-organizational discipline*—and, relatedly, an ethical focus on organizational effectiveness born of a close connection to 'the work itself' and 'the situation at hand'. Deploying the term classical organization theory in this way, to refer to a stance, attitude, or comportment, and an associated persona that bears it, we highlight this particular approach to formal organization as one with a distinctively practical focus and ethos, that differs considerably from many contemporary approaches, not simply in organization studies, but also in sociology and

---

[3] Clearly, these 'organizational reality devices' (one classic example of which—the heuristic of a 'primary task' as developed in the work of the Tavistock Institute of Human Relations—is discussed later in this chapter and is also a key focus of Chapter 5) will inevitably bear the imprint of the contexts in which they were elaborated, and the specific cluster of concerns to which they were addressed. However, this does not mean that they are anachronisms with no potential to address pressing matters of contemporary organizational concern. Just as, according to Dewey (1938), you can't know a priori how property should be distributed after a social upheaval, so you can't know in advance what you might need to draw upon or where you might need to find it to generate an appropriate solution to a pressing organizational problem. Ultimately, this is an empirical matter.

other branches of contemporary social and human science ostensibly focusing on and interested in organizational life, for instance (a point we return to in some detail in Chapter 2).

The Practical Focus of Classical Organization Theory

The classical tradition in OT is often seen to be composed of a disparate group of figures including, among others, Henri Fayol (1841–1925), Mary Parker Follett (1868–1933), Chester Barnard (1886–1961), and Lyndall Urwick (1891–1983). As we indicated in the Introduction to this chapter, one common feature of their work is that it departs from within organizational life, rather than from academia per se. In other words, the classicists were working within the orbit of that which they also sought to study, and it was from this direct practical confrontation that they pursued ambitions of identifying and clarifying principles of good administration and management. In their different ways, they regarded organization and management as crucial for both industrial and societal life to thrive. They also saw a need for establishing 'administration' (the umbrella term deployed at the time) as a practical science in order to cultivate a broader recognition of its importance. For them, good administration was not an issue exclusive to the operation of an enterprise in a technically or instrumentally efficient manner, but a key ethico-political concern (O'Connor, 2012). Parker Follett's principle of 'dynamic administration'—and the issues of authority, power, leadership, conflict, and conciliation that flowed in its wake—for instance, was not something she considered of significance only to business:

> It is a part, and a significant part, of the wider field of human government. Business men have a great deal to learn from organized activities outside their own firms and industries, and other branches of human organization can learn much from what is best in business. The world of to-day needs new relationships among its groups.   (Quoted in Metcalf and Urwick, [1940] 2013: 29)

In this way, the classical scholars were not simply narrow instrumental practitioners, but posited a connection between sound organizational practice and societal thriving.

In the pursuit of 'general principles of administration', the classical scholars were trying to formulate concepts and theories about organization and management, but were also aware of the inherent limits of this attempt. Even though the scholars differed in their focus and in the manner in which they wrote, their work was characterized by a constant interweaving between the attempt to put forward general principles of organization and a concern for discussing the practical limitations or considerations associated with such general principles. Consider, for example, the following quote from Fayol's discussion of the role of plans in administration:

> No one disputes the usefulness of a plan of action. Before taking action it is most necessary to know what is possible and what is wanted. It is known that the absence of plans entails hesitation, false steps, untimely changes of direction, which are so many causes of weakness, if not disaster in business [...] But there are plans and plans; there are simple ones, complex ones, concise ones, detailed ones, long- or short-term ones; there are those studied with meticulous attention, those treated lightly; there are good, bad and indifferent ones. How are the good ones to be singled out from among the others? Experience is the only thing that finally determines the true value of a plan, i.e. on the services that it can render to the firm, and even then the manner of its application must be taken into account. There is both instrument and player. Nevertheless, there are certain broad characteristics on which general agreement may be reached beforehand without waiting for the verdict of experience.
>
> (Fayol, [1949] 1955: 44)

On the one hand, it was assumed that administration rested upon and embodied a set of basic principles that could be articulated and systematized into a 'theory of administration'. On the other, the classic scholars were cautious about crude generalizations. In their texts, they gave numerous examples of the manner in which basic principles cannot be uniformly and uncritically imposed across organizations, but that careful analysis of the specific administrative arrangement and situation in which they are to obtain is required so that such principles might be applied appropriately. They generally agreed that organizations should be understood as cooperative systems, and that the division and coordination of work among those employed in an organization forms the key principle for this cooperation to work:

> Every large-scale or complicated enterprise requires men to carry it forward. Wherever many men are thus working together the best results are secured when there is a division of work among them. The theory of organization, therefore, has to do with the structure of co-ordination imposed on the work-division units of an enterprise. (Gulick, [1937] 1977: 3)

At the same time, it was emphasized that the specific ways in which work shall be divided and coordinated is essentially pragmatic: 'Does the division work out? Is something vital destroyed or lost?' (ibid.: 5). This is not something that can be decided simply by accident or once and for all, but should be determined through intelligent, persistent and organized effort. While there will always be more than one opinion about the way to organize work—some managers prefer to work and think about such matters primarily top-down whereas others approach it bottom-up—it is important to keep in mind the fact that 'the problem of organization' must be approached from both top and bottom in order to balance the risks of each of the two approaches:

> Those who work from the top-down must guard themselves from the danger of sacrificing the effectiveness of the individual services in their zeal to achieve a model structure at the top, while those who start from the bottom, must guard themselves from the danger of thwarting co-ordination in the eagerness to develop effective individual services. (Ibid.: 11)

Some authors advocated approaching 'the problem of organization' as a 'technical problem' (Urwick, [1937] 1977), that is, as a matter of using the principles developed inductively from the study of human experience of organization to help govern organizational arrangements of different kinds. Others used the notion of 'structural principles of organization' to emphasize that organization is not reducible to the administration and management of persons, but concerns the collective job of an organization and the coordination of all effort necessary to this end: 'The job as such is therefore antecedent to the man on the job, and the sound co-ordination of these jobs, considered simply as jobs, must be the first necessary condition in the effective coordination of the human factor' (Mooney, [1937] 1977: 92). The choice of these terms—'technical' and 'structural'—may explain why the classic scholars were later thought of as subscribing to a 'machine metaphor' of the organization: advocating a strong belief in standardization and requiring little creativity and intuition from the individual worker (Morgan, 2005). However, it is important to recognize that those terms were used to emphasize the importance of approaching organization as a complex whole comprising an arrangement of relations between parts, while, at the same time, insisting that practical organization is also an art and a craft. A closer look at one of the tools of this 'technical' but, at the same time, pragmatic and intuitive approach, the organizational chart, may be useful in this regard.

While Taylor and the scientific management movement had focused attention on analysing and planning individual job elements and the matching of specific employees to specific tasks, the discussion of the emerging administrative science revolved around the broader question of division and coordination of work in the organization as a whole. The organizational chart was a key tool for illustrating and thinking through this relationship. In today's terms, the organizational chart served as a 'reality device', that is, as a tool for outlining the organizational as a specific practical whole of parts and providing a map of the proximal relations and territories of each unit—in effect, their organizational reality (see footnote 3). Through the means of the organizational chart, the divisions and subdivisions of work, the lines of authority, and the channels of communication and accountability were to be presented: sometimes for the purpose of instructing new members about

	HEALTH DEPARTMENT	EDUCATION DEPARTMENT	POLICE DEPARTMENT	PARK DEPARTMENT	
	Director Assistant Directors	Superintendent Assistant Superintendents	Chief Assistant Chiefs	Commissioner Assistant Commissioners	
CLERICAL AND SECRETARIAL SERVICE — Director	Private secretaries Stenographers File clerks Clerks Messengers	Private secretaries Stenographers File clerks Clerks Messengers	Private secretaries Stenographers File clerks Clerks Messengers	Private secretaries Stenographers File clerks Clerks Messengers	
FINANCE DEPARTMENT — Director	Budget officer Accountants Purchasing officer Statisticians	Budget officer Accountants Purchasing officer Statisticians	Budget officer Accountants Purchasing officer Statisticians	Budget officer Accountants Purchasing officer Statisticians	Other finance activities including tax administration, controlling accounts, etc.
	Personnel manager Lawyer	Personnel manager Lawyer	Personnel manager Lawyer	Personnel manager Lawyer	
ENGINEERING DEPARTMENT — Director	Engineers Architects Repair force Janitors	Engineers Architects Repair force Janitors	 Repair force Janitors	Engineers Architects Lendacape staff Repair force Janitors	
	Physicians Dentists Nurses Psychologists	Physicians Dentists Nurses Psychologists	Physicians Psychologists		
	Bacteriologists Inspectors	Laboratory assistants Gardeners Classroom teachers Special teachers Librarians Recreation leaders Playground supervisors Traffic supervisor	Crime laboratory staff Police school staff Uniformed force Detective force Traffic force Jail staff Mounted force Veterinarian	Plant laboratory staff Gardeners Recreation leaders Playground supervisors Park police Traffic force Zoo staff veterinarian	
	Switchboard operator	Switchboard operator	Communications staff	Switchboard operator	
MOTORIZED SERVICE — Supt.	Motorized service	Motorized service	Motorized service	Motorized service	

Vertical network — Purpose departments
Horizontal network — Process departments

Figure 1.1 From Gulick's 1937 [1977] chapter, Notes on the theory of organization, showing the interrelations of different departments in a city administration.

the existing formal structure of the specific organization for which they worked (Figure 1.1); at others, for identifying potential problems or possible alternative forms of organizing, for example, in terms of span of control or degree of specialization (Figure 1.2).

Figure 1.1 is taken from Gulick's ([1937] 1977) chapter 'Notes on the theory of organization', and shows the interrelations of different departments in a city administration: just as coordination is a crucial concept—a core object— in classic OT, so is 'purpose', as Gulick calls it. The chart shows how this particular city administration has four coexisting purposes: to deliver health care, to educate, to police, and to maintain city parks, and that each of the distinct departments involved in securing these purposes is equipped with the type of staff needed for accomplishing them. It also shows how the purposes are dependent on a number of general services from other departments—the

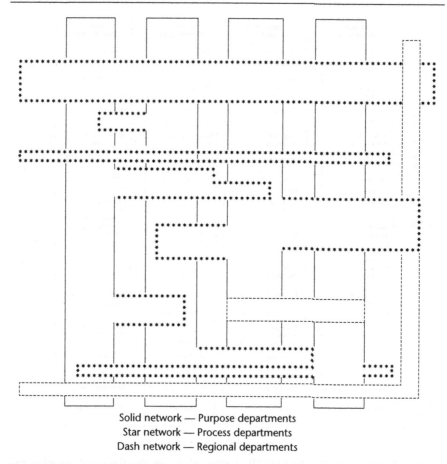

Solid network — Purpose departments
Star network — Process departments
Dash network — Regional departments

Figure 1.2 From Gulick's 1937 [1977] chapter, Notes on the theory of organization, showing the fabric of organizational interrelations.

secretarial service department, the finance department, the engineering department, and the motorized service department—and where their activities intersect.

In a subsequent chart, Gulick shows how such departments, established on quite different principles, may be 'woven together to form a single fabric' as he formulates it, by carefully arranging different ways of working together across units and divisions. In this way, the chart was not only meant as a formal representation, but also as a resource for conducting analyses and thought experiments concerning the role of different units and divisions of the organization and how they could be tied together in relevant ways. The organizational chart, it was argued, permitted the viewer 'to seize at a glance, better than we could with a long description, the organization as a whole' (Fayol, [1937] 1977: 106). It also served to 'bring out major questions and considerations which arise in the practice and theory of organization' (Gulick, 1937 [1977]: 20). One consideration could, for instance, be: Is there any advantage in placing specialized services like private secretaries or filing clerks in each department as part of a cross-unit team, or should they be located in a specialized unit and work from there? The act of visualizing organization in terms of functions, relationships, coordination, and lines of command was not about providing a 'blueprint' for the organization, but about establishing a resource for pragmatically describing, analysing, and balancing organization as a whole of parts.

For the classical scholars, the problem of organization was both a scientific and practical question. The ambition was to develop and promote a practical science of organizing in which administrative phenomena could be documented and analysed using 'standard nomenclature and rational concepts' (ibid.: 194). This would provide explanations of phenomena and events and thereby inform the practical arts of organization and management, which often failed 'to take into account all the elements of the situation as a whole' (Barnard, [1938] 1968: 290). It was also recognized that a scientific interest in organization would have to be anchored in rich knowledge of organizational practice—in organization as a way of life—without attempting a full rendering of the specific circumstances: '[T]here is required in order to manipulate the concrete a vast amount of knowledge of a temporary, local specific character, of no general value or interest, that it is not the function of science to have or to present and only to explain to the extent it is generally significant' (ibid.: 291). Rather than positioning themselves clearly as 'scientists' vis-à-vis practitioners or the other way round, the classic scholars described their work and interests as being located at the intersection of science and practice. They were presenting concepts, axioms, and arguments, but also giving numerous concrete examples and pointing to practical questions and contingencies that would help determine how one principle or the other should be concretely employed depending on the circumstances. In this, the classic scholars were not rejecting scientific methods and concepts but constantly treating them as part of an organizational casuistry.

Writing not simply from practice to theory or vice versa, the classicists sought to articulate organization and management as a 'practical science': a systematic gathering and analysis of practical experience and wisdom not easily placed within the dichotomies of basic/applied science or theory/practice. Instead, OT emerged in the writings of the classic scholars as an amalgam of practical and scholarly activity, standing out as a self-contained and designated area and discipline alongside other fields such as psychology, sociology, and economics. Their effort to develop concepts, tools, and principles for an emerging OT were not considered as essentially different from specifying and improving operational competence, but deeply associated with and supportive of a balanced, casuistic managerial practice. Likewise, they did not operate with the dichotomy of 'practice' versus 'theory', but considered conceptual and theoretical artefacts as means to nuanced organizational and managerial action.

This particular point can be further elaborated by a brief engagement with the work of Chester Barnard and Wilfred Brown, whose reputations in the field of OT are largely premised on their *theoretical* contributions. Barnard is routinely represented as an exemplary 'classicist' in conventional chronologies, whereas Brown—an experienced and successful manager, executive, minister of state, and organizational analyst, who rose to prominence in the field of organizational theory as a result of his involvement in the first major research project undertaken by the Tavistock Institute of Human Relations in the UK after the Second World War: the Glacier Project—only published his first monograph shortly after Barnard's death. Brown is therefore clearly outside the parameters of the 'classical canon', as conventionally understood. In addition, his work is, today, largely forgotten. Apart from both being successful executives who took on a remarkably extensive range of organizational responsibilities across private, public, and so-called 'third' sectors, what unites these two seemingly disparate organization theorists, we argue, is the stance they adopt to 'organization and management theory'. This stance is 'classical' in the manner indicated at the beginning of this section, not least in the sense that their 'theory' is nothing in the abstract; it needs to be seen in terms of the *practical* road travelled to reach it, and to which it is in turn directed, and its 'formative' purpose for those (including its authors) at whom it is aimed—those involved in the practical activity of organizing. Significantly, we argue, the 'stance' they adopt, and the concepts, maxims, and examples they elaborate, are useful and important today, without any need to update them. We build on this point, and further elaborate the notion of classical OT as a practical science of organizing, one with continuing relevance, by introducing two representatives of the classic stance—Chester Barnard and Wilfred Brown—and their reflections upon conducting organization theory as a practical science. We then briefly explore two particular organizational 'reality devices' elaborated by practitioners of the classical stance: Barnard's concept of 'purpose', and Miller and Rice's concept of 'the primary task'.

Organization Theory as a Practical Way of Life: Chester Barnard and Wilfred Brown

> One of the members of the Graduate School of Arts and Sciences calls it Machiavellian because we did try to influence behaviour . . . I thought that was the purpose of education.
>
> Chester Barnard

Fritz Roethlisberger, one of the authors of the canonical account of the Hawthorne experiments, *Management and the Worker*, once remarked that the organization theorist and practising manager, Chester Barnard, was 'the only executive in captivity who could not only run a successful organization, but could also talk intelligently about what he was up to in the process' (quoted in Wren, 2005: 321). Barnard, of course, figures large in accounts of the history of OT, not least as the originator of a theory of formal organization as a cooperative system—what John Kenneth Galbraith once described as 'the most famous definition of an organization'—in his *The Functions of the Executive*, one of the acknowledged classic texts of OT generally, and a key accomplishment of 'classical organization theory' in particular. In commentary on the text, much is made of Barnard's supposed surpassing of the concerns of the scientific management movement, and, indeed, of the so-called rationalistic theory of organization attributed to Henri Fayol, for instance, both of which are deemed important but inherently limited contributions to understanding 'organization' (Wren, 2005). The presumed superiority of Barnard's work in relation to its predecessors is therefore premised upon its being the first to offer 'a total theory of organization' (Andrews, 1968: x). The conventional building blocks for the history of OT as a progression towards 'the essential copy' that we alluded to in the Introduction to this chapter are, therefore, all in place. Barnard's work is a progression from what precedes it, its major contribution is to be represented in theoretical terms, and it is to be appraised not least in how systematically and closely the theory gets to the 'truth' of organization in its totality ('the essential copy').

While it would be ludicrous to suggest that Barnard is uninterested in matters of form, system, conceptual clarity, and explanatory reach, it is also quite clear that he is not interested in constructing a theoretical edifice in and of itself. Indeed, the clues to an alternative understanding of what his major work is doing can be discerned if one is disposed to look. In the preface to *The Functions of the Executive*, we find Barnard stating that one of the key motivations in writing the text was that 'nothing of which I knew treated of organization in a way that seemed to me to correspond either to my experience or to the understanding implicit in the conduct of those recognised as adept in executive practice...' (Barnard, 1968: xxviii). Experience, here, is crucial for Barnard, as Ellen O'Connor (2012: 114), for instance, has made clear: Barnard used writing as a means of recording, organizing, and testing his experience as a manager and an executive, and as a 'tool to explain his "mental processes"', and explore his organizational conduct, to himself. He particularly reacted to 'theorising' as an end in itself, and criticized those whose habitus devalued knowledge obtained from practical experience, particularly academics and intellectuals (Barnard, 1968: 301–22). While 'book learning' could be indispensable, it was not the be all and end all for Barnard.

Rather, 'local and personal knowledge of the everyday and commonplace matters' of organizational existence, which 'many people are unwilling to grant is knowledge at all' is 'absolutely indispensable for the acceptance and discharge of responsibility for all and any action, and the capacity for responsibility is a vital component in the execution of useful work' (Barnard, quoted in O'Connor, 2012: 114). Barnard set out to live this maxim in his own organizational conduct, seeking constantly to secure significant experience and to develop himself and his capacities through taking on an extraordinarily wide range of organizational roles and responsibilities in a variety of contexts.[4] As he put it, 'significant experience is secured largely by adapting one's self to varieties of conditions and by acquiring the sense of the appropriate in varieties of action'.[5] When once asked about his extensive and intensive professional obligations, Barnard replied 'Look, every one of these things I get connected with has two things: one is the immediate, practical, pragmatic question of what you can do...the second is, it's always a laboratory for me.' This was where he found out how things worked and, as he indicated, '[Y]ou have to be on the inside to do that' (ibid.). *The Functions of the Executive* is therefore not a theoretical text on organization, in the narrow sense of 'theory' as an objectifying epistemic pursuit. While the text does pertain to the genre of an academic treatise, its epistemology is voluntarist, in the sense that, on the one hand, it does not privilege the 'theory' format of what knowledge and opinion are like, and, on the other, it allots a crucial role to experience and volition;[6] in effect, Barnard adopts an indirectly *protreptic* method, one designed as much to form people as organizational persons—to develop 'organizational character'—as to inform them. Overall, Barnard rewrote the book sixteen times, and, as he stated, 'there is scarce a word that has not been thoroughly weighed', reworking it in effect throughout the course of his entire adult life. In one of his final interviews, held two months before his death in 1961, we find Barnard still revising the text, exhorting himself to test it against reality as he finds it, and appraising its reach and relevance for himself and for those similarly charged with 'co-ordinating and directing the activities of others'. *The Functions of the Executive*, as Ellen O'Connor (2012: 137) has persuasively argued, is a text 'that derives from

---

[4] In addition to leading New Jersey Bell Telephone from 1927, Barnard completed two terms as the head of the New Jersey Emergency Relief Administration during the Depression, and ran the United Services Organization (president for three years) and the Rockefeller Foundation (president for four years) among many other organizational roles and responsibilities.

[5] Here the similarities to Weber's work on the 'ethics of office', and, specifically, his focus on the conduct of life (*lebensführung*) in different life orders (*lebensordnungen*), also become apparent (du Gay, 2008). Whether Barnard was at all influenced by Weber's work is a moot point. However, it appears that he had read Weber in German (Wren, 2005: 313).

[6] We may detect something like this, of course, in ancient philosophy, as outlined by Hadot (2011); more contemporaneously, however, it can be traced in the stance adopted by the American pragmatists (Van Fraassen, 2002: 77 and 83).

and demonstrates the personal basis of organizational knowledge and the organizational basis of personal knowledge for Barnard personally'. For Barnard, organization was a choice of life, and in his major work, as well as the other modes of address through which he developed his thinking on this choice of life, such as his commencement speeches (O'Connor, 2013), he was concerned to indicate what such a choice entails, not least characterologically, and what dispositions and capacities it was necessary to cultivate in oneself if one was to live up to the demands of this particular vocation in a conscious and responsible, as well as efficient and effective manner.

Wilfred Brown on Organization and Judgement

> This book is not a theoretical one. It states a large number of concepts which may prove very useful to managers in ordering their daily work. Concepts are tools which enable people to think in a straight line about the problems they have to handle, so long as those concepts are reasonably well aligned to the situations with which we have to deal. If they are not well aligned those concepts direct our efforts to non-solutions, they confuse our thinking . . . (Note to self on line one: 'Purpose and Intention')
>
> Section entitled 'Concepts for Managers' (Marginal Note: 'Too general. Needs to start with an example')
>
> Wilfred Brown, Draft Notes for a Book to be entitled *The Grammar of Organization* ('Concepts Book'), 1977

Like Chester Barnard before him, Wilfred Brown was, as Alistair Mant succinctly put it, 'in the great tradition of pioneers of industrial practice, in staying within the problems, devising empirical solutions, and developing theory the while' (Mant, n.d.). Indeed, in his report on the draft manuscript of Brown's *Exploration in Management* for the publisher W. Heinemann, Professor Leonard Sayles of Columbia University explicitly linked Brown's work to Barnard's *The Functions of the Executive*, both in terms of content, and in relation to the stance adopted to the 'nature of on-going human organisation' (Sayles, 1960). Like Barnard, Brown could not stomach theorizing for its own sake, and tended to be similarly intolerant of what he considered the 'nonsense' on the topic of organization emanating both from academics and from people of ample organizational experience (Mant, n.d.).

For Brown, the 'customary view' within OT of bureaucracy as a dysfunctional mode of organizing was one such dogmatism, and he was at pains to indicate just how easy it was to slip into, and how much inner distance and self-discipline it took to avoid these sorts of trap, not least for practising managers (Brown, 1971: 114).

Brown's two major monographs, *Exploration in Management* (1965) and *Organization* (1971) are, as he indicated on many occasions, attempts to put down in writing everything he had learnt from his management and executive experience in industry and government. Experience is therefore at their heart, as it was also in the handwritten notes for his planned book, *The Grammar of Organization* (Brown, 1977), an excerpt from which was given as the epigraph for this section. Again, like Barnard, Brown used his writing and his numerous speaking engagements as ways of recording, organizing, and testing his experience of managing and organization, and as means of judging the adequacy of his own thinking and organizational conduct. Brown's monographs, articles, speeches, and television and radio programmes, circle the same terrain—analysing the nature of authority in an executive system, exploring the relationship of organization to work, assessing how managers should go about judging the performance of their subordinates—time after time, always with a view to enhancing practical understanding, and cultivating a conscious and responsible attitude to the matter of organization and management. As he noted at the outset of his planned text, *The Grammar of Organization*, 'this is not a theoretical book'. Rather, its concepts derive from a continuous engagement with experience and are aimed specifically at those in similar situations: those for whom 'organization' is a practical way of life. Thus, the intention is as much characterological as it is to enhance 'theoretical understanding'—in other words, and once again, to form as much as it is to inform. Continuous reflection on his own experience of organizing is the basis of Brown's writing. The books, which are remarkably similar, almost identical, in fact, in content and attitude, are designed, as Alistair Mant put it, to overcome a temptation, to re-emphasize the importance of a particular attitude, to conduct a real therapy, in order to change the life, not only the beliefs, of the interlocutor; the latter obviously includes Brown himself. The aim is clearly to form the mind of those engaged in organization, to teach it to recognize problems and methods of reasoning in a certain way, and thus to cultivate a particular attitude towards managing and organizing. Of crucial importance for Brown, as indeed for Barnard, is to be 'on the inside', because close and repeated proximity to 'the situation at hand' is a key component of the exercise of judgement, which both prize highly, not least because it is fundamentally concerned with decision-making where there is insufficient or ambiguous factual evidence (Brown, 1971). Principles and factual evidence are indeed important, but as assessment is required, practical experience becomes the soul of wisdom. For Brown as for Barnard, the hard work aimed at acquiring experience of 'the sense of the appropriate', and thus of learning to exercise responsible situational judgement, is crucial.[7]

---

[7] In a remarkable set of highly personal, and extraordinarily self-critical, unpublished typescripts concerning his own exercise of judgement, and written between February and September 1979, Brown recalls and describes in some detail a number of 'hard cases' he experienced at Glacier, from

Through the prism of Brown and Barnard's work, the now commonplace philosophical opposition between universalist deontology and consequentialism, and its 'organizational' manifestations in the seemingly mutually exclusive doctrines or principles of the right (*honestas*, or the 'human factor') and the useful (*utilitas*, or 'the production side'), make little to no sense. We can see the casuistical dissolution of such principled distinctions very clearly in the work of Brown (1971), for example when he considers the structuring and conduct of manager–subordinate relations within employment hierarchies.

For Brown (1965b: 308), all work, and thus all work roles, no matter how ostensibly routine or circumscribed, requires 'decision-making' by those performing it. He defines work as 'the totality of discretion which a member is expected to exercise, and the proscribed acts he must discharge, in carrying out the responsibilities of the role he occupies' (ibid.). By discretion, Brown refers to an act or course of action adopted by an organizational member in a specific role, where the policy set for that role leaves alternative courses of action from among which that member has to choose. By proscribed acts, Brown means an act or course of action performed by a member in undertaking their work role, where the policy set allows that member no choice. In framing employment work in this manner, Brown is keen to highlight that the main basis on which the assessment of the performance of such work is to be undertaken is how an organizational member uses experience, knowledge, and judgement in making decisions, rather than on the *apparent results* of their use of such experience, knowledge, and judgement. As he puts it:

> We too readily agree that chief executives should be assessed on the basis of the profit and loss account, that the factory manager should be solely assessed on the volume of output, or the civil servant on the speed with which they can introduce arrangements that put into practice a change in Government policy. But these achievements—profit, volume of output, speed—are the end results of processes that involve not only the quality of the decisions made . . . but also a host of other variables outside their control. It would be very convenient if these were objective parameters of the performance of people, but they are not. Many find this so distressing that they sometimes fail to face up to it and go on trying to assess the work done by subordinates or others on a quite unreal basis. The reason for their distress is that instead of the relatively easy task of looking, for example, at the output volume achieved by the factory manager and accepting the figures as an index of their performance they must, instead, take their whole experience of their performance over a period of time into account and use their own judgment in

the earliest days of his career until his departure to join the Labour government in the 1960s. In these notes to himself, he remorselessly puts his own organizational judgement and conduct under the microscope, indicating where, how, and why he failed to live up to the ideals he publically professed, and what he felt he should have done differently under the circumstances in question (Brown, 1979).

coming to a decision as to whether their performance is good, bad, or indifferent. Judging the performance of subordinates is, in a very real sense, hard work.

(Brown, 1974: 110–11)

This 'hard work' is a form of casuistical reasoning where practical judgement is crucial. The quality of assessment depends on judgements concerning the significance of situational factors. In the case of the chief executive, for instance, the profit and loss account is itself affected by variables outside the control of any one member of the organization, such as the state of the market, the changing costs of raw materials, changes in government policy, the decisions of the Board about such things as capital investment, and so on and so forth. The existence of these variables is obvious enough, so the question then is: Exactly how useful or practical is it to undertake assessment of a chief executive's performance in terms of financial results alone? For Brown (1971: 111), the answer is clear:

> This is an important example of fantasy thinking.... This particular fantasy can lead to organizations setting up 'profit centres' so that they can have what they think is a basis of assessment. Quantitative indices such as profit, output, volume of sales and so on, are very important, but in using them as the basis of an assessment of performance, it is essential to consider the other variables that have affected them, and to assess how far they are a function of a manager's performance.

Moreover, as Brown (1974: 112) continues, '[I]f one introduces the time element, the fallacy is compounded.' To the extent that profits are affected by the decisions of the chief executive, the effects virtually never show up during the year in which such decisions were made, and for which the profit and loss account is constructed. The chief executive may take decisions in one year. The results may not appear until several years later. The larger the organization, the longer the time span of the chief executive's discretion is likely to be. If it is decided to develop a new product line, for example, it may be some years before sales in volume result. In the intervening years the profit and loss account will include all the costs of a plan that has yet to introduce any revenue. How can it then be said that the chief executive's efforts can be assessed in terms of profits in those intervening years?

Brown (1974: 112–13) argues that:

> [F]allacious perceptions like this about how to assess an individual's work exist at all levels in employment hierarchies and are widespread in society. Factual results are very important, but they must be used intelligently. Their crude use as sole criteria of success not only results in injustice to individuals but can also bring about decisions that damage the future of companies.

However, he continues, if managers encourage their subordinates to discharge the tasks allotted to them by precisely cultivating and deploying their practical, situational judgement, in, for instance, deciding how best to distribute work among their own subordinates, how to devise new methods of obtaining results when normal methods have failed, how to keep things on schedule, how to deal with personnel difficulties, how to train people to do their jobs, how to match changes in the environment in which they work that no one foresaw with initiatives that nobody ordered them to take, then the fallacy can be avoided:

> [If] we realize that we have to judge subordinates on the way they use their judgment, then we will realize that *our* judgments of *their* work are based on experience over time and on our *use* of intuition and judgment. There is no easy formula. (Ibid.: 114)

For Brown, an effective and equitable assessment of a subordinate's performance must, of necessity, be mediated by a principle of specific judgement:

> It is only by considering a subordinate's work in this way that a manager can help him. It is no help to him to say: 'Your output has fallen, there must therefore be something wrong about your approach to running the factory and you must do better.' You can help him only by pointing to examples of errors or marginal errors of judgment, and to do that you must have a pretty extensive knowledge of the types of decisions that his work involves. (Ibid.: 114)

As with Weber (1994), with whom, alongside Barnard, he is often compared (see Kelly, 1968: ch. 10), Brown roots almost everything to *Fraglichkeit der situation* ('the uncertainty of the situation'). As Weber's work can be seen to reside within both a classical tradition of political judgement and an 'ethics of office' (du Gay, 2009), so too can Barnard and Brown's work be located within the classical stance of organizational theory as a *practical science of organizing*.

Organization Theory as a 'Practical Science'

Throughout this chapter we have argued that classical OT is best understood as a practical science—in the manner of ethics or medicine—one focused on the structured ways of arranging for the coordinated performance of tasks and thus on 'maintaining the organization in operation' (Barnard, 1968: 215–16). In making this case, we have also suggested that there is much to be gained for contemporary OT in reconceiving itself as a practical science of organizing in the manner of its classical antecedents, and thus in cultivating a renewed interest in a particular stance towards its own core object and 'canon' of concepts and tools, norms and techniques of conduct. In making this case, we find that we connect with some of the arguments articulated by Paul Adler (2009) in *The Oxford Handbook of Sociology and Organization Studies: Classical*

Foundations, but end up inflecting them in a rather different direction. Adler (2009: 7) argued that organization studies ignored its classical *sociological* foundations at its peril, not least, he suggested, because the latter 'provide us not only with paradigms for rigorous engagement with big issues, but also with powerful concepts for making sense of these kinds of issues'. The pertinence of the classical sociological heritage to the explanatory power, reach, and relevance of contemporary organization studies, he argued, was clear and present. We suggest that a reconnection with classical OT has a not dissimilar potential for the field of organization studies. Indeed, these twin moves can, to some extent, proceed hand in hand. However, there are points at which they clearly part company. While certain forms of classical sociology, not least that of Max Weber 'reconstructed' by Wilhelm Hennis (1988, 2000, 2009),[8] have considerable affinity with the programme for organization studies as a practical science that we have begun to articulate here, others operate in an entirely different register, and, as such, are not easily recuperable to such a programme.[9] Much as practising the sociology of science and working on natural science are not the same (they involve quite different tasks, and their respective 'facts', 'discovery' procedures, mechanisms of justification, and so on are therefore non-reducible, even if the boundaries between them can and do shift over time) (Collins, 1992), or undertaking contextual empirical history and philosophical history are different moves in different games (Fish, 1994; Pocock, 2004; Hunter, 2009a), so, too, conceiving of organization studies as a practical science of organizing necessitates exercising a degree of care when it comes to the appropriation of theories and concepts from other disciplines, such as sociology and social theory, for instance. To put it bluntly, while organization studies will undoubtedly continue to borrow and translate theories and concepts from other fields, if it is to approximate to a practical science in the manner we suggest, not just any old (or new) theory or concept will do. This is an important point, because the sorts of concepts appropriate

---

[8] Indeed, Hennis's (2009) collection of essays is entitled *Politics as a Practical Science*. In chapter 9, 'Political Science as a Vocation: A Personal Account', Hennis states how, in the 1950s, he finally got it: 'I had finally realized why in Göttingen the *Politica* volumes were shelved alongside books on equine distemper and the proper management of farmhands...politics was a...*practical science*...It was now clear to me why I so much disliked the new political science and its weakness for "theoretical" fashion...I have never been as impressed as their proponents have been with those "theories" that have flourished in my discipline, be they critical, system-theoretical, or communicative' (Hennis, 2009: 240–1).

[9] Many of the most powerful criticisms levelled at 'classic' OT, for example, have come precisely from those committed to certain forms of 'social explanation'. The practical orientation of much classic OT—the tool-making job it undertakes to assist organizations in engaging in more effective action, no matter what direction this may be inflected—often appears less than savoury ('amoral', 'instrumentalist', 'ideological'—think of various sociological critiques of scientific management, or indeed, its apparent antithesis, human relations) from the perspective of a stance committed to highlighting the social construction of organizational reality, the better to claim that a given state of affairs could have been and indeed can be otherwise.

to or requisite for the conduct of organizational analysis as a practical science differ considerably from several of those that have permeated many disciplines and interdisciplinary fields in the social sciences and humanities in recent years, not least as a result of the proliferation of what has become known as 'the moment of theory' (Hunter, 2006, 2007; du Gay and Vikkelsø, 2013).[10]

The shared attitude, deportment, or stance characteristic of this 'moment', which, as we shall suggest throughout this book, is largely 'metaphysical' in orientation, has had the effect, as an intellectual activity within the field of organization studies, of advancing the disappearance of its core object, 'formal organization'. In contrast to the 'metaphysical stance' characteristic of so much recent and ongoing theorizing within this field, we argue that a crucial concern of OT as a practical science is to develop a set of concepts that have a pragmatic reference to the situation at hand. In order to specify more precisely what we mean by this, we briefly introduce two particular concepts that exemplify this 'classical' stance.

Conceptual Tools for Organization

Many of the conceptual tools developed by practitioners of the classical stance in OT no longer loom large in contemporary discussions of organizational life. As we indicated in the introductory chapter, and elaborate further shortly, both mainstream and critical voices, consultant and academic, are preoccupied by different sorts of concepts and concerns, or so it would at first appear, to those enunciated by practitioners of the classic stance. Some 'classic' concepts have become little short of dirty words in many forms of organizational analysis, popular and critical (with the latter's mutual obsessions with 'empowerment', 'change', 'innovation', and so forth, though couched in diametrically opposed, and equally underdescribed, normative terms); concepts such as 'authority' and 'authorization', and 'command', 'office', 'hierarchy', and 'bureaucracy', for instance. In this section, we explore two 'concepts' (or organizational reality devices), not typically seen as having distinctive commonalities, yet sharing the idea that 'requisite', or 'effective and 'responsible', organization is something that can be put together or, in the contemporary idiom, 'assembled', even if 'requisite', 'effective', and

---

[10] Following Hunter (2006: 81), we suggest that the various intellectual developments referred to as the 'moment of theory' (which includes, most obviously, forms of 'structuralism' and 'post-structuralism') are unified neither by a common object, nor by a single or agreed upon theoretical language, but rather by a shared intellectual deportment or 'stance', albeit to differing degrees. This stance is sceptical towards empirical experience (in a more or less Kantian way), but also towards a priori formalisms, which it regards as foreclosing a 'higher'-level (transcendental) experience—and hence seeks to cultivate openness to 'breakthrough' phenomena of various sorts.

'responsible' are contingently understood in relation to the particular 'situation at hand'. Indeed, the two conceptual tools outlined—Barnard's concept of 'organizational purpose', and Miller and Rice's concept of 'the primary task'—share a number of family resemblances, with the latter being, in a certain sense, literally inconceivable without the pioneering work of the former. Let us begin with Chester Barnard once more, and certain formulations outlined most famously in his *The Functions of the Executive*.

For Barnard, the essence of an organization is its nature as a cooperative system, that is, an aggregation of people tied together around a particular goal or objective, though his preferred terminology is 'purpose'. Individuals have their own purposes (in fact Barnard saw 'purpose' as a defining feature of the personal too), yet what binds together people in organizations, or 'cooperative systems', is the addition of a common purpose; something which can only be achieved through an organized effort. Without a common purpose, an organization withers away and leaves people with only their personal purposes; a truth which is simultaneously self-evident and elusive. At the same time, the cooperative purpose has a dual nature as seen from each organizational member's point of view, comprising both a 'cooperative' and a 'subjective aspect', that is, the general purpose and the particular significance which the cooperative purpose has for each cooperating person. Those two aspects may, over time, drift apart to a point where individual understandings of the cooperative purpose are no longer overlapping:

> [A] purpose can serve as an element of a cooperative system only so long as the participants do not recognize that there are serious divergences of their understanding of that purpose as the object of cooperation. If in fact there is important difference between the aspects of the purpose as objectively and cooperatively viewed, the divergences become quickly evident when the purpose is concrete, tangible, physical; but when then the purpose is general, intangible and of a sentimental character, the divergences can be very wide yet not recognized.
>
> (Barnard, [1938] 1968: 87)

Accordingly, Barnard sees the purpose of an organization as something that must continually be framed and communicated in order to establish the very premise of the cooperative system with its few or many individual participants. Yet it is an inculcation that requires both a moral stance of the executive, since personal motives and organizational purpose can easily be mistaken for each other, and a constant analysis of the organization as a whole and its possibilities and limitations:[11] '[I]t should be noted that, once established, organizations

---

[11] '[W]e have to clearly distinguish between organization purpose and individual motive. It is frequently assumed in reasoning about organizations that common purpose and individual motive are and should be identical (. . .), this is never the case; and under modern conditions it rarely even appears to be the case' (Barnard, 1968: 89).

change their unifying purpose. They tend to perpetuate themselves; and in the effort to survive may change the reasons for existence. I shall later make clearer that in this lies an important aspect of executive functions' (ibid.: 89).

To Barnard, 'purpose' designated a crucial concern of the executive function, but also, in a broader sense, a defining premise of the organization as a distinct entity. The clarification of this, was, on the one hand, a continuation of the agenda successfully introduced by F. W. Taylor and the scientific management movement, that it is necessary to develop a clear understanding of the practical work to be undertaken in an enterprise and the role of management in guiding the accomplishment of this work; on the other, it also instantiated a conceptual and practical realization that the enterprise was not simply providing the physical and economical framework for the management of the worker, but that the relationship between activities, workers, foremen, and managers, for instance, constituted a larger cooperative system, which posed a wealth of managerial concerns not covered or perhaps even understood by advocates of scientific management. The notion of 'purpose' was not simply an addendum to Taylor's programme, but helped, conceptually and practically, to constitute the reality of an enterprise as an *organizational* reality or, as Barnard preferred it, as a 'cooperative system'—a reality surrounding and pervading the individual work tasks and employees, tying them together into an overarching 'purpose'. Through the insistence that the many activities and elements of an enterprise were to be understood as parts of a whole arising around a common purpose, Barnard established the 'organizational' or 'cooperative reality' as a distinct entity in its own right, which the executive must systematically address, monitor, and intervene into if necessary, and without which an enterprise is nothing but a more or less incidental collection of individuals.

Barnard's focus upon 'purpose' as a core characteristic of organizations was not unique. He borrowed from others (including, notably Mary Parker Follett), just as others have borrowed from him. Barnard's conception, though, had considerable resonance. In particular, it was to be revived in distinctive ways by two rather different, yet contemporaneous schools: 'the contingency theory' school, on the one hand, and 'the socio-technical systems school', on the other. In the first, as we indicate in more detail in Chapter 4, it would turn into something of a core axiom that there was no 'one best way of organizing' an enterprise, but that any organization must be structurally arranged and managed depending on a number of 'situational factors': for instance, its core technology, and, completely in line with the above argument, its basic task (Burns and Stalker, 1961; Lawrence and Lorsch, 1967). In the latter, the notion of 'primary task' acquired an even more pivotal role, and we will briefly seek to show how, for writers in this tradition, any statement of task objective became basically synonymous with a full statement, or precise specification, of the task itself.

In 1951, two members of the Tavistock Institute of Human Relations published an article in *Human Relations* entitled, 'Some Social and Psychological Consequences of the Longwall Method of Coalgetting' (Trist and Bamforth, 1951). As a contribution to social science of the time, it was unusual in two respects: it provided a detailed, precise description of the technical characteristics and operation of the partially mechanized coal-mining situations with which it was concerned, a level and type of specification which was considerably in advance of much that had gone before (or has since) in sociology and organization studies; and it stressed the interrelation between technology and social relations, for instance, in a way that challenged many of the then-prevailing conceptualizations of the place of 'the human factor' at work. As one of the authors reported in later work, the article basically argued that 'socio-psychological factors are in-built characteristics of work-systems rather than additional—and possibly optional—features to do with "human" relations' (Trist et al., 1963: xii). The focus, then, was on the organization as a 'socio-technical system'—rather than on one side or another of a set of a priori distinctions, between 'formal and informal', instrumental rationality and affective sociality, or 'production' and 'the human factor', for instance—and, while this designation did not feature in the original article, it came to explicitly frame a series of studies that followed in its wake.

For the next two decades, members of the Tavistock Institute followed the lead offered by Trist and Bamforth's paper to develop the notion of 'socio-technical systems' as the appropriate framework for analysing and intervening in organizational life, whether at the level of the enterprise conceived of as a 'whole', divisions and departments therein, or indeed the primary work group. The most significant empirical studies were those in coal mining (ibid., 1963) and in the textile industry in India (Rice, 1958).

The most notable applications of the socio-technical systems concept or 'tool' were in the empirical examination of work groups, but the 'tool' was also applied to analyses of the supervisor and management functions which coordinate the work of such groups, and of organizations as 'wholes' with particular reference to their 'structure' or 'design'. A key concept in such analyses was the heuristic of 'primary task' (a detailed discussion of the centrality of 'task' to 'formal organization' is the subject of Chapter 5). For the Tavistock writers, the identification of the primary task of an organization, or some part of it, has been the starting point for investigating, evaluating, and seeking to reform an organization's structure or design, and hence improve its effectiveness, in the light of its 'purpose': in Barnard's terms, the various task properties of the work it performs in relation to this purpose and the context(s) in which it operates.

The notion of a socio-technical system was initially conceived of as one 'that exists, and only can exist, by exchanging materials with its environment. It imports materials, converts them, and exports some of the results. Its outputs enable it to acquire more intakes, and the import-conversion-export process is the work the enterprise has to do to live' (Rice, 1958: 25). Taking inspiration from Wilfred R. Bion, a British psychoanalyst and one of the directors of the Tavistock Institute, the socio-technical systems writers suggested that these activities are all connected to a fundamental basic task: a 'primary task'. This primary task is the task an organization must perform in order to survive. Thus, for example, the primary task of a commercial airline can be defined as to make profit from the transport of passengers and/or cargo. However, the concept is not to be understood as a fixed, technical matter: 'The primary task is essentially a heuristic concept, which allows us to explore the ordering of multiple activities (and constituent systems of activity where these exist)' (Miller and Rice, 1967: 25). There might be organizations which have more than one primary task, e.g. (a university or a teaching hospital. Or, for example, a prison service in which three primary tasks of 'punishment, confinement, and rehabilitation' are all equally important (Rice, 1963: 189), entailing that these organizations have particular challenges in balancing the different tasks against each other or reconciling them. Moreover, the primary task(s) may change over time. For the practicing manager—as well as the organizational scientist—the concept of primary task is crucial in order to understand, evaluate and adjust a particular organizational arrangement. The basic focus is practical rather than normative: 'We do not say that every enterprise must have a primary task or even that it must define its primary task; we put forward the proposition that every enterprise, or part of it, has, at any given moment, one task which is primary. What we also say, however, is that if, through inadequate appraisal of internal resources and external forces, the leaders of an enterprise define the primary task in an inappropriate way, or the members—leaders and followers alike—do not agree on their definition, then the survival of the enterprise will be jeopardized, (Miller and Rice, 1967: 28).

Despite the brevity of this argument, we hope to have indicated that the use of a 'primary task' in socio-technical systems theory bears a clear family resemblance to Barnard's emphasis on 'purpose' as a defining element of organization. In spite of differences in metaphor and vocabulary, both approaches insist that 'organization' invariably must be seen in connection with an overall aim or objective—whether phrased as a 'purpose' or a 'primary task'. To conceive of and theorize about 'organization' without this basic awareness, they both suggest, is to treat the topic in a tangential, and perhaps even mystifying, way. Yet, despite the similarities of their conclusions, born of practical experience and definitional precision, their message was treated rather casually by their contemporaries—something that both Barnard and Rice and Miller regretted. In fact, we will argue, it is a message that is even less recognized today. Within organization studies, the term 'organization' is often underdescribed (e.g. by sociologically inclined scholars treating it as an 'actor' among other actors in 'institutional fields', 'business systems', or 'networks'; or as a black box pervaded by or reacting to social forces) or treated as an end in itself (e.g. as Luhmann-inspired analyses have it, as an 'autopoietic system' or, as is standard within 'process ontological' approaches to organizations, a 'becoming entity') rather than as a 'dispensable means' (ibid.: 196). One could speculate whether the contemporary situation in the eyes of Barnard and Rice and Miller would look like one in which there is much theorizing, yet little practical understanding.

In addition to the shared focus upon 'purpose' or 'primary task', there is another point in which the work of Barnard and the socio-technical systems school come together in a way that contrasts markedly with much contemporary organizational analysis. This, once again, concerns the role of theory in the understanding of organization. In contrast to many scholars within organization studies today, Barnard and the Tavistock writers did not set out to generate 'theory' as a goal in itself, but to articulate a conceptual repertoire and set of systematized experiences to assist managers and members of organizations in understanding, investigating, and reflecting upon their duties. The basic conceptual apparatus is not treated as is often standard in scientific disciplines, as the ultimate and pure grasping of a phenomenon. Rather, as Wilfred Brown (1977: no page numbers) put it, the aim was not to construct a 'theory', per se, nor to apply one to something, but rather to develop 'concepts' as tools in situ which would enable those for whom organization was a practical way of life or habitus, 'to think in a straight line about the problems they have to handle'. This would only be achieved, of course, if those concepts were 'reasonably well aligned to the situations with which we have to deal'. Concepts were therefore not something to be 'applied' willy-nilly, but were developed in situ to help deal with practical issues—the concept of the primary task, for example, emerged in the course of Miller and Rice working with clients to help clarify their problems:

> In the analysis of organization, the primary task often has to be inferred from the behavior of the various systems of activity, and from the criteria by which their performance is regulated. One may then be able to make such statements as: 'This enterprise is behaving as if its primary task were . . .'; or: 'This part of the enterprise is behaving as if the primary task of the whole were . . .'
>
> (Miller and Rice, 1967: 27)

Concluding Comments

Emerging from an interest in formulating and systematizing concepts and principles of 'administration', classical OT was, at the outset, intimately connected to a practical interest in the operation and management of 'cooperative systems'.[12] Nowadays, across theoretical communities, OT is defined as an almost exclusively scholarly discipline, whether this is couched in terms of a 'rigorous' organization science on the one hand, or via an emphasis of 'reflexivity' in organization studies, on the other. Its past anchoring in practical administration and management is frequently portrayed as a 'naïve' or 'instrumental' starting point, which has gradually and rightly has been left behind. For practitioners of the classical stance, the purpose of engaging with a systematic and detailed investigation of organization and management was not to reach a deeper, general truth or a higher intellectual vantage point from where organizations can be understood, but to facilitate an efficient, balanced, and ethical practical organization of cooperative efforts. Many of the reality devices developed by these practitioners, and the concerns animating them, are deemed to possess little explanatory traction in the present, possibly because a different terminology is deemed more supple, subtle, and possessing greater 'theoretical' reach (the classic focus on 'task' has, for example, been superseded by the contemporary turn to 'practice'— especially communities thereof—and 'process', for instance, as we indicate in Chapters 2 and 5), or because some of these artefacts seem so much part and parcel of the flotsam and jetsam of organizational life they no longer appear worthy of sustained discussion, even if the precision with which they are understood and used often leaves a lot to be desired (e.g. 'manager', 'role', 'performance'). However, while many of the concepts, maxims, and dictums developed by practitioners of the classical stance are now deemed anachronistic, out of step with the demands of the present, it is interesting to note how they frequently appear in the here and now, not least in the context of recent corporate scandals and 'crises'. Thus, Barnard's concern with executive 'personal responsibility' and 'purpose' resonates with the debacles at Enron and Lehman Brothers, or, most recently, in the parliamentary investigation into HBOS in the UK: 'The corporate governance of HBOS at board level serves as a model for the future, but not in the way in which Lord Stevenson and other former Board members appear to see it. It represents a model of self-delusion, of the triumph of process over purpose' (Parliamentary Report on Banking Standards—Fourth Report, 2013). Likewise, Brown's concern with the 'judging of performance' echoes debates about the conduct associated with 'shareholder value' and its organizational effects, and with the anxiety and stress experienced by organizational members generated by contemporary

---

[12] However, as this interest was taken up by academic scholars in the USA and transposed to the institutional settings of universities and laboratories, the focus upon guiding principles and specific, situational circumstances was gradually replaced with efforts to produce general theories about organizations, and, more recently, general theories of *organizing* per se.

performance management regimes. If the classic concepts and tools and the concern they represented are deemed irrelevant and outdated, it also seems that the present can't entirely do without them. This leads us to suggest that there might be something to be gained from making that unacknowledged 'dependence' on the classical heritage more explicit. Perhaps the assumption of the present having 'moved beyond' its concerns is somewhat overblown, or even misplaced? Perhaps contemporary matters of organizational concern are not so far removed from those animating the practitioners of the classical stance? Could it be that their conceptual (and ethical) toolkit is not quite so anachronistic as we might assume? Maybe their highly formulated knowledge of 'what makes up good organization' (Brown, 1965b: 32) is still relevant? That it is indeed possible to answer these questions in the affirmative is a key contention of this book. As Hadot (2009: 68) put it—in relation to a different context, but the point holds true for our argument here:

> One must distinguish from the ideology that justified the attitude in the past, the concrete attitude that can be actualized. In order to actualize a message from Antiquity, it must be disengaged from everything that denotes its period; it must be demythologized...One must try to go straight to the inner process, the concrete attitude it implies.

So, too, with the classical stance in OT. Far too much academic attention has been spent focusing on 'the ideology' of classical OT, for instance, and considerably less on the attitude or stance it embodies and expresses.[13] Like the moral schools of antiquity, we suggest that classical OT, viewed as a *stance*, can be seen as an experimental laboratory from which we can, usefully, circumstantially, apply the results today. Unfortunately, the idea that the classical stance has anything of significance to offer contemporary organization studies is rarely countenanced by those working in the field. Rather, organization studies today is increasingly devoid of 'an object', having spent much of the last half-century actively 'disappearing' it—the it, in question, being, of course, 'formal organization'. In Chapter 2, we seek to show how organization studies became progressively sceptical about and antithetical towards what used to be its key concept and object of study. Of crucial significance here, we suggest, is the rise to prominence within the field of what van Fraassen (2002) termed a 'metaphysical stance'.

---

[13] The manner in which Braverman's *Labour and Monopoly Capital* set the agenda for the understanding of the work of F. W. Taylor for a whole generation of 'critical' scholars of organization, would be a case in point. For a more recent text that positions the classicists, in terms of ideology and power, above all else, see Hoopes's (2003) *False Prophets*.

2

'Outside Organization'

The Idea of a 'Metaphysical Stance' in Organization Studies

In *The Empirical Stance*, the philosopher of science, Bas van Fraassen (2002: 3) seeks to answer the question: How has so much work in contemporary philosophy reverted to the once moribund *vieux jeux* of metaphysics? This is not a question that is unique to philosophy; it could be equally applied to a number of other academic fields, including contemporary organization studies—popular, mainstream, and 'critical'. In this chapter, we explore the rise of what we term, following van Fraassen, a 'metaphysical stance' within organization studies, indicating the differences between this and the 'classical' stance' outlined in Chapter 1. In so doing, we also chart the manner in which this metaphysical stance dissolves or renders obsolete the idea of formal organization. Clearly, as we argued in the Introduction, stances can encompass a wide range of theoretical vernaculars, so we should not expect the metaphysical stance in organization studies to be identifiable through a shared language, set of beliefs, or normative commitments, for example. Rather, as the historian of ideas, Ian Hunter (2006, 2007, 2008) has suggested we might begin to describe such a stance in terms of the shared intellectual comportment and attitude that comes to characterize a range of distinctive and non-reducible positions within a field. At first sight, it seems hard to pinpoint any such shared comportment or attitude within the field of organization studies, broadly defined—a particular disposition somehow encompassing shareholder value or stakeholder theory, for instance, on the one hand, and process theory, critical management studies (CMS), or neo-institutional theory, on the other. And yet, as we will argue, such a shared attitude can be discerned if one is predisposed to look for the clues as to its existence. One such clue we suggest, lies in the idea, implicit in much contemporary scholarship in organization studies, that one can get a better purchase on the intelligibility of matters organizational by looking beyond 'organization'; that what was once deemed to lie 'outside organization'—its margins, contingent context, or backdrop, for example—is now deemed central or constitutive to an understanding of what 'organizational life' is all about. It is this focus on the 'outside' or 'extrinsic vantage point' that provides us with some important clues to the presence of a shared intellectual attitude or stance within organization studies, one we describe as 'metaphysical' in orientation. Having outlined the key characteristics of this shared attitude and established its provenance within contemporary organization studies, we then proceed to examine the implications of such a 'metaphysical stance' for the enterprise of analysing, and, indeed, performing organization, comparing and contrasting this with the 'rival' classical stance introduced in Chapter 1.

On the Immanent Rationality of Organization (Studies)

> Metaphysical theories purport to interpret what we already understand to be the case. But to interpret is *to interpret into* something, something granted as already understood.
>
> Bas van Fraassen, The Empirical Stance, 2002

Unless a particular academic enterprise—sociology, literary criticism, law, history, economics—is bent on suicide, it will usually present itself, both to its own members and indeed to the 'outside world', as uniquely qualified to undertake a particular task. It is this task that gives the enterprise its distinctiveness (furnishing it with a determinate content and its purposeful differences from other enterprises). As we indicated at the end of Chapter 1, organization studies is currently perceived by its own membership to possess a less than distinctive identity as an academic enterprise, and this is both a source of celebration for some, as well as a cause of considerable regret for others. Whether organization studies should be considered bent on suicide is, of course, a moot point. What seems evident, though, is that implicit in much contemporary scholarship is the idea that organization studies embody or should embody some goal that can be specified *apart from* an analysis of formal organization itself, and which can serve as the standard by which matters organizational are to be evaluated and judged. Such an idea is not exclusive to organization studies. It can be found in many different disciplinary domains. If we turn briefly to the field of law, and specifically to an argument made by a legal scholar whose question is not 'What is organization studies as an activity?', but rather 'What is the law of torts?',[1] we can begin to furnish ourselves with some methodological guidelines for grasping what is at stake in this move, and why it might be plausibly designated as 'metaphysical'.

In his essay, 'Legal formalism: on the immanent rationality of law', Ernest J. Weinrib (1988) voices his concerns about the manner in which so much legal scholarship seeks to approach, analyse, criticize, and evaluate the law from a vantage point extrinsic to it. Weinrib takes one branch of the law—tort—as a means by which to assess the effects of this move. He begins his endeavour by stating that:

> When we seek the intelligibility of something, we want to know what that something is. The search for 'whatness' presupposes that something is a this and not a that, that it has, in other words, a determinate content. That content is determinate because it sets the matter apart from other matters... (Ibid.: 958)

It follows from this, Weinrib (1988: 358) continues, that 'nothing is more senseless than to attempt to understand the law from a vantage point extrinsic to it', on the reasoning that any such attempt is more likely to give rise to an understanding of that 'extrinsic vantage point' (whatever it may be) and not of the law. For Weinrib (1988: 958), legal understanding is an immanent (internal) affair, and 'legal phenomena' will come into view only under the pressure of a legal analysis; otherwise they would not be legal phenomena but something else.

'Immanent understanding', as Weinrib describes it, is not to be apprehended by itemizing features of the internal landscape, but by grasping the coherent set of *purposes* that confer value and significance and even shape on those features. It is that set of purposes, when they inform an insider's perception, for instance, that is responsible for her or his sense of what is and what is not 'intuitively plausible' in the consideration of any legal problem. As Fish (1995: 21), for instance, has argued, when a legal practitioner listens to a client's story, she listens with legal ears and what she hears is quite different in its emphases from what the client hears when he offloads his story on her. The client may stress a moment or an action that appears to him to be defining of his cause only to hear the legal practitioner say that it is not something that can be brought under categories with which and within which the law thinks.

What this means is that justification—the process by which a move in a game is declared valid—is always internal and is never a matter of looking for confirmation to something outside of the law's immanent intelligibility. The client who complains that their experience of an event has not been accommodated by the law's understanding or interpretation of it will remain

---

[1] 'Tort' refers to a wrongful act, other than a breach of contract, for which a civil action for damages can be brought.

unhappy because 'the crucial consideration is not what happened, but how one is to understand the justificatory structure that is latent in the legal arrangements that might deal with what happened' (Weinrib, 1988: 985). Weinrib (1988: 985) indicates that this account of justification renders it somewhat circular, since it 'does not strive for any standpoint beyond the law, the most it can do is plough over the same ground in ever deeper furrows'. However, he regards this inherent circularity as a source of law's considerable strengths rather than as a weakness, not least because, 'if the matter at hand were to be non-circularly described by some point outside it, the matter's intelligibility would hang on something that is not itself intelligible until it was in its turn integrated into a wider unity' (ibid.: 975).

If we are to avoid such an infinite regress, Weinrib (1988: 956) argues, we have to see the law not so much as an 'instrument in the service of foreign ideals but as an end in itself, constituting as it were, its own ideal'. He elaborates his argument by reference to the example of tort law, which he describes as a continuing meditation (by tort law itself) on 'the relationship between tortfeasor and victim' (ibid.: 969)—that is, between someone who wrongfully inflicts an injury and someone who suffers it; the unfolding of that meditation will necessarily induce considerations of fault, causation, duty, foreseeability, and proximity. It is of course always possible to view a tort case through the lens of a different complex of concerns—a desire to redistribute wealth as evenly as possible regardless of any finding of fault or demonstration of loss, for example; but if a case were decided in the name of such a foreign ideal, it would be a tort decision in name only, for a 'conception of tort liability in which the plaintiff can recover from the defendant for injury in the absence of wrongdoing, or in which the defendant is liable to the plaintiff for a wrong that does not materialize in injury, would be a "conceptual monstrosity"' (ibid.: 969). It would be employing the language of tort law while bypassing and destroying the very rationale (internal and immanent) for having a tort law in the first place. In this regard, it would be analogous to a situation in which a goalkeeper in a football match, aware that the opposing striker is in danger of losing his job and unhappy at the prospect of contributing to his loss of livelihood, allowed a goal past him rather than saving it; the criticism would not be that he was playing badly but that he was not playing the game at all.

If, as Weinrib argues, the source of the law's validity lies within the legal system itself—that is, it is 'immanent'—in the legal norms regulating legislative and judicial decision-making, then the source of 'legal personality' or 'standing'—what we can term 'personhood'—will lie firmly within the legal system too. In other words, the statuses and attributes of legal personality will be seen to be inseparable from the definite yet limited parameters of particular legal systems. Legal personality, then, cannot usefully be viewed as an expression of human subjectivity in some general sense. It is an artefact too particular and specialized to be counted as 'the individual', 'the subject', or 'the person'. The specificity of legal forms of personality and their non-reducibility to a trans-contextual or universalist conception of the individual, subject, or person can be most clearly evidenced by the simple legal truism that not all individuals are legal persons and not all legal persons—corporations or states, for instance—are human beings. As this extract from *Black's Law Dictionary* (1968: 61–2) makes clear, a legal person:

> [I]s such, not because he is human, but because rights and duties are ascribed to him. The person is the legal subject or substance of which the rights and duties are attributes...Every full citizen is a person; other human beings, namely subjects who are not citizens, may be persons. But not every human being is necessarily a person, for a person is capable of rights and duties, and there may well be human beings having no legal rights...

For legal purposes, then, any entity, whether human or not, whom the law regards as capable of bearing rights and duties, is a person. An entity which is not so capable in the law's eyes, again, whether human or not, is not a person for legal purposes. In legal terms, persons are nothing but the substances of which rights and duties are the attributes. Only in this respect do persons possess juridical significance. Thus, legal personality 'refers to the particular device by which the law creates or recognizes units to which it ascribes certain powers and capacities' (*Black's Law Dictionary*, 1999: 1162–3). Considered in this light, it becomes clear that the statuses and attributes of legal personality are inseparable from the norms, techniques, and practices of the legal system. They are not universal modes of 'being human'; they cannot be unproblematically equated with the 'individual', the 'subject', or any other such designation.

As Mark Cousins (1987: 119) argued precisely in this regard:

> If legal personality is not of a piece, and moreover if it is comprised of differentiated elements in respect to the type of legal action, then it is not a ticket that permits the holder to walk in to and out of legal actions as a member of humanity at law. Rather, it is that law designates in particular actions what forms of legal personality are appropriate for joining or being joined in particular actions. What is important is what form of agency the law recognises/constitutes as the appropriate subject. Sometimes, this can be a person, a man or a woman as defendant, sometimes it might be a man as father or a women as mother, sometimes it might be a man or a woman as representative, agent or servant of a corporate body... [T]he point is that the materiality of these legal categories, of the distribution of types of agent that appear within the law, cannot be made reducible to men and women and their identities.

This is an important argument, not simply in relation to the problems attendant on approaching 'law' from an extrinsic point of view, but equally in relation to approaching 'organization' in the same way. After all, the distribution of types of 'person' that appear within formal organizations (and which often have juridical and not simply organizational significance, as is the case with corporate 'officers' such as CEOs, or presidents, for example) are equally irreducible to individuals and their identities, something which dominant theories of the firm fail to appreciate just as much as do post-structuralist-inspired studies of workplace resistance or identity formation. If we take the former, for instance, we note quite quickly that authors writing about the firm constantly rely upon and deploy legal concepts: contract, property right, and corporation, for instance. The problem, as Jean-Philippe Robé (2011: 7), has pointed out, is that the legal provenance of these terms is occluded or even completely disappears in most dominant theories of the firm, in favour of definitions and meanings that derive from other forms of discourse 'outside law', not least economics, and whose deployment in effect creates a parallel universe (a simulacrum, in fact), somewhat removed from the world as we know it—the world of formal organization, where entities are developed using legal instruments, among many other devices, and 'in which the terms of all economic exchanges obtain their binding effect via law', and thus 'where the builders of real life firms are bound to take into account the legal characteristics of property rights, contracts or corporations to structure firms. For them, law matters' (ibid.: 7–8). In other words, by deploying their own sectarian meanings of what property rights, contracts, or corporations are, or more frequently, should be, and by not recognizing the actually exist-ing legal meanings of these terms, theorists of the firm engage in a form of metaphysical transubstantiation in which carefully crafted, technically limited, and practically focused (*corporate legal*) concepts are stripped of their precise meanings and turned into natural kinds to be deployed at will and across all areas in the manner of the elixirs sold at county fairs by quack doctors (Jensen and Meckling, 1976; Fama and Jensen, 1983). As Weinrib (1988: 969) put it, this is indeed 'a conceptual monstrosity'.

Like many others before them (such as the sociological theorists discussed in Cousins (1987)), influential theorists of the firm dismiss the juridical sig-nificance of the corporation—its possession of 'legal personality', in particular—as a 'legal fiction', for similar reasons, not least of which is that only 'human beings' ('individuals' in their favoured conception) are deemed to be real persons. Of course, as Cousins's comments illustrate, all legal con-cepts are 'fictions' in the sense of being 'artificial' rather than 'natural' kinds, but that does not make them 'illusions'.[2] Rather, the illusion comes in failing

---

[2] King James I of England famously argued that he could not see why he shouldn't adjudicate cases in his own courts because, after all, law was about reasoning and he and other human beings had reason just as much as judges did. His Chief Justice, Sir Edward Coke, is reported to have replied (apparently on his knees) that while his monarch clearly possessed mental capacities second to none:

to take legal personality seriously, as an important corporate reality device, because it does not happen to comply with certain a priori assumptions (philosophical, economic, sociological, or whatever they might be) concerning, for instance, what a person is (always a human), or what an organization is (a nexus of contracts between individuals). As Jean-Philippe Robé (2011: 3) has indicated, precisely because of the a priori assumptions they hold, many theorists of the firm are constitutionally incapable of recognizing that, in our sorts of societies, 'firm' and 'corporation', for instance, are not legally and thus not practically synonymous. In the world as we know it, corporations possess legal personality while firms do not, and much flows from this. First, contracts only exist between legal persons. If not all organizations are corporations, then they cannot reasonably be represented as if they were first and foremost a nexus of contracts because they possess no legal capacity to contract. This applies equally to the individuals held to be at the centre of this nexus. Individuals have no natural capacity to contract. They are equipped with such agency only by legal means. As Cousins (1987: 119) makes clear, the distribution of types of agent that appear within the law, and thus within organizations formatted and framed by law, cannot be made reducible to individuals and their identities. Second, and relatedly, property rights, rules, regulations, liabilities, and so forth are only allocated and applied to legal persons. The capacity to undertake certain aspects of economic activity, for example, is therefore not a 'natural' kind. Quite the contrary, in fact. It is precisely not a capacity that an entity without legal personality—such as a firm—can possess. Rather than an illusion or an irrelevance, the possession of legal personality is a crucial element in the capacity of formal organizations to exert economic agency—to own property, incur debts, accumulate assets, contract, sue, be sued, have recourse to the courts, and so on and so forth. Such agency is in no sense a 'natural' capacity that the law, for instance, either recognizes or fails to so recognize. Rather, the so-called 'legal fiction' of the corporation, far from being negligible in organizational analysis, as theorists of the firm argue, is actually fundamental to it. It is problematic then to suggest, as agency theorists have, that:

> [M]ost organizations are simply legal fictions. This includes firms, and even governmental bodies such as cities, states . . . The private corporation or firm is simply one form of legal fiction which serves as a nexus for contracting relationships . . . it makes little or no sense to try to distinguish those things that are 'inside' the firm (or any other organization) from those things that are 'outside' of it. There is in a

'His Majesty was not Learned in the Laws of the Realm of England, and Causes which concern the Life, or Inheritance, or Goods, or Fortunes of his Subjects are not to be decided by natural Reason but by the artificial Reason and Judgement of Law, which requires long Study and Experience before that a man can attain to the cognizance of it . . .' (quoted in Simpson, 1990: 832)

> very real sense only a multitude of complex relationships (i.e., contracts) between the legal fiction (the firm) and the owners of labor, material and capital inputs and the consumers of output. (. . .) The firm is (. . .) a legal fiction which serves as a focus for a complex process in which the conflicting objectives of individuals (. . .) are brought into equilibrium within a framework of contractual relations. In this sense the 'behavior' of the firm is like the behavior of a market, that is, the outcome of a complex equilibrium process.   (Jensen and Meckling, 1976: 310)

As their elementary failure to distinguish between firm and corporation attests, the sense here is of the authors articulating the 'true reality' of 'the firm'—as fundamentally a nexus of contracts—that lies beneath, behind, or somehow outside of, what they regard as the (illusory) superstructure of corporate legal definition and instrumentation. The audacity of this thesis is only an extreme version of the widespread academic tendency to assume that the skills, capacities, and concepts attending one's own discipline or practice are basically indispensable to any and all disciplines and practices (Fish, 1995: 73).[3] Regardless of how legal instruments actually format and frame organization in practically significant ways, Jensen and Meckling (1976) assume that their own favoured conceptual repertoire, which is represented essentially as a 'natural kind', can dispense with such legal meanings because it is itself cognitive—not least by dint of its capacity to reveal the truth (regardless of surface appearances) of organizational existence—and is thus capable of acceding to knowledge of *all* aspects of that existence. This is evidence indeed of a 'metaphysical stance' as far removed from the pragmatism of the 'classical stance' as could be imagined. Unsurprisingly, perhaps, the practical application of such metaphysical theoretics to the world of actually existing organization has been predictably unfortunate (Ghoshal, 2005; Dobbin and Jung, 2010; Davis, 2011; Stout, 2012). To disregard the existence of the corporation as a legal person, for instance, and to insist on treating it as the object of property rights, expresses not only an ignorance of the legal constitution of organizational structure and functioning, but also the importance of such legal mechanisms for the operation of the economy more generally (Thompson, 2012, 2014). And that is not the worst of it: aggressively promoted theories based on such ignorance have assisted precisely in 'forcing the

---

[3] This 'good for all ills' syndrome has been a particularly noticeable tendency within philosophy. The latter has regularly, and for the longest time, sought and often managed to convince practitioners in other fields that whatever capacities and dispositions might appear to be necessary for the fulfilment of particular tasks, the true ability, underpinning all others, is philosophical. The assumption here is that philosophy is not really a specific form of practice, *per se*, but rather a natural kind that is fundamental to the conduct of any given task—to managing formal organizations as much as to explicating Kant. More recently, economics has played a not entirely dissimilar role. The less-than-benign effects of the syndrome, though, are remarkably similar, regardless of where the claim originates.

concentration of management's efforts on the promotion of the sole share-holders'. The latter are being:

> wrongfully presented as 'principals', as owners: 'the whole purpose of modern corporate law was precisely to sever any property right connection between the shareholders and the assets used in the operation of the firm. It is only because agency theory disregards the reality and importance of the legal instruments used to structure large firms-as-they-are that a widespread ideology that 'shareholders-own-the-firm-so-management-must-maximise-profits' could develop...A disclaimer should accompany its use for the treatment of real world issues...it has toxic consequences.   (Robé, 2011: 63–5)

This brief engagement with discussions concerning the 'immanent rationality' of law provides us with two methodological axioms for charting the emergence and effects of a metaphysical stance in organization studies. First, that organizational understanding, like legal understanding, is an *immanent* affair; organizational phenomena only coming into view under pressure of an *organizational* analysis. This is a point that practitioners of the classical stance, such as Barnard (1968) and Brown (1974), frequently made, but which seems to have lost its explanatory reach in recent years, not least because what passes for organizational analysis today often appears to have little to do with 'organization' (King, Felin, and Whetten, 2010). Second, and relatedly, that attempts to approach organization, like law, from a vantage point extrinsic to it, at best say more about the extrinsic viewpoint than they do about formal organization, and at worst completely disappear formal organization by interpreting it into something else; this 'something else' then serving as the basis by which organization is to be understood and assessed. Such a move, we argue, evident in agency theory and its discussion of the firm, for example, corresponds precisely to a key element of the 'metaphysical stance' outlined by van Fraassen (2002: 3): that metaphysical theories interpret something already understood into something altogether different, and then specify that we cannot do without it. This metaphysical enterprise, we suggest, subverts or occludes an understanding of formal organization by its development of an often highly elaborate, ornate, and intricate understanding of simulacra that pass under the same basic name. This occlusion or disappearance of 'organization' and its simultaneous replacement by theoretical simulacra (such as 'the nexus of contracts', but, equally, 'rationalized myths', 'action nets', and so on (the list, as ever, is very long)) characterizes the metaphysical stance through and through. In so doing, it seems to honour the letter—talking organization—while losing the spirit and significance of the subject entirely. In what follows, then, our task is to try and show it up for what it is, and to bring to light the ways in which its strenuous labours address simulacra of considerably less significance than its advocates believe. We begin this endeavour by returning to the field of organization studies and tracing the ways in which the 'outside' of organization has come to be imported to the very centre of its inside, in the process disappearing 'formal organization' as a discreet or enduring object of analysis.

A(n Endless) Series of Problematizations

Some years ago, Raymond Hunt (1976: 99) remarked that, for all its self-styled sophistication in relation to earlier, predominantly 'classical' organization theory (OT), the 'open-systems' oriented approaches to organizational analysis that proliferated from the 1960s had been accompanied by something of a decline of concern with the 'work itself' (by which he meant a focus on an organization's tasks, the latter's properties, and the manner of their coordination in relation to the securing of overall organizational purpose). He stressed that whereas F. W. Taylor and other 'historical figures' whom March and Simon (1958), for example, somewhat patronizingly termed 'physiological organization theorists', had paid considerable attention to 'the work itself', contemporary forms of organizational analysis had neglected the organizational role of such work to the point where it had increasingly disappeared from view. This neglect, Hunt (1976: 99) continued, was somewhat ironic because, if organizations existed for the coordinated performance of particular tasks, a not unreasonable assumption, he felt, then it would be plausible to assume that certain 'basic effects upon their processes and outputs' would be traceable to 'variations in the properties of the tasks they were performing'. The avowed sophistication of 'open-systems' thinking in OT, he contended, had led some organizational analysts of this programmatic persuasion to be 'disinclined in their thinking' about the practical, situated determinants of organizational matters such as task properties and performance—'the work itself'—and thus about enhancing 'organizational effectiveness' (which Hunt saw as most likely to flow from 'a better understanding of the essential task based nature of organization') in favour of more 'exotic and even self-congratulatory ingredients'(ibid.: 113, 116). In its own way, Hunt's analysis testified to the declining standing of the 'classical stance' in OT and the emergence of an alternative disposition or attitude, which, among other things, privileged the 'outside' as a key source for understanding organizational matters. As his analysis hints at, though, the 'outside' can come to displace the very thing it is seemingly designed to more clearly explicate—what makes organization—and instead lead to the development of often highly elaborate simulacra under the same basic name. In so doing, as we have indicated, the 'outside' seems to honour the letter—understanding organization—while losing the spirit and signifi-cance of the subject entirely.[4]

Enter 'the Environment'

One of the first and most significant 'outsides' to be brought to the centre of organization via an 'open-systems' theoretical vernacular was, of course 'the environment' (Lawrence and Lorsch, 1967; Scott, 1981). Clearly, the term environment was not unknown to organizational theorizing prior to its enthronement as a key concept for understanding organization, as 'open-systems' thinking was held to trump so-called 'closed system, rational actor' thinking in the field. Barnard (1968), for instance, is often described as being ahead of his time in organizational theorizing precisely because he is deemed to have broken with 'closed-system' thinking in his major work, referring to organization–environment interactions and viewing 'organizations as open systems that included investors, suppliers, customers, and others' (Wren, 2005: 448). 'Environment', though, is not a count noun; while it always denotes something, it does not denote the same thing in every context of use. In each example of the latter it seems that we could take that something to not exhaust all there is, but rather to encompass what we might term some relevant class or region. The 'environment', then, will come to mean some-thing in relation to a particular context, including a specific domain of discourse. For Barnard (1968), deployment of the term is related to the stance adopted both towards organizational analysis and to the conduct of organ-ization itself, as an activity. Rather than being an open-systems theorist manqué, we suggest Barnard's use of the term 'environment' and his concern with investors, customers, and so forth is indicative of his attitude or com-portment towards organization as a practical concern and indeed as a way of life. Could you be engaged in conscious and responsible executive work 'inside organization'—that specialized effort of 'maintaining the organiza-tion in operation' (ibid.: 215–16)—and not be concerned with such matters (including the corporate legal instruments outlined by Robé in the section 'On the Immanent Rationality of Organization (Studies)', come to that)? Here the term 'environment' resides in a context of executive work and a domain of discourse focused on the practical activity of organization as a way of life.

Such a practical focus also attended the initial development of contingency theory—not least the pioneering work of Lawrence and Lorsch (1967)—that

---

[4] A point made precisely by Lopdrup-Hjorth (2013) in relationship to the phenomenon of 'co-creation', but having a wider resonance within organization studies, as he argues (see esp. pp. 109–23).

school of thought which did so much to establish the provenance of 'the environment' at the heart of OT. As Greenwood and Miller (2010: 86) argue with specific reference to the work of Lawrence and Lorsch, 'contingency theory was birthed not by scholars setting out to invent new theory, but rather in the attempt to solve organizational problems'. Even here, then, 'the environment' points to a context of use and domain of discourse that is resolutely 'inside organization', or 'immanent'; in other words, that is part and parcel of a practical ('classical') organizational stance towards establishing effective organizational design for the 'situation at hand' or the 'work itself' (Lawrence and Lorsch, 1967: 209). This particular deployment of the phrase does not position 'the environment' as an 'extrinsic vantage point' that trumps or otherwise transcends a practical focus on 'internal structures and processes'; yet this is precisely what 'the environment' did end up doing.

Without using the term 'metaphysical', Perrow (1986) points to two general trends within post-open-systems organizational theorizing that resulted in a gradual occlusion of the organization as a unit of analysis, and, relatedly, a significant depreciation in its own practical applicability. On the one hand, he outlines a growing engagement with issues of 'motivation', 'leadership', and 'productivity', for example, 'where the variables are now so numerous and complex'—not least because so many more can be introduced once the organization is opened up to anything and everything—that it is barely possible to talk about organization anymore at all (ibid.: 95). On the other, he refers to the growing popularity of supra or meta-organizational analysis, where the focus has shifted to over-arching designations such as 'the environment', 'organizational fields', or 'populations' and 'networks', but where the result is the same—the disappearance of organization as an object in and of itself. From the latter perspective, as Scott and Davis (2007: 106) suggest, not without approval, the 'outside' not only comes to be viewed as 'vital to the continuation of the organization', but, more significantly 'the source of order itself'.[5] Here we come face to face with an 'extrinsic point of view' in the manner posited by Weinrib (1988) as a 'foreign ideal', or by van Fraassen (2002) as a 'simulacrum'. Let us explain. The focus on 'the outside' as constitutive of 'the inside' of organization, and of the 'impossibility' of the latter's 'autonomy' as a discreet object, is, in a sense, a classic constructionist move *avant la lettre*; it assumes that, once it is recognized, any and every 'organization' is manifestly dependent upon, makes use of, and invokes, materials derived from 'social' ('cultural', 'economic', 'political') locations, spheres, discourses, and so on and so forth (the list is endless) 'outside' of itself; thus, its 'autonomy' as a discreet

---

[5] In the language of post-structuralism, for instance, we find a similar idiom: 'the constitutive outside' (see, for instance, Laclau, 1990).

object is compromised.[6] However, the reasoning informing such assumptions only holds if organization is deemed to be a once-and-for-all condition of hermetic self-sufficiency, a view that classical OT as a 'closed-system' programme has often been accused of promoting (especially, perhaps, the scientific management movement (Witzel, 2012: 189)), not least by advocates of 'open-systems' theory programmes (Scott, 1981). However, if one approaches classical OT as a stance, then so-called 'closed-system' presuppositions begin to take on a rather different character. Again, the idea of 'immanent intelligibility' proves a useful starting point.

'Closed Systems' Are Not What You Think

One of the key criticisms levelled at classical OT concerns what we might term using a contemporary idiom, its 'self-referentiality'. In the customary history of OT, referred to in Chapter 1, for instance, it has frequently been argued that most 'classical' organizational theories were based on 'closed-system' models or assumptions—from Weber's 'theory' of bureaucracy, through Taylor's principles of scientific management, to Fayol's administrative axioms, and beyond—where the dominant 'tropes' and 'metaphors' were more or less mechanistic (Morgan, 1997). Closed-system thinking is here deemed 'self-referential' and thus constantly in danger of fostering 'closed minds' as a result; the focus on internal ordering leading, inter alia ,to system–environment misalignment, lack of flexibility, erosion of adaptiveness, loss of purpose, and so on.

As we noted earlier in this chapter, such (critical) charges of self-referentiality have been regularly pinned on the law too as a 'closed system'. Weinrib's (1988: 973–5) point, though, was that, in the absence of such self-referentiality, a legal practitioner would have little grasp of what they were doing, or why they were doing it. Tort law's 'circularity', he argued, is precisely its strength, not a fatal weakness, because, as we noted previously, 'if the matter at hand were to be non-circularly described by some point outside it, the matter's intelligibility would hang on something that is not itself intelligible until it was in its turn integrated into a wider unity'. The same applies to 'classical organizational theory' when it is seen as a *practical science*. 'Classical' schools of thought, such as scientific management, have been the subject of scathing criticisms within organization studies and the wider social sciences— much of this opprobrium focusing on the inhuman effects of the techniques derived from its so-called mechanistic, 'closed-system' mentality (Braverman,

---

[6] As Scott (2014: 262) puts it in relation to the institutional theory programme 'the "figure" (organization) is often de-focalized to stress the centrality of the "ground" (environment). In many institutional accounts, "the figure is not simply embedded in, but also penetrated and constituted by the ground".'

1974). As Perrow (1979: 15) has argued, though, the force of these sorts of criticism quickly peters out when one realizes, for instance, that these were among the first efforts to both analyse and create tools for organizing and managing 'a new animal that had lumbered onto the industrial...and governmental...landscape and which promised to be an exceedingly large and complex beast indeed': the 'formal' organization. These 'efforts' constituted a practical task, based on experience, observation, and trial-and-error experimentation of and theorizing about organizing, and were not, first and foremost, objectifying epistemological pursuits or attempts to build 'totalizing' conceptual edifices in and of themselves. It is hardly surprising then, that scientific management was 'self-referential'. How could it be otherwise? The work of Frederick Taylor, for example, is regularly represented within contemporary organizational studies and the wider social sciences as simplistic, 'normative' not empirical, and narrowly mechanistic, yet, for all their presumed sophistication and explanatory power, contemporary academic analyses have rarely managed to achieve the significance and lasting prominence in relation to organizational behaviour and functioning that Taylor's work has done, not least because of its 'immanent intelligibility' in relation to, and hence congruity with, pressing problems of management and organizing (and not just 'capitalism') (ibid.: 16, 1986: 52–3). Taylor's clear and present focus on task properties as crucial and distinctive features of both performance and modes of organizing, for example, stand in stark contrast to the lack of importance attributed to 'the work itself' and its implications for organizational design, in many prominent contemporary organizational theories, whether they be neo-institutionalism (DiMaggio and Powell, 1983; Scott, 2014) on the one hand, or 'dynamic capabilities' (Teece, Pisano, and Shuen, 1997; Teece, 2009) on the other.

Because classical OT as a stance is characterized, inter alia, by a focus on organization as a practical activity and upon organizational effectiveness in relation to specific purposes, its rationale is internal and immanent—'circular' or 'closed', if you prefer. That does not mean it is static or unresponsive, for organization as a practical activity is necessarily an accomplishment; it is not a once-and-for-all achievement, something that happens one time and then just 'is'. This is often what 'closed system' appears to mean to those committed to an extrinsic point of view, but if 'closed' simply (as if it was simple) means having immanent intelligibility, then it is clear that the classical stance in OT is not unconcerned with nor antithetical to the 'outside', but will relate to that precisely in terms of its own immanent and internal criteria and purposes. In a sense, this is what Lawrence and Lorsch (1967) show happening in *Organization and Environment*, for example. Rather, the problem comes, we suggest, when you move from actually undertaking a practical science of organizing, in the manner of 'classical organization theory', to examining, say, the network of relations and forces that underlie, constitute, or otherwise provide the 'conditions of existence of' that performance, or of 'organizing' itself. Those organizational theories that operate with what we have described as an extrinsic point of view, focus their attention on the latter rather than the former, but still appear to assume they are contributing to the former as well as the latter (Scott, 2014). In this way, they employ the language of 'organization' but lose the very spirit and significance—immanent and internal—of the subject entirely. It is, after all, no easy task to be involved in a practice ('organization', or what Scott (2014: 262) calls the 'figure') and, at the same time, to be self-consciously in touch with the conditions that enable it (what Scott (2014) calls 'the ground', which, of course, also happens to constitute 'the figure'). Despite all its protestations to relevance and practical organizational utility, for instance, the remarkably popular neo-institutional theory suffers precisely from this confusion or delusion (Thornton, Ocasio, and Lounsbury, 2012; Greenwood et al., 2013; Lounsbury and Beckman, 2014). It talks the language of 'organization', but its inherently extrinsic point of view—a 'core idea' of which is that 'organizations are deeply embedded in social and political environments' such that 'organizational practices and structures are often reflections of or responses to rules, beliefs, and conventions built into the wider environment' (Powell, 2007)—denies it the sort of 'immanent intelligibility' in relation to practical matters of organization possessed by the 'classical stance' in OT. We could even go so far as to say that neo-institutional theory isn't actually *organizational* at all, precisely because OT is an immanent or internal affair, and neo-institutionalism departs from an extrinsic point of view, one which dispenses with 'organization' substantively if not as a word, in favour of concepts such as 'logics', 'fields', 'rational myths', and so forth. This may seem a harsh and, to some, even a ridiculous claim to make. After all, how could one of the most popular schools of thought in contemporary organization studies not be 'organizational'? Without too much difficulty, we suggest. And in this, as we will further argue, it is far from alone.

As we indicated, neo-institutionalists clearly believe they are exploring, and indeed providing, important and practically relevant analyses of pressing matters of organizational concern (Scott, 2014: ch. 9). In a recent article, Greenwood and Miller (2010), for instance, deploy various neo-institutionalist axioms in seeking to revive interest in organization design, which they view as a core concern of OT,[7] and by extension, to return OT to its proper object, namely, to a concern with formal organization. Greenwood and Miller (2010: 84) argue that a fundamental cause of the neglect of classical preoccupations with

---

[7] 'There is growing recognition that, over the past several decades, we have neglected a vital challenge that should be a core, perhaps even *the* core, of organizational theory: understanding the management of collective effort through organizational design' (Greenwood and Miller, 2010: 78).

organization design within contemporary organization studies is a shift of 'focus, empirically and theoretically, from the organization to the field, population, and community ... [A]ssociated with the shift was a move ... from the recognition of subtle and substantial differences across types of organizations to generalization to *all* organizations.' The shift, in other words, to an extrinsic point of view leads to a neglect of organization as a discrete entity or object, and as a practical activity and accomplishment: in other words, it effectively 'disappears' formal organization. They suggest that OT can only (re)establish its relevance and usefulness by focusing on 'organizations' as entities, and 'their managerial and organizational challenges' (ibid.: 87). The core assumption, they state, 'is that a focal interest of organizational theory must inevitably be the understanding of how to organize people and resources in order to collectively accomplish desired ends' (ibid.: 78). While their diagnosis of the problems confronting contemporary organizational analysis, and their ambitions for a revived OT, are in broad alignment with those animating this book, the approach they take to the problems they identify, and the manner in which they envisage their ambition for OT being fulfilled, is not. This is in large part due to how they understand what OT is or should be as an activity. As we have argued, for practitioners of the 'classical stance', OT is a practical science, one expressive of a distinctive 'way of life' or 'habitus', and largely developed within the orbit of organization itself (Chapter 1; du Gay, 2015). It tends to 'reason from cases', in Jonsen and Toulmin's (1988) or Becker's (2014) sense of that term, rather than rely upon or construct 'Big'—grand, general, abstract—theory, or seek to derive practical guidance about specific types of cases (or 'organizations') from such theory. For Greenwood and Miller (2010: 81), on the other hand, organization analysis is predominantly a *theoretical* endeavour, one in which substantive organizational reasoning seems to involve the selection and deployment of preformatted general theories that can be picked off the shelf and deployed in various ways and combinations to address any given 'organizational and design problem at hand', rather than emerging from what Parker Follett (1982), for instance, termed a 'conscious and responsible' attitude to a particular organizational dilemma, to 'the situation at hand'.[8] True, for Greenwood and Miller (2010: 83), the situation at hand might lead to a diminution in the authority of any one theoretical perspective, but the matter is still framed in terms of theoretical activity per se: 'to illustrate how the use of theories in concert can help unlock the daunting complexity of contemporary organizational designs, we apply three theories—contingency theory, the resource dependence view,

---

[8] 'Close observation' or 'detailed description' (see Chapter 3) 'invariably shows that, even in the most ordinary situations, more than a few easily measured variables are at work and that everything in the situation has some effect' (Becker, 2014: 2).

and institutional theory—to the transnational professional service firm (PSF)'. The word 'recipe' comes to mind—mix these three 'virtual' ingredients together, *et voilà*, your PSF design issues are sorted out.[9] The first ingredient is contingency theory, which is recommended because 'it would anticipate that each relevant axis of an organization should be represented in its organizational design'. Fair enough. However, and sadly, contingency theory can't manage alone, not least because 'the level of the theory's generality (designed to apply to all organizations) limits its utility when confronted by the complex reality of a particular organizational type' (Greenwood and Miller, 2010: 83–4). As abstract 'theory' perhaps this is the case; as a practical stance, *à la* Lawrence and Lorsch (1967), probably not. To make up for what Greenwood and Miller conceive of as contingency theory's initially helpful, but ultimately flawed 'theoretical approach', we are advised to add a good dose of 'resource dependency' ('look what happens when we add another perspective', they write (Greenwood and Miller, 2010: 84)). This ingredient, it transpires, provides much needed assistance for prioritizing 'organizational axes by determining which axis defines the organization's critical advantage and thus should be afforded primacy, and which axes should be sub-ordinated to that axis in order to secure realization of that advantage/capability' (Greenwood and Miller, 2010: 84). This is deemed to lend 'greater clarity to the design task by providing clues as to how to structure accountabilities and orchestrate collaboration through human resources and information processes' (ibid.: 86). But 'even these theories, taken together', are regarded as 'incomplete' ('in theory'—how can we know 'in practice'?). Enter 'institutional theory', whose formulations concerning, for instance, the manner in which behaviour is affected by 'institutional logics', and whose focus on the role of 'discourse and language', is argued to aid understanding of 'members' perceptions and portrayals of organizational design and the meanings they have for organizational members. Organizational designs are both responses to these perceptions and their determinants' (ibid.: 84). Thus, the design challenge is complete. At least, 'in theory' it is. And this is the problem. While eschewing the world of meta-organizational analysis, generalization, and high abstraction, and in fact insisting that proper organizational analysts shouldn't live in such places, Greenwood and Miller nonetheless end up residing there. It isn't clear what follows, practically, from the analysis proffered, in terms of precise modifications of concrete organizational phenomena, not least because the 'multiple relevant theories' they deploy operate, in their hands, at such an elevated level themselves. While certain resource-based scholars, for example, may declare that managerial skills are critical to building, maintaining, and modifying firm

---

[9] A similar aura permeates Lounsbury and Beckman's (2014) discussion of the contemporary 'dynamism' and 'flourishing' of OT and its practical usefulness in undertaking 'organization'.

capabilities, what this means concretely, practically, in a given context is not always obvious; this lack of precise specification and an associated rigorous definition of operating procedures is intensified when those skills are held to include building *dynamic capabilities*: sensing and shaping opportunities and threats, internal and external, enhancing and altering the firm's intangible and tangible assets:

> Dynamic capabilities include difficult to replicate enterprise capabilities required to adapt to changing customer and technological opportunities. They also embrace the enterprise's capacity to shape the ecosystem it occupies, develop new products and processes, and design and implement viable business models.
>
> (Teece, 2009: 4)

What exactly the determinate content of these 'dynamic capabilities' may be, is a moot point. They can appear to embrace so many variables, including a large and diverse number of 'external resources and competencies', variously and baggily termed 'reputational assets', 'external linkages', and 'institutional assets', among which are included, for instance, 'the system of higher education and national culture' (Teece, Pisano, and Shuen, 1997: 515), that the focus on organization as distinctive and manageable entity is lost. This occlusion or disappearance of 'organization' and its simultaneous replacement by theoretical simulacra ('institutional assets' and so forth) is, as we argued earlier in this chapter, characteristic of a metaphysical stance in organization studies. It appears to honour the letter—talking organization—while losing its spirit and significance. This is equally true of institutional theory as well. After all, as institutionalists are keen to emphasize, their theoretical enterprise is not really interested in or focused on 'organization' per se, but on 'the wider drama, rather than the individual player' (Scott, 2014: 262). This wider drama is of course the 'social context' within which organizations are embedded and through which they are constituted. It is this rather ill-defined and baggy focal point from which institutional analysis departs. In other words, institutionalism adopts an extrinsic point of view to matters organizational. Quite why Greenwood and Miller (2010: 86) would therefore position it as a crucial means through which to analyse and perform organization design as a practically relevant activity is not clear. After all, it is not at all easy, perhaps even impossible, to make specific and positive statements concerning the practicalities of organization—to undertake an organizational 'tool-making job' (Trist, 1960: 21)—through the medium of supra- or meta-organizational discourse. The assumption that such an endeavour is possible confuses two very different practices, the organizational and the meta-organizational, by assuming in fact that they are 'really' doing the same thing. They are not, and the belief that they can be reconciled or rolled into one will lead only to a form of metaphysics. The concepts developed within institutional theory—

'institutional logics', 'organizational fields', 'rationalised myths', 'institutional work', and so on and so forth—are the product of an extrinsic point of view and cannot be put to work in way that would make them particularly useful to those for whom doing 'organization' is a way of life. They are devoid of operational meaning and have no traction for OT when seen as a practical science of organizing. In this sense, as we indicated, institutional theory is not *organizational*, in much the same way that the theory of 'dynamic capabilities' is not either.

As Perrow (1986: 265) noted, neo-institutionalism is at heart a modern variant of the old 'critique and expose' form of institutional enquiry within organization analysis. Indeed, as some neo-institutionalists attest, viewing the bulk of institutional scholarship over the course of the last fifty years would lead one to believe that organizations are constitutively failing entities, constantly unable to achieve their avowed purposes. What institutional theory itself fails to do, though, is indicate how good organization can be made up and maintained, practically (Kraatz, 2009). Rather, neo-institutionalism has been keen to: 'delegitimate power, expose hidden forms of domination, and reveal fragmentation and hypocrisy in the actions of organizations and their elites. It says very little about how to govern, reform, or productively improve any given existing social institution' (ibid.: 85–6). In other words, it says nothing about organization as a practical science. Kraatz goes on to suggest that neo-institutionalists should attend more to the work required to design and defend organizational structures, including developing a fine-tuned attention to the crucial importance of 'mundane administrative systems' that are deemed to be the bedrock of 'precarious organizational values' (Kraatz, Ventrusca, and Deng, 2010: 1521). Sadly, this is not something institutionalists can easily do, as long as they stay wedded to the institutionalist language game; in other words, while they comport themselves as institutional scholars. Indeed, in engaging with Kraatz's *cri de coeur*, one of the elder statesmen of the field, Scott (2014: 274), indicates precisely why this might be the case. As he puts it, if institutionalism has 'taught us anything, it is that organizations are sub-systems of wider systems. Institutional work is required to not only at micro but macro levels—in sub-groups, organizations, organization fields, and societal systems'. Quite how anyone could hope to act in relation to all of these, and simultaneously, or to imagine that the deployment of 'institutional theory' would enable such a radiating effect is difficult to imagine, practically speaking. The ambition remains, though, and is conducted in sentences such as the following, for instance, which purports to examine something called 'the work of meanings in institutional processes and thinking':

> The emphasis on specificity, contexts, and politics brings to the fore the multiplicity of the institutional order. We have multiple meaning systems, multiple actors

who hold multiple interests and who work in relation to multiple contexts. They may or may not share the same understandings, and they instill institutional structures and practices with meanings, at least part of the time, to further their own interests. Thus, institutionalization is understood as fluid and dynamic, as an on-going process rather than an endpoint. Meanings are central to our understanding of institutionalism as work-in-progress.   (Zilber, 2008: 159)

It is tempting to subject this kind of discourse to a 'close reading', but, for the sake of brevity, we will simply point to the manner in which the prose deployed here signally fails to allow itself to settle anywhere, and thus cannot make positive statements in relation to any specific object that might be amenable to empirical observation.[10] It has to be so unsettled and 'in process' precisely because that which it seeks to conjure up is of a 'higher order' ('institutionalisation as a work in progress')—it is metaphysical—and not empirical.[11] This meta-organizational, highly abstract, and basically metaphysical stance is in marked contrast to the classical stance outlined in the Introduction and Chapter 1 of this book.

For Barnard, Brown, and indeed for Miller and Rice and other members of Tavistock Institute (in their early work), for instance, 'theory' was not something to aim for in and of itself, or to assist practitioners in reaching a deeper 'Truth' behind the immediately present. Nor was 'Theory' to be 'applied' *à la* Greenwood and Miller; rather, it consisted in conceptual approximations, incomplete and often seemingly simple, to a whole that was to be grasped through habitual familiarity with and empirical specification of its 'total arrangement' and its effects and imbalances. Completeness, in this sense,

---

[10] If we contrast chapter 5 of *The Sage Handbook of Organizational Institutionalism* (2013), 'The Work of Meanings in Institutional Processes and Thinking', from which this passage is drawn, with chapter 5 of the *US Army Ranger Handbook* (SH 21 76), 'Patrols', we get a clear sense, not only of how the meaning (and physical weight) of Handbooks has changed, but also how 'Organizational Handbooks' can express very different 'stances'. Consider the paragraph reproduced from Zilber (2013) with this from the most recent edition of the classic *Ranger Handbook* (2011: 46):

This paragraph provides the planning considerations common to most patrols. It discusses task organization, initial planning and coordination, completion of the plan, and contingency planning.

A) Task Organization. A patrol is a mission, not an organization. To accomplish the patrolling mission, a platoon or squad must perform specific tasks, for example, secure itself, cross danger areas, recon the patrol objective, breach, support, or assault. As with other missions, the leader tasks elements of his unit in accordance with his estimate of the situation, identifying those tasks his unit must perform and designating which elements of his unit will perform which tasks. Where possible, in assigning tasks, the leader should maintain squad and fire team integrity. The chain of command continues to lead its elements during a patrol. Squads and fire teams may perform more than one task in an assigned sequence; others may perform only one task. The leader must plan carefully to ensure that he has identified and assigned all required tasks in the most efficient manner.

[11] As Wittgenstein (1998: 49) remarked: 'For when I began to speak of "the world" (and not of this tree or table), what did I wish if not to conjure something of the higher order in to my words? ... [O]f course, here the elimination of magic itself has the character of magic.'

was a condition of accurate description, but such completeness was not to be achieved by exhaustiveness per se, but by relevance to the determination of what was to be done: to the 'purpose' or 'primary task' at hand:

> It has repeatedly been made evident to me by inquiring students that this subject is the most difficult so far as the approach to concrete situations is concerned, although intellectually it is grasped easily. Probably the reason is that a sense of a situation as a whole can usually only be acquired by intimate and habitual association with it, and involves many elements which either have not been or are not practically susceptible quickly to verbal expression by those who understand them .[...]. All of our thinking about organized efforts tends to be fallacious by reason of what A. N. Whitehead calls 'misplaced concreteness'. Analysis and abstraction we must and do make in everyday conduct of our affairs; but when we mistake the elements for the concrete we destroy the usefulness of the analysis.   (Barnard, 1968: 239)[12]

The basic conceptual apparatus, the theoretical doctrine, and the subset of propositions are not treated as the ultimate and pure grasping of a phenomenon. Rather, they should be understood as heuristic concepts that, exactly because of their 'empirical character', that is, their immediate intelligibility to the participants in the activity that they seek to describe, have the potential to instigate an investigation of or conversation about 'the situation as a whole':

> One point that needs to be made is that such effectiveness as Rice had as a change agent did not come from applying a general theoretical framework of organization to specific situations. His concept of the primary task... emerged in the course of working with clients to help clarify their problems.   (Miller, 1976: 10)

Similarly, as we indicated in Chapter 1, for Wilfred Brown the aim was not to construct a 'theory', per se, or to apply one to something, but rather to develop 'concepts' as tools in situ which would enable those for whom organization was a way of life or habitus, 'to think in a straight line about the problems they have to handle'. This would only be achieved, of course, if 'those concepts are reasonably well aligned to the situations with which we have to deal'.[13] Here, the locus of OT as substantive organizational reasoning and judgement still remained the specific case, the concrete problem, the particular set of circumstances.

---

[12] Or, as Conal Condren (2006: 351–2) put it in another context, 'for theoretical constructs with the virtues of abstraction, elegance, and explanatory suggestiveness, a little detail goes a long way... the elegance of any model screens out material, thereby accentuating a pattern, but once the model is treated as evidence, or embedded beneath it, differing forms of difficulty become apparent. Models as underlying truths become shibboleths and metaphysical principles to be defended and rescued by so much tinkering to accommodate deviant evidence that their virtues are lost in defensive tautology and anachronism.'

[13] According to Simon (1946: 62), for instance, 'administrative' concepts 'must be operational, that is, their meanings must correspond to empirically observable... situations'.

Concluding Comments

In this chapter we have begun the task of outlining the remarkably pervasive presence of a shared deportment, attitude, or stance within the field of organization studies, broadly conceived, which we have described as metaphysical in orientation, and of indicating the less-than-benign consequences of this stance for both analysing and performing formal organization. Our initial discussion of the 'immanent rationality' of law furnished us with two methodological axioms for charting the emergence and effects of a metaphysical stance in organization studies. First, that organizational understanding, like legal understanding, is an *immanent* affair and it therefore follows on from this that organizational phenomena only come into view through an *organizational* analysis. This is a point that practitioners of the classical stance elaborated, but which has lost both its standing and explanatory reach in organization studies in recent years, as what passes for organizational analysis has less and less to do with 'organization', and more to do with almost anything but (Miller, Greenwood, and Prakash, 2009; King, Felin, and Whetten, 2010). Second, and relatedly, that attempts to approach organization, like law, from an extrinsic point of view, say more about that extrinsic viewpoint than they do about organization, and often obscure formal organization by interpreting it into something else; this 'something else' then serving as the basis by which fromal organization is to be understood and assessed: 'the nexus of contracts', 'institutional fields', 'action nets', 'assemblages', 'the episteme', and so on and so forth. Such a move, we argued, is evident in any number of 'schools of thought' within the broad church of organization studies, from agency theory, on the one hand, to neo-institutional theory and CMS, on the other. In Chapters 3 and 4, we seek to indicate how the shared 'metaphysical' deportment informing these and other contemporary 'organizational' schools of thought, and the 'core' concepts they elaborate, format and frame particular matters of concern, such as those relating to the practice of 'change management' and 'organizational learning', in ways that subvert or occlude *organizational* understanding by the development of a set of simulacra that pass under the same basic name. The subsequent occlusion or disappearance of 'formal organization' and its simultaneous replacement by theoretical simulacra characterizes the metaphysical stance in organization studies. In so doing, as we have argued in this chapter, it seems to honour the letter—talking formal organization—while losing the spirit and significance of (and, indeed, actively 'disappearing') the subject and object entirely. In Chapters 3 and 4, then, our task is to bring further to light the ways in which the strenuous labours of practitioners of the metaphysical stance in organization studies address simulacra of considerably less significance, and create more practical havoc, than those self-same practitioners imagine;

in so doing, we also seek to indicate how and why the comportment, attitude, and stance characteristic of 'classical organization theory' offers a considerably more plausible and indeed ethically appropriate modus operandi for addressing the very real problems of organization and management that metaphysical designations such as 'change' and 'learning' point to, but manage to elude or occlude. We begin this endeavour by focusing on the ubiquity of 'change' discourse in contemporary organization studies.

3

Metaphysical Speculation in Organizational Theorizing

On the Lost Specification of 'Change'

Introduction

Strange as it may seem to modern minds, there was a time when the terms 'officious' and 'officiousness' could commend the proper, prudent, exercise of authority, and the term 'innovation' had purely negative connotations, signifying excessive novelty, without purposes or end (Condren, 2006; Lepore, 2014).[1] No longer. One of the most salient symptoms of the presence of a metaphysical stance in contemporary management and organizational discourse is the continuous reference to 'change', 'innovation', 'disruption', and 'reinvention' as indisputable ontological premises within the field (Peters, 1987, 1992; Kanter, 1989; Champy, 1995; Christensen, 2011; Linkner, 2014). 'Change', and the other signifiers to which it is invariably attached, is frequently represented as an organizational imperative that increasingly appears to trump all other concerns. Managing change is therefore seen as a, if not the, crucial feature of the business of organizing, and it is from this basic premise that organizational theory (OT) and practice must depart. Certainly, this call to arms has not been ignored. No shortage of often antithetical, theoretical, and practical approaches to 'change' have emerged within the field of organization studies, broadly conceived. Across the differences, however, 'change' is seldom specified in detail, but treated as a general and basic premise from which to theorize. Furthermore, 'change' is often treated as something that is in itself good or bad (Clarke and Newman, 1997; Morgan

---

[1] Edmund Burke described the French Revolution as a 'revolt of innovation', for instance, while the federalists were self-styled 'enemies of innovation' (Lepore, 2014). The relationship between 'office' and 'innovation' features in the discussion of 'authority' and 'authorization' in Chapter 6.

and Spicer, 2009). Accordingly, cases of change are routinely introduced and analysed as examples of general theoretical or epochalist axioms, rather than as specific, concrete instances of reorganization from situation A to situation B. In other words, change is typically conceived of and represented as a generic entity, which is more or less desirable and manageable depending on the point of view adopted.

The inclination to address change both as an existential absolute and in a broad and general fashion seems to coincide with a declining interest in other topics in OT. As 'change', 'innovation', 'disruption', 'process', and 'flux' have grown in theoretical prominence, traditional key concepts such as 'core task', 'distribution of work', and 'exercise of authority' have correspondingly fallen out of favour. Such terms are increasingly considered as at best anachronistic, and at worst, fundamentally misguided, being based, it is assumed, upon a nostalgic idea of the organizational world as in some sense stable, and upon an equally quaint view of OT as a practical science that positively defines, describes, and evaluates this world. In much contemporary OT, as we argued in Chapter 2, the object of analysis is less the organization as a distinctive entity than ongoing, multifarious, and often ephemeral processes of 'organizing'. Here, organizations are never fully established, but always in the process of 'becoming'; tasks are not given bundles of activity to be undertaken, but the occasional result of interpretative processes; and actors are not engaged in practical, recurrent work, but in making sense of, experimenting with, and enacting an unstable environment.

The framing of 'change' as a basic ontological premise offers a classic instance of the 'extrinsic point of view' characteristic of the metaphysical stance in organizational studies that we discussed in Chapter 2. 'Change is inevitable. You need to decide. Will you drive that change or be driven away by it? Will you disrupt or be disrupted?', Linkner states in the advertisement to his paean to change and disruption, *The Road to Reinvention* Linkner (2014). Following clearly in the 'visionary' religious and romantic footsteps of popular management and organization theorists such as Peters (1987, 1992), Osborne and Gaebler (1992), Champy (1995), and Christensen (2011), for example, Linkner lists a number of external forces (almost the same ones as the earlier authors articulated) that combine to make something euphemistically called 'business as usual' an impossibility for each and every organization, no matter what its 'core task' might be, and thus radical 'reinvention' an absolute necessity: 'Fickle consumer trends, friction-free markets, and political unrest... dizzying speed, exponential complexity, and mind-numbing technology advances' (Linkner, 2014: 1) all coalesce to produce a generalized context of panic, fear, asymmetry, and disorder in which only those willing to constantly 'disrupt' can effectively survive. Or, as Tom Peters (1987) put it almost thirty years earlier (in almost identically evangelical terms), organizations and managements are operating in an increasingly chaotic environment that has the capacity to destroy them if left unrecognized and unconfronted. The enemy, in the form of globalization, new technology, hard-to-please consumers, or unprecedented competition, is at the gates and threatens to lay waste the promised land which has been betrayed by unwieldy organizational forms (most notably, of course, the bureaucratic form) and complacent, self-satisfied managements. If organizations and the persons who work for them are to survive and flourish in a 'world turned upside down' they need to completely alter themselves and their modes of conduct. The old order is passing away, the traditional ways cannot work, and there is a need for radical change and reinvention. However, salvation is at hand if, and only if, you receive the prophet's spirit and 'face up to the need for revolution' and 'achieve extraordinary responsiveness' (ibid.: 3–4).

Using this sort of evangelical rhetorical strategy (one that will be familiar to readers of Christensen and Linkner), Peters sets up a dynamic of fear, anxiety, and discontent. An atmosphere of generalized threat is articulated—what could be more threatening but less specific than 'chaos'?—whose veracity cannot be questioned or tested, but simply accepted or rejected (the founding statement that the world is now chaotic is a profoundly religious assertion). Recasting specific circumstances into general polarities that create polemical comparisons out of non-comparable terms (as in Christensen, Linkner, et al.), an aggressively polarized world is conjured up in which organizations are either conspicuously successful—those adept at change so they can 'thrive on chaos' (disrupt, innovate, reinvent), or doomed to failure. There is nothing in-between. The idea that forced options are often false options is never countenanced. As Ronald Moe (1994: 111) put it in relation to the operationalization of Osborne and Gaebler's (1992) (Tom Peters-inspired) reinvention agenda in the US federal government—the National Performance Review (NPR)—'a theological aura' permeates contemporary programmes of organizational 'change' in both the private, public, and not-for-profit sectors. Focusing specifically on the NPR, Moe argued:

> The report largely rejects the traditional language of administrative discourse which attempts... to deploy terms with precise meanings. Instead a new, highly value-laden lexicon is employed... to disarm would be questioners. Thus... there is a heavy reliance on active verbs—reinventing, reengineering, empowering—to maximise the emotive content of what has been a largely non-emotive subject matter... The administrative management paradigm with its emphasis on the Constitution, statutory controls, hierarchical lines of responsibility to the President, distinctive legal character of the governmental and private sectors, and the need for a cadre of nonpartisan professional managers ultimately responsible not only to the President but to Congress as well is depicted as the paradigm that failed. This paradigm is the cause of the government being broken in the eyes of

the entrepreneurial management promoters. It has not proven flexible enough to permit change to occur at the speed considered necessary in the new information-driven technological world. The report argues, somewhat deterministically, that the entrepreneurial management paradigm will prevail in the future. Those who question this paradigm are not merely incorrect, they have no place in the government of the future.   (Moe, 1994: 113–14)[2]

Similarly, with Christensen and Linkner's claims concerning 'disruptive innovation', Lepore (2014) writes,

Disruptive innovation as the explanation for how change happens has been subject to little serious criticism, partly because it's headlong, while critical inquiry is unhurried, partly because disrupters ridicule doubters by charging them with fogeyism, as if to criticize a theory of change were identical to decrying change; and partly because, in its modern usage, innovation is the idea of progress jammed into a criticism-proof jack-in-in-the-box.

Like Peter's millenarian 'chaos', 'disruptive innovation' holds 'out the hope of salvation against the very damnation it describes: disrupt and you will be saved' (ibid.).

The work of Peters, Moss Kanter, Christensen, Linkner, and so forth explicitly states that the contemporary 'epoch' of fast and unpredictable change requires new organization theories and new organizations. The old adages and axioms, and the organizational reality devices or arrangements associated with them, are simply irrelevant to the present and future. However, in this chapter we will argue that the phenomena gathered together under the contemporary heading of 'change' are not absent from the canon of classical OT, but addressed there in rather different ways. In the tradition of 'organizational design', for instance, change is not viewed as an overarching norm (whether good or bad), but in terms of the chosen adjustments in the relations between an organization's goal or purpose, its organizing mode, and its integration policies (Galbraith, 1977). In many classic texts on organization and management, 'change' is not represented as an abstract entity—a thing in itself, that an organization must relate to or 'acknowledge'—but a relevant concern insofar it designates a specific modification of an organization's key features: its core tasks, work roles, product line, authority structure, or its allocation of resources, for example. Throughout this chapter we seek to provide examples to substantiate our hypothesis that detailed specification of particular organizational arrangements, rather than 'change' as a general and epochal assumption or assertion, is the best—indeed, the only possible—starting point for organizational analysis and action. In other words, to adopt a useful and realistic stance towards organizational analysis as a practical science requires

---

[2] We focus on the case of the NPR in more detail later in this chapter.

scholars and practitioners to both provide and work from precise specification rather than highly general or abstract assertions or assumptions about organizations and their environments.

Basic Assumptions on the Nature of Change

While there are, of course, a number of practitioners of the classical stance in organizational theorizing whose work one might invoke to advance this argument concerning the importance of specificity to the conception and practical management of organizational change, we begin by turning to certain formulations developed and deployed by the British psychoanalyst Wilfred R. Bion. Bion has been an important source of inspiration for OT, influencing, for instance, the work of the Tavistock Institute of Human Relations and Edgar Schein's notion of organizational culture, though his ideas are seldom referred to in mainstream OT today. A key interest of Bion's was to try and advance a method for sorting out phantasmagoric or 'magical thinking' from a realistic and practically focused understanding of the situation at hand, such as the challenges facing an organization. He argued that groups tend, over time, to develop certain unwarranted, 'psychotic' assumptions concerning, for example, their raison d'être and need of leadership. These basic assumptions, as he termed them, serve to comfort group members and reduce anxiety; however, they also prevent proper assessment of reality as it is. According to Bion, three types of basic group assumptions are often at play, all equally illusory. The first he called 'the dependency group'; the second 'the pairing group'; and the third 'the fight–flight group', each nurturing certain fixated beliefs. Although they may appear both reasonable and recognizable, they tend to overshadow a practical and realistic assessment of a group's task and possibilities for action.

While it is a moot point whether organizations need to or indeed do actually engage in 'change initiatives' more often today than in the past (Kaufman, 2007), the manner in which 'change' is typically addressed in the literature on organization—as a general and omnipresent phenomenon with 'deep consequences' of various sorts—suggests that basic assumptions rather than detailed descriptions are at work. In fact, the proliferation of change theories and change management concepts seems in many ways to resemble the way in which the phenomenon of so-called 'organizational myths' spread (Christensen et al., 2007), that is, through processes of: *authorization* (stories of change typically anchor their relevance through employment of anecdotes and examples from big companies and societal phenomena such as the Internet); *universalization* (change is depicted as something that affects all kinds of organizations and can be handled by tools that work equally well everywhere);

commodification (the market for easy-to-read-literature on change and for change management consultancy and education has grown significantly); *timing* (the notion of change is presented as coinciding with issues such as global competition and digitalization); *harmonization* (change is often portrayed in a way that will equally challenge or be an opportunity to all organizations and their members); *dramatization* (the narratives related to change are often compelling and emotionally laden); and *individualization* (despite the broad and generalizing terms in which change is addressed in the literature, organizations are still interpolated as individually possessing the capacity to 'break the code of change').

In the following we will address a broad selection of literature on change, organizational change, and change management and show how there are indeed some types of selective attention and preferred assumptions at play there, which might be usefully brought to light using Bion's analytical framework, and which, as we suggested in the introductory chapter, are indicative of a metaphysical orientation or comportment towards organizational phenomena.

'Change' as the Invocation of Dependency

According to Bion, the dependency group (which can arise in any type of organization and at any moment—peacetime or wartime) is convinced that it is basically a vulnerable organism, which needs a leader to provide it with security. This means that one person in the group is always felt to supply this need and the rest of the group seeks shelter in a position in which their needs are supplied for them by this person (Bion, 1961: 74). The group concentrates on establishing a doctor–patient relationship between the leader and the group, and anything that doesn't support this relationship is ignored. The impulse of the group is to shy away from what it considers a 'hostile object', whereas the leader's is to go towards it, and this symbiotic relationship serves to protect the members from certain aspects of life for which they do not feel prepared. The dependency group often chooses as its leader the most unwell member (in the sense of being 'psychiatrically disordered'), as the group typically believes that it is possessed of a demon or is mad, and needs to be led by a 'deity' who can counter this insanity (ibid.: 122).

Even though the object is not the group but the organization, the dependency assumption, with its key figures of vulnerable clients and rescuing helpers, seems to be present in the change management literature too. In particular, it seems to find expression in the intellectual discourse that emerged as the idea of 'organization development' became increasingly synonymous with psychological dimensions of organizational change and abandoned its original interest in the organization as a 'total system'.

The tradition of organization development arose in the period after the Second World War, when social science had become increasingly focused on the small group as a unit of analysis, and on democratization and societal prosperity as two sides of the same coin. Informed by developments such as the Hawthorne experiments, the growth of industrial psychology, and the open-systems perspective on organizations, the notion of organization development became an umbrella for diverse sets of ideas and approaches to planned organizational change with different foci and loci of intervention (Ganesh, 1978; Grieves, 2000).

A small book series from Addison-Wesley provides a good starting point to describe two different approaches to organizational development (OD), advanced at the end of the 1960s. In the first of these, organization development was presented as a general strategy aimed at increasing organizational 'effectiveness and health through planned interventions in the organization's "processes", using behavioural-science knowledge' (Beckhard, 1969: 9). The term 'total system' suggests that organizations should be examined as complex systems with a unique character, and Beckhard describes the combined examination and development effort embodied by this approach with the keywords: 'planned', 'organization-wide', and 'managed from the top'. In the same book series, Lawrence and Lorsch presented a vision of OD, which aimed to 'change the organization from its current state to a better-developed state' (1969: 4), by emphasizing the interdependency between elements of the system and the ability of the system to change itself. Departing from their 'contingency model' of the organization, they positioned organization development as a systematic description and evaluation (diagnosis) of three equally important dimensions: the organization–environment relationship (e.g. fit between aspects of the environment and the attributes of organizational units); the group-to-group relationships (e.g. collaboration between specialized units to obtain organizational goals); and individual–organization relationships (e.g. alignment of personal effort and organizational goals).

In both books, OD is presented as a programme that includes the role of a 'change agent', whose primary task is 'to facilitate the improvement of organization effectiveness and health through providing interventions, development activities and programs for organization improvement' (Beckhard, 1969: 20). The change agent occupies a triple role of educator, diagnostician, and consultant: someone who can focus on educating and enhancing the ability of top managers to identify organizational problems themselves and 'more fully understand all the dimensions of the problems and not just the obtrusive symptoms which they observe' (Lawrence and Lorsch, 1969: 96). However, the authors add that 'constant reliance on a consultant by management should be a warning signal that something is missing in their own resources for maintaining the health of the organization' (ibid.: 98).

A third book by W. G. Bennis in the series sketches a rather different approach that foreshadow future tendencies within OD. Bennis presents three basic propositions: (1) unparalleled changes are taking place which make it necessary to rebuild organizations; (2) the only viable way to change organizations is to change their 'culture'; (3) a new type of social awareness is required by people in organizations along with 'its spiritual ancestor, personal awareness' (Bennis, 1969: v). Here, in contrast to Lawrence and Lorsch's position, OD is viewed as a response to change itself: 'a complex educational strategy intended to change the beliefs, attitudes, values and structure of organizations so that they can better adapt to new technologies, markets and challenges, and the dizzying rate of change itself' (ibid.: 2). From this perspective, the change agent is an external professional behavioural scientist who works with the 'client system' on the 'exigency or demand the organization is trying to cope with' (ibid.: 11). An outside change agent is better able to affect the power structure in organizations, Bennis argues, because of 'the aura' created by such an external (often highly paid) consultant, but also related to this person's ability to 'see' more clearly 'the problems which insiders have long learned to avoid or overlook and most certainly regard with anxiety' (ibid.: 13). Organization development consultants work on the basis of a social philosophy that governs their responses to the client system, and which they believe will ultimately lead to not only more humane and democratic, but also more efficient, systems. The key challenge is to transgress dominant bureaucratic values: 'These values, basically impersonal, task-oriented, and denying humanistic and democratic values, lead to poor, shallow, and mistrustful relationships [...] Without interpersonal competence or a "psychologically safe" environment, the organization is a breeding ground for mistrust, intergroup conflict, rigidity and so on' (ibid.). Through various types of interventions the consultant will challenge the behaviour, assumptions, and traditions that hinder the organization in seeking alternative possibilities and thus bringing its culture under 'deliberate management'.

By coupling OD to 'change' as an epochal characteristic, and by defining the purpose and locus of intervention as the change of organizational culture, Bennis's approach departs from the total system approach put forward by Beckhard and by Lawrence and Lorsch. It is also representative of the wealth of 'people approaches' to organizational change that proliferated in the 1950 and 1960s, particularly in relation to what Leavitt calls the 'power-equalization approach':

Besides the belief that one changes people first, these power-equalization approaches also place major emphasis on other aspects of the human phenomena of organizations. They are, for example, centrally concerned with affect; with morale sensitivity, psychological security. [...] Thirdly, they place much value on human growth and fulfilment as well as upon task accomplishment; and they have often stretched the degree of causal connection between the two.

(Leavitt, 1965: 1154)

As such ideas began to proliferate, the classic focal points of OT (task, structure, technology, etc.) receded into the background. The topic of change became pivotal and organizational consultancy was increasingly seen as a matter of change facilitation: helping members of organizations to become more reflexive and flexible, and, thus, able to cope and thrive on change as a permanent condition. Organizations were increasingly viewed as cultures (Handy, 1976; Schein, 1985), learning (Argyris and Schön, 1978), and sense-making systems (Weick, 1979). Interest in the 'production side' was, by and large, left to researchers within operations management, and the emerging tradition of quality improvement, which, with inspiration from the Japanese Kaizen system and the spread of information technologies (IT), launched change programmes such as the total quality movement and business process re-engineering.[3]

As change theory increasingly preoccupied itself with the 'people side', the role of the external change agent also shifted in a subtle way. Grieves, for instance, depicts the history of organization development as a:

> movement from centralization to decentralization, a focus on the flexible firm by disaggregation or outsourcing, a movement from long-term strategic planning to short-term tactical planning, the emergence of down-sizing and restructuring with teams as the central mechanism for innovation and change [and] the movement from training (typifying the division of labour) to organizational learning, personal growth and development.   (Grieves, 2000: 429)

Whereas organizational consultants were previously seen as specialists in describing and analysing the organization as a totality of variables, they became increasingly depicted as 'process consultants' (Burke, 1982) or 'change facilitators' (Bennis, 1969), focused on the cultural or psychological mindset of the organization. Through their competency as skilled 'interpreters', they could probe 'the readiness to change' of the organization and help to confront and sort out dominating assumptions in the organization so these could be reassessed, as well as 'search for alternative ones', 'mobilize energy', and 'release human potentiality'. This required persons with mercurial competences: 'The role of the change agent is protean, changing, difficult to grasp and practically impossible to generalize'; however, 'in short, the change agent should be sensitive and mature' (ibid.: 49). Likewise, the transformation process they bring about is one of 'grace, magic and miracles' (Lichtenstein, 1997: 393).

---

[3] Interestingly, a shared characteristic of both the 'people' and the 'production' approaches was the focus on change as an epochal condition and on the assumed superiority of 'flexible', 'reflexive', and 'organic' organizational systems.

The potted history of OD we have presented charts a movement away from a focus on the efficiency of an organization as a totality of specific elements to a focus on its 'change readiness'. Simultaneously, the OD consultant changed status from what might be termed a 'problem solver and educator' to a 'healing visionary'. Returning to Bion's characteristic of the dependency assumption, it is striking how the language of OD gradually became one of rescue and salvation by an esteemed figure. Tools and methods were no longer deployed to make organizations specify their particular challenges, but, on the contrary, to help them 'transcend' their current situation: to free their eyes and minds from narrow present-day conditions and considerations—from 'the hostile object' in Bion's term—to the promise of a democratic, flexible, and loving culture. It is perhaps no coincidence that the image of OD consultants as inspired interpreters emerged alongside a growing discourse of 'uncertainty' and 'ambiguity'. This discourse seems to rouse feelings of perplexity and helplessness in organizations, and to nurture the assumption that organizations depend for their future upon the courage and comfort of a change consultant, rather than on collaborative description and authoritative analysis of the here-and-now situation.

Change as a Call for Pairing

Bion also describes how a group can develop the assumption that it exists for the purpose of allowing a 'Messiah'—that is, an omnipotent creature or a magnificent idea—to be born. This type of group will seek to nurture an atmosphere of hope and is occupied with finding the pairing that will be able to produce such a miracle. The life of the group revolves around some supposedly future events, but the crux of the matter is not the latter but rather the immediate present—the idea of hope itself, which rescues the group from feelings of hatred and despair directed at itself or at another group. In order to sustain this feeling of hope, Bion argues, it is crucial that the 'leader' of the group remain unborn, since the messianic hope must never be fulfilled: 'Only in remaining a hope does hope persist' (Bion, 1961: 151). The danger is, on the one hand, that such a group will either 'suffer through excess of zeal' and thereby interfere with genuine work–group functioning or, on the other, that it will allow itself to be forestalled—for example, by allowing somebody to realize a vision or idea—and then be 'put to the troublesome necessity of liquidating the Messiah' and recreating the messianic hope (ibid.: 152).

The hopeful, yet peculiarly aimless optimism of the pairing group can also be found in key texts within the change literature. In particular, the discourse of 'emergent change' appears to nurture the assumption that change offers the prospect of generating bright ideas and amazing innovations if only organizations could create the right spirit and atmosphere. By depicting change as instituting a promising yet ambiguous moment, an intangible *kairos*, this literature works to divert the attention of scholars and practitioners from the specific and practical to the abstract and ethereal dimensions of organizational life.

Within OT, a large body of literature became preoccupied with what was depicted as a mismatch between the 'rigidities' of (mainly bureaucratic) organizations, which were stifling initiative and continuous readjustment and the 'acute need for change' (Beer and Nohria, 2000: 2). The dominant trope became one of a hyper-turbulent environment and the imperative for organizations to align with and exploit the possibilities of ever-changing markets, rapid globalization, and transformations in information and communication technologies. A discourse of survivability and inventiveness attested to the need for a shifting locus of control in organizations: from managerial hierarchies to spontaneously forming centres of innovation. Under these conditions, it was argued, the key to survival was the ability to seize opportunities, cultivate streams of creative initiative, and dissolve barriers that stifle exploration and experimentation. On a conceptual level, a key focus was that organizations should abandon classic preoccupations with design parameters, organizational structure, and control mechanisms and instead focus on 'processes' of organizing—on the continuous flow of action and knowledge as carrying the seeds of new organizational tomorrows. 'Stamp out nouns... stamp in verbs' became a catchphrase in the work of Karl E. Weick (1995: 187) and, under the rubric of 'emergent change', he argued against the idea that organizational structure was something that could or should be adjusted to changes in the environment through a 'planned change approach'. Instead, people in organizations should be allowed to dynamically update and organize their activities: 'When people reaccomplish the coordination that ties activities together, they tend to alter it slightly so that it fits better with changing demands from internal and external sources. This continuous updating tends to produce units that change just as rapidly as their environment' (Weick, 2000: 230). Here, the key to 'effective emergent change' is not controlled intervention, but 'sense-making':

> It makes no difference what program they choose to implement, because any old program will do—as long as that program: (1) *animates people* and gets them moving and generating experiments that uncover opportunities; (2) *provides a direction*; (3) *encourages updating* through improved situational awareness...; and (4) *facilitates respectful interaction*. (Ibid.: 233; original emphasis)

The work of Rosabeth Moss Kanter developed a similar approach. Departing from a pessimistic assessment of the US economy, Kanter argue that there was a pressing need for innovation: 'We face social and economic changes of unprecedented magnitude and variety, which past practices cannot accommodate and which instead require innovative responses' (Kanter, 1983: 19). The key to success is to trust the creative capacities of people in organizations and allow 'idea power' to thrive. If organizations dare to give up the assumption that all change is a threat and that the appropriate response is to 'segment' and 'control', they can discover that loss of control and increased turbulence might lead to innovations: 'Change can be exhilarating, refreshing—a chance to meet challenges, a chance to clean house' (ibid.: 63). Control is not the key to success, flexibility is: react quickly, combine people across categories, and create a climate that encourages new possibilities.

In contrast to a classic focus on system imbalances and breakdowns, lack of fit between organizational elements, and quality of output, Weick and Kanter argue that successful leaders of change must have a different focus. In a fast-moving world, old virtues such as 'control' and 'administration' stifle the creative forces on which the organization's future depended. Managers must be visionary facilitators inspiring people to innovate. Likewise, change agents are first and foremost fertilizers of a creative and open climate, where experimentation is naturally encouraged and the human spirit allowed to unfold without having rigid criteria imposed in the vulnerable moment when ideas are conceived. This is not to be confused with 'revolutionary change' or with change as a 'planned process':

> The hyperbole of transformation has led people to overestimate the liabilities of inertia, the centrality of managerial planning, and the promise of fresh starts, and to underestimate the value of innovative sensemaking on the front line, the ability of small experiments to travel, and the extent to which change is continuous.
>
> (Weick, 2000: 223)

The influence of Weick, Kanter, and cognate scholars on the theorization of organizational change and innovation can hardly be overstated. The tropes of creativity and emergence are dominant in current change literature (and in much social theory as well). Indeed, Weick's call to replace nouns with verbs seems to have been heard very clearly. The new vocabulary of nouns clusters around a small set of generic entities such as 'actors', 'contexts', and 'processes'—and their theoretical interrelations—thus indicating a diminished interest in specific elements and relationships in organizations. However, the salience of verbs also seem to suggest that the literature on 'continuous change' is not very preoccupied with any endpoint of change, and is remarkably vague, even pessimistic, when it comes to describing the actual practices or competencies needed for turning 'change' into a moment of opportunity: 'The danger lurking in many discussions of organizational change is that the whole thing starts to sound much simpler than it is' (Kanter, Stein, and Jick, 1992: 4). For Kanter and colleagues, the problem is not simply the difficulty of describing the complex ways in which organizations manage to seize the occasion presented by change. Rather, the art of becoming a flexible and innovative organization is a rare miracle. It is 'difficult to find practical examples of organizations not born that way that have fully transformed themselves to attain this ideal' (ibid.). Weick also points to the vulnerability of 'effective emergent change': '[a]nimation, direction, attention, respectful interaction—are crucial for adaptation, learning, and change in a turbulent world. But they are also the four activities most likely to be curbed severely in a hierarchical command-and-control system' (Weick, 2000: 234). Furthermore, it takes special abilities to recognize the right sort of changes in the melange of available change cues: 'Our ability to recognize changes may be largely limited to the immediately obvious and therefore superficial ones, while ultimately more powerful factors are hidden from our view' (Kanter, Stein, and Jick, 1992: 5).

In this way, the message of emergent change as an opportunity is also replete with reservations—an ambivalent promise indeed. On the one hand, the seeds of new tomorrows blow in the wind of change. On the other, the impulses to flesh out and 'segment' these seeds must be curbed in order to stay animated and attentive, and to 'break the code of change'. Rather than thinking in terms of the classic Lewinian 'unfreeze-change-refreeze', Weick argues, successful emergent change is a matter of 'freeze-rebalance-unfreeze' (Weick, 2000: 236). On closer inspection, the key difference between the two sequences seems to be that the first entails a movement—small or lengthy—from one specific situation to another; whereas the second—the continuous change approach—suggests a leap into abstract hope through a process of critical reflection, reflexive cleansing of the mind, and a resilient aspiration towards unknown potentialities. The basic dynamic of this advice, and of the conceptual framework underpinning it, seems remarkably close to Bion's characterization of the pairing group. In order to avoid feelings of disaster and hatred, the group engages in a collective cultivation of hope. A type of hope, however, whose nature is not to find the specific way in which hope can be fulfilled, but rather to sustain itself as an abstract refuge or a metaphysical ideal.

Change as a Call for Fight or Flight

The fight–flight group is the third of Bion's three basic assumption groups. Whereas the dependency and the pairing group coalesce around the belief that their purpose is, respectively, to be protected and to produce a wonder, the fight–flight group acts on the assumption that it must either fight or flee from an enemy. Accordingly, the group seeks to build the notion of a hostile force or menace, and often it chooses as its leader a person who is able to single one out. This leader is, Bion says: 'Usually a man or a woman with marked paranoid trends; perhaps if the presence of an enemy is not immediately obvious to the group, the next best thing is for the group to choose a leader to whom it is' (Bion, 1961: 67). The leader of the fight–flight group will prompt the group to find ways to avoid, escape, combat or beat an imagined danger. 'If he makes demands that do not do so, he is ignored' (ibid.: 152). Whereas the group provides security for its members to the extent that individuals demonstrate courage and self-sacrifice, the cost is that a realistic assessment of the group situation is difficult to obtain.

The fight/flight dynamic can also be detected in contemporary theories of change. In one form, it is evident in the 'best practice' literature. In another, it surfaces in critical management studies (CMS). Although neither of the two forms operate with explicit notions of an enemy or menace, they revolve around the idea that 'change' calls either for the mobilization of strength and acumen against counterforces, or is an situation saturated by power. We will exemplify both assumptions and argue that they deploy accounts in which change is treated with unquestioned normativity or suspiciousness.

Within the field of strategic change management, the work of John P. Kotter occupies an influential position. In the book *Leading Change*, Kotter (1996) argues—in line with the dominant trope—that change is a crucial necessity in contemporary business life because of macroeconomic forces pushing organizations to reduce costs, improve quality, increase productivity, and locate new opportunities for growth. However, he continues, many change efforts suffer from lack of competent execution, which results in a vast number of failed change programmes with disappointing results and frustrated employees. The reasons for the poor results are, on the one hand, that 'pain is always involved' whenever people have to adjust to shifting conditions; on the other, that 'leaders of change' typically make a number of basic errors when trying to transform organizations. Kotter outlines the eight most common types of errors and suggests how they can be avoided: (1) allowing too much complacency; (2) failing to create a sufficiently powerful coalition; (3) underestimating the power of vision; (4) undercommunicating the vision; (5) permitting obstacles to block the new vision; (6) failing to create short-term wins; (7) declaring victory too soon; and (8) neglecting to anchor changes firmly in the corporate culture. As the phrasing of these eight errors suggest, Kotter adopts a war-like rhetoric: to take a lead on change means to start a battle against complacency by invoking a sense of urgency and offering strong ideals. It also means building alliances with powerful players, the removal of obstacles, and the securing of both short- and long-term wins.

The right leader for such a struggle may not necessarily be the most charismatic or 'leader-like' person, but the one who sustains a 'competitive drive and life-long learning':

When hit with an unexpected downturn, he [sic] would often become angry or morose, but he would never give up or let defensiveness paralyze him...he watched more closely and listened more carefully than did most others...he relentlessly tested new ideas, even if that meant pushing himself out of his zone of comfort or taking some personal risks.   (Kotter, 1996: 180)

In order to direct the battle for change, 'leadership' rather than 'management' is needed. Change does not happen through classic managerial virtues such as planning, budgeting, organizing, and so on, but through 'attacks' that enable organizations to 'break out of the morass' and gain the 'victory'. Bureaucracies are one of the generic obstacles to change, Kotter argues, and leadership is rarely found in them. However, 'only leadership can blast through the many sources of corporate inertia. Only leadership can motivate the actions needed to alter behaviour in any significant way' (ibid.: 30). Drawing a picture of organizations as caught between, on the one hand, the dead hand of bureaucracy and, on the other, a widespread complacency, Kotter depicts change as, simultaneously, an unquestionable necessity and a matter of unremitting struggle. The content and direction of change is of less importance than the persistent fight for the organization's freedom and capability to change. Change is a call to fight against red tape and indolence.

Where Kotter promotes the idea of change as an occasion for fight and constant endeavour, the literature on change within the field of CMS advances the opposite idea: change is an occasion for deep scepticism and flight from dominant belief.

CMS is an umbrella term for a diverse set of ideas and approaches united around the contestation of the 'traditional imperatives of mainstream management research and practice' (Tadajewski et al., 2011: 1). Drawing upon a potent and eclectic brew of Marxism, critical theory, post-structuralism, feminism, and other traditions of critique, critical management scholars seek to question the 'taken-for-granted', detect hidden dynamics of power and ideology, confront the claims of rationality and objectivity and reveal the interests that these conceal, and work towards an emancipatory ideal (Reynolds, 1999). The issue of change and change management is consistently viewed from these vantage points by CMS scholars. For instance, Morgan and Spicer (2009: 254) depict the notion of change as something that needs to be 'de-naturalized', that is, disclosed as belonging to certain discourses or theoretical assumptions about reality: 'Change only becomes a socially meaningful and political efficacious phenomena when it is "fixed" and explicated through a set of ideas and theories about change.' Change theories are never neutral representations of reality, but: 'partial and "interested" representation[s] of reality' that 'construct the change processes they claim to describe' (ibid.). Accordingly, 'change' is never something that can simply be explored and described, since the descriptive vocabulary and the selection of details are always theoretically, hence politically, loaded. Instead of such description,

CMS seek to 'politically engage' with change processes by juxtaposing actors' accounts and views of change against each other, thereby indicating how actors struggle around the direction of change processes: 'They open up the study of change to considering how the models of change which are propagated by business schools, consultants and other carriers of ideas do not just describe change processes, but actually play a central role in directing these processes' (ibid.: 259). Thus, by employing a methodological repertoire drawn from ideology critique, discourse analysis, and semiotics, for example, CMS depict 'change' as an occasion for suspicion, unmasking, and problematization. Change is invariably political, and the proper response is political as well, although it is of a different kind than that undertaken by change agents who are enmeshed in the processes of change themselves. The critical management theorist takes a step back from direct implication and monitors from a distance the movements and rhetorical tactics of the involved parties. Through 'reflexivity' and 'critique', CMS scholars seek to displace attention from specific change situations—and their own potential part in these—to an abstract multiplicity of powers at play behind the immediately real. This strategy can, depending on the critical theoretical point of view adopted, be seen as either a flight from description and practical engagement with specific change situations, or as a sophisticated fight against attempts to define and direct such instances.

Whereas Kotter represents 'change' as an occasion for fighting against complacency, CMS frame 'change' as a battle to reveal hidden politics and simultaneously as a flight from direct involvement. In both approaches, however, the basic figure of change remains remarkably underspecified, either because change is seen as a self-evident necessity, or because it is regarded as an empty signifier, that cannot be described without politicization.

Managing on the Basis of Unwarranted Change Assumptions

Viewed through Bion's analytical framework, the contemporary literature on change seems to rest upon and nurture a set of basic assumptions which works to preclude the detailed description and assessment of organizational reality, and instead invoke a number of normative and absolutist change recipes. We will now highlight the practical consequences of this normative and theoretical closure by examining the way the change tropes serve to inspire and legitimize organizational reforms, and do so in a manner which is, at best, quite problematic and, at worst, potentially damaging in its lack of precision and contextual specificity.

Change, Epochalism, and Organizational Reform

> For when I began to speak of 'the world' (and not of this tree or table), what did I wish if not to conjure something of the higher order in to my words? ...of course, here the elimination of magic itself has the character of magic.

Ludwig Wittgenstein, Culture and Value, 1998

As we have argued, contemporary discourses of organizational change tend towards being both absolutist (change is undeniable, it is everywhere and you can't escape it) and highly abstract (its imperatives require flexibility, innovation, creativity, enterprise: the list is as endless as the practical operationalization of its imperatives remains remarkably underspecified). While it is clear that such discourses have some intuitive rhetorical appeal—offering, for instance, a powerful set of generalizations that can act as a catalyst for 'transformation'—it is not at all obvious how such abstract injunctions are to be acted upon practically, and whether their lack of precision and specificity has some serious implications for the appropriateness of particular changes in different organizational settings. After all, as Peter Drucker (quoted in MacDonald et al., 2006: 271) once argued: 'the function of management in a church is to make it more church-like, not more business-like', thus begging the question as to the appropriateness of applicability of generic change 'recipes' to the 'core tasks' of different sorts of organizations.

It was a key maxim in classic OT that the nature of the management task, and the appropriateness of the management methods deployed, can be defined only in relationship to the particular purposes or 'core tasks' of the organization to be managed. When it comes to 'change', the differences between organizations—their distinctive missions, their varying obligations to differing constituencies, and their typical ways of specifying and addressing ethical questions, for instance—are as vital as their similarities. It is unlikely that they will experience 'change' in an identical manner—as an abstract phenomenon—but rather as a particular matter of concern, with distinctive characteristics and practical implications related to the conduct of concrete aspects of their activities. If this is indeed the case, then it is unlikely that a generalized set of 'change' injunctions or recipes would be appropriate to them all. Indeed, without a clear sense of what an organization's core tasks are, and equally precise concepts through which to formulate the conditions of their attainment, generalizations about and injunctions to 'change' are at best somewhat gestural or gratuitous, and at worst potentially quite destructive.

In order to elaborate our point, we turn briefly to a specific case. In their highly influential book, *Re-Inventing Government*, Osborne and Gaebler (1992) posited the need for a complete transformation in the ways in which the US federal government conducted itself, and in the ways in which people conducted themselves within government departments and agencies. They did so on the basis of a loose agglomeration of abstract imperatives of 'change'. Amongst the latter were cited: a generalized crisis in governmental authority, the dislocatory effects of an increased deployment of new information and communication technologies, and the logics of 'globalization'. These and other imperatives were then lumped together to constitute what the authors pictured as an environment characterized by uncertainty. It was this uncertain environment which was deemed to problematize the established 'values' and operating procedures characterizing the workings of the federal government and thus to demand their radical transformation. Failure to respond could only lead to disaster:

> Today's environment demands institutions that are extremely flexible and adapt-
> able. It demands institutions that deliver high-quality goods and services, squeez-
> ing every more bang out of every buck. It demands institutions that are responsive
> to the needs of their customers, offering choices of non-standardized services; that
> lead by persuasion and incentives rather than commands; that give their employ-
> ees a sense of meaning and control, even ownership. It demands institutions that
> empower citizens rather than simply serving them.   (Ibid.: 15)

If uncertainty was the problem, making established practices untenable, then 'entrepreneurial government' was the solution. It was held to offer the only viable means through which a 'broken' public administration could be effect-ively 'reinvented' and the core tasks of government thus continue to be fulfilled. Unsurprisingly, perhaps, the key tenets of this 'new entrepreneurial-ism' were represented as the very antithesis of those held responsible for getting government into such trouble in the first place. The latter were simi-larly lumped together under one heading: the 'bureaucratic paradigm'. In contrast to this slow, inefficient, morale-sapping monster, signally lacking in the capacity to respond to the imperatives of change, entrepreneurial govern-ment was represented as efficient, flexible, fast, and responsive.

While such narratives and oppositions—which we term 'epochalist'—pro-vide a simple and easily digestible set of slogans through which to catalyse the demand for 'change', problems invariably arise when it comes to the specifi-cation of actually effecting practical changes within governmental institu-tions based on such general categories. After all, we will suggest, judgements about the wisdom of certain forms of organizational change, arrived at in the concrete circumstances of a practical case, can no more be abstracted from their detailed circumstances than can medical judgements about the present condition of individual patients. As Amélie Rorty (1988: 8) has argued in this regard: judgements are given their sense and direction by the particular context within which they arise. Yet it is precisely the specificity of circumstances that epochal approaches render insignificant or invisible, and herein lies their practical danger. In so far as they neglect the specificity of circumstances, attempts, such as Osborne and Gaebler's, to generalize 'entre-preneurial principles' to all forms of public organizational conduct may well end up serving to incapacitate a particular organization's ability to pursue its specific purposes or 'core task' by redefining its identity and hence what its purposes are. A brief examination of the Clinton administration's NPR in the USA and subsequent report—*From Red Tape to Results: Creating a Government That Works Better and Costs Less*—gives a flavour of just how such a slippage can occur when absolutist diagnoses form the basis of practical organizational 'change' interventions in the area of public administration.

Reinventing Government: The National Performance Review

The centrepiece of public administrative reform under the Clinton presidency in the USA was The National Performance Review (NPR), chaired by then-Vice President Al Gore. In launching the NPR in April 1993, Gore indicated that 'our long term goal is to change the very culture of the federal government'. This was to be achieved through a process coined reinventing. The origins of this phrase are not hard to trace. It is Osborne and Gaebler's bestseller, and their epochal pronouncements and diagnoses, that clearly inform the value premises and practical goals of the NPR. Indeed, David Osborne played a major part in drafting the NPR's final report (1993).

Osborne and Gaebler's text picked and mixed ideas from a number of different locales—from the voluminous privatization literature of the 1970s and 1980s, to the populist business motivation literature of the 1980s and early 1990s. The result was a heady brew that could appear acceptable to liberals and democrats who wanted to save government from the worst excesses of neo-conservatism but who also wanted a more 'responsive' gov-ernment that catalysed all sectors of society and, importantly, cost less to run. Such a government was realizable, Osborne and Gaebler argued, if there was a 'cultural' shift away from the 'bureaucratic paradigm' towards 'entrepreneurial government'. This epochal designation was taken up by the NPR and consti-tuted the inspiration for its basic organizing framework.

According to the NPR, the idea of reinventing government rested upon 'four bedrock principles' of entrepreneurial management (NPR, 1993: 6–7). These were remarkably similar to, indeed pretty much a distillation of, Osborne and Gaebler's ten principles of entrepreneurial government. First, effective entre-preneurial managements cast aside red tape and moved away from systems where people were accountable for following rules to ones where people were accountable for achieving results. Second, entrepreneurial managements were customer-focused and insisted on customer satisfaction. Third, entrepreneur-ial managements transformed their cultures by decentralizing authority and encouraging the front line to make more of their own decisions and to take responsibility for solving their own problems. Finally, entrepreneurial managements constantly sought to do more for less, through 're-engineering' their work systems and processes.

These 'principles' were never presented as propositions subject to empirical disproof but simply asserted. Objections and questions concerning the wisdom of these assertions—was being against red tape (e.g. bureaucratic regulation) really a useful organizing principle for the administration of government given its sovereign politico-legal role? (Kaufman, 1977)—were suppressed in advance through the continuous invocation of the impossibility of the status quo. 'Change' was the given, being unamenable to challenge within the terms of reference of the Gore report.

This epochal schema in which 'bureaucracy' or 'administration' are reduced to a simple and abstract set of negativities contrasted with an equally simple and abstracted, but positively coded, set of 'entrepreneurial' principles, systematically evacuates the field of public administration of any of its characteristic, we might say 'positive', content. How could anyone be for bureaucracy if it is defined simply as a dysfunctional, outdated, and inefficient organizational form? However, when attention is focused on the specific purposes of public administration and the particular political and constitutional constraints framing its activities (Wilson, 1994), the generalized articulation of bureaucracy with the outmoded and dysfunctional is less obvious and the generalized superiority of 'entrepreneurial principles' more problematic. As a number of commentators have argued, the implementation of the NPR's proposals raised a host of constitutional problems, and yet the Gore report was characterized by an almost complete absence of the language of constitutionalism (Moe, 1994; Rohr, 1998). At one level, this seems shocking, given the role of the public bureaucracy as an institution of government, yet it is not that surprising when one remembers the epochalist terms in which the NPR is framed, and the fact that, as a result, it never describes the field of public administration in any specific or detailed sense.

The NPR sought to institute a highly pluralistic organizational and management structure upon the executive branch of government, in keeping with its model of best 'entrepreneurial' practice. Congress was represented here as a relatively unimportant, and, indeed, largely negative, factor in this new paradigm. The president, in turn, was seen more as a catalytic policy entrepreneur than as the legal agent of sovereign power. Thus, the entrepreneurial management paradigm sought to reverse the thrust of prior constitutionally based organizational management initiatives in government, in which the institutional presidency was considered central to the management of the executive branch of government, and to devolve management responsibility to the lowest practicable levels (Moe, 1994: 117). As a consequence, primary accountability was no longer to the president through departmental lines and central management agencies, but to the customer. This was a shift of remarkable constitutional importance and yet its merit was taken for granted simply because it conformed to 'good' entrepreneurial management and not 'bad' bureaucratic practice.

The NPR, and the ideas informing it, derived from Osborne and Gaebler's *cri de coeur* for radical 'change' in governmental administration, operated at a highly abstract level. As Moe (1994) has suggested, Osborne and Gaebler's epochalist assumptions, the use of argument by faith and assertion rather than through precise formulations, and the rigorous definition of operating procedures, lends their prescriptions a metaphysical 'aura'. In Wittgenstein's (1998) terms, by failing to go beyond the form of substantive assertion, and operating at the heights of abstraction, the NPR, and Osborne and Gaebler's tract, conjure 'something of the higher order' into their dreams and schemes. In the process, specificity is lost or made to disappear.

Jaques, Bureaucracy, and 'Change'

An absolutist or epochalist designation only achieves whatever rhetorical power it is presumed to possess by virtue of underdescribing that which it seeks to excoriate. Indeed, despite the widespread view that bureaucratic forms of organization kill initiative, undermine enterprise, and crush creativity, and are no more than anachronisms in the contemporary organizational landscape, they remain remarkably resilient (Alvesson and Thompson, 2005). This in turn suggests that approaching any existing bureaucracy a priori as bad or useless, as many contemporary advocates of 'change' have a tendency so to do, is neither practically useful nor in accordance with the dictates of a classical as opposed to a metaphysical 'stance'. Discussion of change in regard to bureaucracy could, we suggest, benefit from regaining a lost specificity—that empirical grounding in detailed description—as a prerequisite to normative assessment and prescription for effective action. And, once again, insights from classic OT can provide some useful rules of thumb in how such an endeavour might be undertaken. In what follows, we briefly explore the work of Elliott Jaques and Wilfred Brown to elaborate this point.

The first major research project undertaken by the Tavistock Institute of Human Relations was an investigation into joint consultation in industry in the UK. It involved work in one enterprise, the Glacier Metal Company, for two and half years, between 1948 and 1950, and deliberately ranged more widely than reference to 'joint consultation' might suggest. Indeed, over three decades from the beginning of the study, Tavistock's director, Elliott Jaques, and the managing director of Glacier, Wilfred Brown, both individually and collectively developed a distinctive programme that became recognized in its time as having as significant an impact on organizational and management thinking as the Hawthorne experiments. However, Jaques and Brown's programme is now largely relegated to a footnote in the history of OT.

One of Jaques's main tasks was to investigate empirically what would be generally accepted as the right level of pay for a given role. From this evolved a key concept in his repertoire: the notion of 'the time span of discretion'—the idea that the main criterion by which the importance of a job is implicitly judged is the length of time which expires before decisions taken by an person are reviewed and evaluated (Jaques, 1956). He also found that differentials in what he termed 'felt fair-pay'—what people in an organization felt they and others should earn—were highly correlated with objective measurement of differences in time span, so that if a payment system was based on discretion differences between jobs/roles it would generally be seen as 'equitable' (Jaques, 1961). The third conceptual strand in his programme related to bureaucratic hierarchy (Jaques, 1976, 1990), where his research led him to argue that bureaucracy was neither inherently pathological nor dysfunctional but rather, in contrast, a form that could potentially enable an organization to employ large numbers of people and yet preserve both unambiguous work role boundaries and accountability for work conducted by those occupying those roles. A properly functioning bureaucracy, he argued, could allow equitable payment based on measurement of responsibility through time-span capacity to operate economic competition, for example, without the exploitation of labour (ibid.). Despite subtle changes since its inception in the early Glacier studies (1951, 1956, 1961, 1965), Jaques's programme exhibited a remarkable consistency over time. This led to some serious criticisms of it, not least from theorists of organizational change, for whom its focus on 'the organization' as the object of analysis, and on managerial accountability hierarchies or 'bureaucracies' as potentially subtle and supple organizational forms, was indicative of both rigid and anachronistic thinking. Indeed, Jaques was accused of being a 'managerial fascist', a Taylorite, and a mechanistic rationalist (Kleiner, 2001). Gareth Morgan summed up the mood when he was quoted in the *Toronto Globe and Mail* describing Jaques's programme as an irrelevance in the contemporary organizational 'epoch': 'He had a very powerful idea, but it's old economy stuff' (quoted in Kleiner, 2001: 1).

The continuing empirical presence and significance of bureaucracy alone should be reason enough to approach such epochalist claims with a degree of caution (du Gay, 2005; Thompson and Alvesson, 2005). For Jaques (1990), though, the empirical persistence of bureaucracy wasn't a matter of chance, nor could it be seen as evidence of an organizational residue, a 'zombie' phenomenon, in Beck's (2005) loaded term. Rather, bureaucracy can be seen to express two fundamental aspects of 'real work'. First, that work tasks occur in lower and higher degrees of complexity, and, second, that there are sharp discontinuities in complexity that separate tasks into a series of steps or categories. These two characteristics of work enable bureaucracy to meet four of an organization's core needs: 'to add real value to work as it moves through the organization, to identify and nail down accountability at each stage of the value-adding process, to place people with the requisite competence in each of the organizational layers, and to build a general consensus and acceptance of the managerial structure that achieves these ends' (Jaques, 1990: 129). But how exactly do they do so? For Jaques and Brown, the answer lay in specifying the nature of managerial accountability and authority, on the one hand, and measuring levels of work on the other. Hence their preoccupation with describing, clarifying, and precisely delineating roles and role relationships, and the attendant allocation of responsibility and accountability in an organization's 'executive' or 'work role' system.

The starting point for Jaques's analysis was an observed distinction between the 'prescribed' and 'discretionary' demands of specific tasks. Prescribed demands could be precisely and specifically stated, and it was almost unambiguously clear whether or not they had been met. The discretionary elements were those aspects of the work task that involved the exercise of judgement and where a decision as to the adequacy of performance, as to whether it has achieved an adequate balance of pace of work and quality, could only be made by a superior. Jaques and Brown argued that the level of discretion or responsibility in a work role could only be measured in terms of its time span of discretion: the maximum period of time during which marginally substandard exercises of discretion could pass without review by a superior (Brown and Jaques, 1965; Jaques, 1967). This measurement was seen as providing a basis both for organizing work roles hierarchically into a number of definite strata—distinguished by qualitative breaks in the nature of the discretion which is required for their satisfactory performance—and for determining payment at an level 'felt' to be equitable for the time span of work involved.

This argument was developed via a set of relational distinctions concerning organizational 'modes' or 'states'. The first of these relates to 'manifest' organization, i.e. the structure of the organization as it appears in official organograms or charts. The second relates to 'assumed organization': the organizational structure as different categories of person within the organization assume it 'really works'. Both manifest and assumed organization may differ from the 'extant' organization: the situation revealed by systematic empirical exploration and analysis (though it can never be 'completely' known). Finally, 'requisite organization' is 'the situation as it would have to be to accord with the real properties of the field in which it exists' (Brown, 1965b: 47–8). The work of Jaques and Brown entailed both detailed empirical description of extant organization and, elaborating from this, a precise set of prescriptions for the attainment of 'requisite' organization. As Eric Trist (1965) noted in his original introduction to Wilfred Brown's book *Exploration in Management*, the main focus of interest is with the organization as a discrete object, with its internal processes and structures, and with the sources of change that may arise therein. The analysis of the executive system, based as it is on empirical observation and detailed description, remains resolutely concrete, referring to sets of work roles and role relationships, though there is some elaboration in terms of rather more abstractly defined activities at various points. It is this attention to detail though, and the rigorous definition of concepts and operating procedures that follows from it, that grabs his attention and leads him to conclude that the programme Brown and Jaques elaborate 'is one which substantially increases the resources available through which managers in an enterprise can take effective action' (Trist, 1965: 21).

In Jaques and Brown's analyses, bureaucracy emerged as a supple, multifaceted, organizational device in which people and tasks were able to be deployed at complementary levels, where individuals could perform the tasks assigned to them, and where employees in any given layer could add value to the work of those in the layer directly below them (Jaques, 1990: 8). Here, everyone would know their place. To contemporary theorists of change who demand that employees 'drop your tools' in the pursuit of poetic improvisation and bricolage (Weick, 1996), or 'develop a public and passionate hatred of bureaucracy' in the quest for liberation and empowerment (Peters, 1987: 459), nothing could be less appealing or, indeed, more dysfunctional. And yet, as Wilfred Brown suggests, the advantage of knowing your place is that it provides the security required by the individual employee before they can become free to fully develop the discretionary component in their own role. In other words, rigidity and flexibility were not here seen as inevitably antithetical to one another. Rather, the former could be seen as the condition of the latter. It was the relation between the two that was important.

The generalized a priori disdain of bureaucracy (and the equation of bureaucratic rules with the inhibition of individual liberty, creativity, and so forth) to be found in contemporary discourses of organizational change has its counterpart in the practical world of organizations too. Indeed, it may not be too ingenuous to suggest that the former might conceivably be connected in some 'performative' manner with the latter. The cases of Enron, Arthur Andersen, and WorldCom at the beginning of the millennium, and those of Lehmann Brothers and other financial institutions more recently, indicate precisely what can happen if bureaucratic formalities and procedures are viewed simply and irrevocably as tiresome and unnecessary constraints on 'executive freedom to act'. It is salutary then, to return to the work of Brown and Jaques for a more nuanced and subtle formulation of what is precisely and specifically involved in 'executive freedom to act', once the latter is subject to a pragmatic empirical stance, and not simply to the dictates of a priori denunciation. In words that echo our own assessment of many theories of change, Brown (1965b: 118) indicates that close empirical examination and detailed description of executive freedom to act, or 'the environment which gives a manager freedom to make decisions', can lead to the very opposite conclusions of those assumed by more normative and metaphysical assessments:

> Many managers feel that 'freedom' lies in the sort of situation where their superior says to them: 'There are not many regulations in this place. You will understand the job in a month or two and make your own decisions. No red tape—you are expected to take command; make the decisions off your own bat as they arise. I am against a lot of rules or regulations, and we do not commit too much to paper.' In my experience a manager in such a situation has virtually no 'freedom to act' at all. [...]
>
> It is much more efficient to delineate as precisely as possible to a new subordinate all of the regulations he must observe and then say: 'You must take all of the decisions that seem to you to be required, so long as you keep within the bounds of that policy. If, keeping within those bounds, you take decisions which I think you should have referred to me, then I cannot criticize; for such a happening implies that some part of the policy which I wish you to operate has not been disclosed to you. I must, then, formulate that policy and add it to the prescribed content of your job.' If, in addition, the manager can give his subordinate a rounded idea of the discretionary component of his job by stating the types of decision he must make, then that subordinate is in a real position to act on his own initiative in the prescribed area ... In fact, it is only by delineating the area of freedom in this way that a subordinate knows when he can take decisions. The absence of written policy leaves him in a position where any decision he takes, however apparently trivial, may infringe an unstated policy and produce a reprimand.
>
> (Brown, 1965b: 118–20)

In contrast to the assumptions framing contemporary discourses of organizational change, Brown's formulations, based as they are on practical experience and empirical observation, suggest that bureaucratic constraints, formalities, and procedures may be understood, in context, as conditions *for* the existence of executive freedom to act, rather than simply and inevitably as *barriers to* the exercise of such freedom. This point is not simply relevant for the assessment of bureaucracy as an organizational device, but holds a basic warning against the decontextualized importation of any general principle or recommendation. It all depends, seems a useful maxim to hold onto, as does that elaborated by Weber (1989) in *Science as a Vocation*, where he commends detailed empirical description prior to moralizing. For contemporary theorists of change, as for some of their predecessors in organizational analysis, a pre-commitment to values of a certain sort—such as the importance assigned to notions of flexibility, creativity, and adaptability above all else—can only lead them to be always antithetical to bureaucracy in advance of any empirical consideration of this organizational form (Crozier, 1964). That is not necessarily a productive stance to inhabit.

Conclusion

In this chapter, we have pointed to a pronounced tendency within contemporary organizational analysis to treat 'change' as an existential absolute, a generalized epochal condition, and, concomitantly, in a highly generalizing manner. We have suggested that this propensity, which takes a number of different forms depending on theoretical orientation, has had some unfortunate consequences, not least for the empirical grounding and relevance of OT as a practical science of organizing. Utilizing the frame provided by Wilfred Bion's notion of 'basic assumptions', and the empirical investigation of 'requisite organization' undertaken by Elliott Jaques and Wilfred Brown, we have indicated how contemporary representations of 'change' as a generic entity have displaced many of the classical concerns or tropes animating work in the field of OT, as well as the pragmatic spirit informing them, and suggest that this shift of perspective and orientation has little to commend it. In particular, we have stressed the importance of recovering a lost 'specificity' when it comes to analysing 'change'—the revival or recovery of a pragmatic, empirical stance, grounded in the detailed description of content, context, purpose, and tools—as a prerequisite for any normative appraisal or critique.

At present in the field of organization studies, as elsewhere in the social and human sciences, rather less prestige or standing appears to flow to such a stance, and to the idea of 'piecemeal engineering' (Popper, 1985: 304) associated with it, than attaches to more grand and metaphysically inclined theorizing and prescription. This is a pity, we feel, because a strongly contextualist approach, which privileges detailed empirical description over and above theoretical reconstruction or metaphysical speculation, gets us closer to the object (in this case, organizations) we seek to analyse, rather than, as in much contemporary theorizing, spiriting it off the stage entirely. As Bruno Latour has put it: '[N]o scholar should find humiliating the task of sticking to description. This is, on the contrary, the highest and rarest achievement' (2005: 136). In this sense, the stance we advocate does not 'disappear' its object but rather treats it with a degree of concern that more generalized, abstracted, or otherwise 'elevated' theories cannot, because the latter set out their coordinates too far in advance and leave no way out from their terms of reference. This tendency, we suggest—exemplified in 'epochalist' approaches to 'change', such as that characterizing the work of Osborne and Gaebler, for instance—has the effect of rendering certain crucial but often (seen from the heights of grand theory, whether managerial or critical in orientation) seemingly banal empirical details insignificant or invisible. Only by underdescribing and decontextualizing are abstract, generic, and metaphysical approaches to 'change' capable of generating whatever rhetorical power they are deemed to possess. And that power should not be underestimated, for, as we have suggested in this chapter, a certain prestige or standing seems to attach itself to those versed in the arts of metaphysical 'change' talk.

In ordinary, everyday parlance, 'change' can mean a host of different things, depending on context of use and preferred project. Indeed, dictionary definitions of change proceed on the assumption that the term always denotes something, but not the same thing in every instance. This being the case, then, it seems only possible to ask whether such things as 'organizational change' have the same 'structure' or 'identity' under a certain description. This in turn suggests that we must specify the description *before* the question can be identified. This is a crucial point, for it indicates the importance of the classical stance, and of detailed description and specificity, for analysing and understanding any concrete instances of 'change'. And it is precisely such specificity and detailed description that is signally lacking, we suggest, in contemporary theories of change that posit this 'something' as an abstract, generic, and constant entity whose dynamics and effects can be posited 'in advance', whether for or against. However, when 'change' is recontextualized and subject to the classical stance, it can once more be practically related to specific modifications of concrete organizational phenomena (as it was, once upon a time, OT): work roles, authority structures, payment systems, production technologies, and so on and so forth. This may seem a rather boring proposition, especially when viewed from the dizzy heights of many recent theories of 'change' (including 'radical' critiques of 'change', as well). However, we suggest that a revival of the classical stance in organizational analyses of 'change', with its focus on context specificity, detailed description, a dissatisfaction with and devaluing of explanation by postulate, a pragmatist call to experience, and an ongoing rebellion against high theory, offers an important resource, not least because the adoption of such a stance is a precondition both for effective organizational action and for the normative evaluation of such action.

4

Metaphysical Speculation in Organizational Theorizing

On the Expressivism of 'Exploration'

Introduction

Rosa Brooks (2014: BR21) has written of the emergence of a breed of commentator, one coterminous with the development of what she terms 'Davos Man' and the 'TEDification of knowledge', and especially adapted to the corporatized landscape of the modern university and 'media biome'. This persona is distinguished by its proclivity for 'ideas': it feeds upon 'stories, studies, and statistics', but does so in such a way as to 'transform the resulting partly digested mix into brain candy for well-heeled aficionados of Malcom Gladwell and Thomas Friedman' (ibid.), among many others. A particular disposition offers the key to understanding its success. For this persona offers a description of a certain state of affairs without, in the words of Harry Frankfurt (2005: 32), feeling the need to submit 'to the constraints which the endeavour to provide an accurate representation of reality imposes'. It's not that this persona fails to get things right, rather that s/he is not even trying. There is among the commentariat, in other words, some laxity which 'resists or eludes the demands of a disinterested and austere discipline' (ibid.: 23) and that comes with 'a concern with truth' (ibid.: 33; Williams, 2002). And it is this lack of concern with truthfulness per se—an indifference to how things are, this 'not even trying'—that characterizes 'Bullshit' in Frankfurt's technical sense of the term.

As a concern with 'impact' (Collini, 2009, 2012) has become an increasingly important element in university research evaluation and funding,[1] so

---

[1] Where 'impact' is associated specifically with the achievement of 'demonstrable benefits to the wider economy and society', and thus precludes 'intellectual influence' on the work of other scholars and influence on the 'content' of teaching. It has to be impact which is 'outside'

distinctions between academic and 'new' commentariat personas also appear to have blurred. A quick glance at engagement and impact vehicles such as the *Conversation*—very much a product of the contemporary 'media biome'—bears this suggestion out. Unsurprisingly, the field of management and organization studies has not escaped this trend. In a way, it was, not least in its populist managerial variants, a trailblazer in its development. Populist tomes and media commentary *à la* Peters, Hamel, Senge, Linkner, and so on, and the work of their 'semi-scholar' (Van Gennep, 1967) siblings, Porter,[2] Christensen, Kotter, and so forth, providing a go-to resource for anyone in the field seeking models for 'impactful behaviour' or, as Collini (2009: 18) puts it, guidance on how to become 'door-to-door salesmen for vulgarized versions of their increasingly market-oriented "products"'. In other words, the 'impact agenda' encourages a particular disposition, one in keeping with Brooks's 'new breed of commentator', for whom, as we have suggested, there is some laxity 'that resists or eludes the demands of a disinterested and austere discipline' (Frankfurt, 2005: 32) that accompanies a concern with truthfulness. In the field of organization studies, as elsewhere, this pertinent mode of laxity cannot be unequivocally equated with simple carelessness or attention to detail, though these are not unimportant. Rather, the mode of laxity, we suggest, is one by-product of the adoption of a metaphysical stance towards organizational analysis. We seek to argue this case by delving into the contemporary fixation with the values of dissonance, disruption, creativity, entrepreneurship, learning, play—often huddled together under the umbrella heading of 'exploration'.

In a now famous paper, James March (1991) argued that establishing a requisite and ongoing balance between what he termed 'exploration' and 'exploitation' is a key facet of organizational survival and flourishing. For March, neither capacity can be ignored, nor indeed privileged in and of itself, on general or a priori grounds, as both are necessary and their combination in practice is crucial. On the one hand, an overemphasis on exploitation can preclude an organization from obtaining new input to its 'code', as he puts it, thus failing to renew itself. On the other, with too little control and an underdeveloped capacity to follow through, an organization can be overwhelmed by too many such inputs, and its capacity to achieve its core tasks will be diminished as result (Levitt and March, 1988). March's proposition was not, in and of itself, a novel intervention: its basic tenets appearing in a

academia, on other 'research users', and must be part of a conscious strategy of engagement with such users: impact cannot simply be equated with the ways various groups and individuals may happen to have made use of those 'findings' (Collini, 2009: 18–19).

[2] Whom *Forbes* magazine called, interestingly, 'The Aristotle of business metaphysics' (Denning, 2013).

number of different guises throughout the history of organization theory (OT) (Simon, 1946; March and Simon, 1958; Lawrence and Lorsch, 1969). However, March's elegant formulation established the basic premise very clearly.

In this chapter we suggest that within contemporary organizational theorizing, broadly conceived, there is a pronounced tendency to ignore his basic premise and to treat 'exploration' as something approximating to an expressivist ideal, by which we mean that the capacities, dispositions, and 'values' routinely huddled together under this heading—innovation, disruption, dissonance, entrepreneurship, risk taking, improvisation, and so forth—have been allotted a *moral* primacy over and above, and indeed, in basic opposition to, those capacities and dispositions March labelled 'exploitation' (Larmore, 1987; du Gay, 2007). This tendency to moralize organizations through the prism of 'exploration' resides not simply in popular and populist management thinking—that work which most readily approximates to a 'commentariat' brew, where a pre-commitment to certain norms (liberty, flexibility, improvisation, and so forth) leads to a denunciation of bureaucratic forms of organizing—it also has its counterpart in critical denunciations of that theorizing and of the organizational forms it seeks to privilege, namely 'post-bureaucracies'. However, this denunciation does not depart from a disinterested and austere assessment of the capacity of such post-bureaucratic forms to effectively combine exploration and exploitation in the manner suggested by March, but rather from an assessment of the failure of such forms to embody the ideals of exploration fully enough. The commentariat disposition towards a certain laxity with truthfulness is also in evidence here. The moral ideals themselves are not problematized, nor is the primacy accorded to them questioned. Instead, post-bureaucracies are accused of surreptitiously enhancing 'exploitation' and thus of not giving full expression to the norms of 'exploration' as they claimed so to do. Once again, exploration functions as an expressivist ideal, and exploitation as its negatively coded 'other'.

In what follows, we investigate this contemporary tendency to privilege 'exploration' over 'exploitation', and examine some of the consequences of this shift of emphasis, not least the resurfacing of a sort of 'one best way of organizing' that it inaugurates. We indicate that a pre-commitment to 'exploration' by certain organizational scholars is indicative of the reappearance of a metaphysical stance within the field. We also suggest some of the explanatory costs of this development through an engagement with two classic, resolutely anti-metaphysical, contributions within OT that are now represented as 'anachronistic' in relationship to contemporary matters of organizational concern: Wilfred Brown's *Exploration in Management and Organization* and Paul Lawrence and Jay Lorsch's *Organization and Environment*. Clearly, we are not alone in elaborating this line of argument, and we make no claims for our originality in so doing. In keeping with others in the field, such as King, Felin, and Whetten (2010), for instance, we seek to 'bend the stick' by highlighting the need for understanding, explicating, and researching the enduring, noun-like qualities of 'the organization', in the face of the metaphysical disappearing of this object in much organizational theorizing concerned with process, networks, learning, and change, for example. In the manner suggested by Simon (1946) many years ago, we are keen to highlight some of the pitfalls associated with attempts to elevate one principle of organizing to a pre-eminent position on the basis of unexamined assumptions or moral pre-commitments. Indeed, we suggest again that a sustained re-engagement with the 'classical stance' in OT offers a productive way of contextualizing, de-dramatizing, and questioning normative claims about the overriding significance of 'exploration'. At the same time, we suggest, such a stance also has the capacity to furnish contemporary organizational analysis with precise 'empirical concepts' that have a clear and pragmatic reference to organizational reality, and which assist in specifying this reality, in order to analyse and assess the types of arrangements and balances between contradictory criteria of (e)valuation that are appropriate to the 'situation at hand'.

The Increasing Emphasis on 'Exploration' and Its Consequences

Over the last three decades within organization studies, as elsewhere within the social and human sciences, there has been a significant upsurge of interest in the values and practices that March gathers together under the heading of 'exploration'. A growing concern with innovation, entrepreneurship, creativity, disruption, dissonance, and related notions has frequently occurred at the expense of, rather than in tandem with, a similar focus on the elements of organization that March labels 'exploitation'. While March's formulation is not without its own drawbacks, as we will show—its explanatory reach being achieved at the cost of a certain lack of empirical specificity and precision in relation to 'the situation at hand'—it has the merit of focusing attention on a recognizable object: the organization. In contrast, many within the field of organization studies no longer appear comfortable with the idea of organization as a discreet or enduring object. An example or two should prove useful. The literature concerned with 'organizational learning', for instance, gives a flavour of the manner in which a renewed focus on exploration is trumping a concern with exploitation. In Weick and Westley (1996), the two key terms, 'organization' and 'learning', are deemed antithetical to one another, the former precluding or otherwise oppressing the possibility of the latter. As a result, March's 'balance' between competing criteria is nowhere to be seen. Exploitation (organization) is represented as inimical to exploration (learning).

In a less dramatic formulation than that advanced by Weick and Westley, but one which nonetheless also trades on distinctions between learning and organization, Argyris (1992: 9; Argyris and Schön, 1996) refers to the differences between 'single-loop' and 'double-loop' learning. The former is deemed appropriate to 'routine, low-level issues' whereas the latter is relevant to 'complex, non-programmable issues'. Clearly, the former is not at all antithetical to organization. The latter, though, is more slippery. Argyris still holds onto the idea of the organization as a discreet entity: double-loop learning may disrupt, disorganize, and pluralize to some extent, but only within specific limits—limits set by organizational authorization. In this way, learning and organization are not antithetical per se, rather 'real' learning (the double-loop *explorative* kind) is deemed inherently antithetical to a particular sort of organization: a bureaucracy (the *exploitative* kind—see also Contu, Grey, and Örtenbald, 2003: 937). This is an important point, for it reconfigures March's formulation, slanting it in a particular direction. March's dictum suggests that *any* formal organization must necessarily cultivate both the capacity to explore and the capacity to exploit. Argyris, and those influenced by him, suggest that the techniques and practices associated with exploitation do entail learning, albeit of a certain limited sort. Double-loop learning, however, cannot be cultivated or found in certain sorts of organization—bureaucracies. Because they are solely focused on exploitation bureaucracies simply cannot accommodate or support double-loop learning. Here, the link between exploration and exploitation in March's sense is sundered. Bureaucracies cannot learn beyond a certain basic level, therefore they are unable to renew themselves (explore) and must of necessity be superseded by new organizational forms (post-bureaucracies) that allow learning to flourish.

Other, more populist interventions within this field of organizational learning, such as those associated with the work of Peter Senge, for instance, have continued to trade on this separation of double-loop learning from bureaucratic forms of organizing. Here, learning organizations are directly counterposed to bureaucratic organizations 'where the wonder and joy of living have no place' (Kofman and Senge, 1993: 22). Emergent learning organizations are represented as harnessing the potential of 'the full human being', whereas bureaucracies connote by contrast, as Boltanski and Chiapello indicate (without endorsement):

[A]uthoritarianism and arbitrariness, the impersonal blind violence of cold monsters, but also inefficiency and squandering of resources. Not only are bureaucracies inhuman, they are also unviable . . . [T]he discrediting of bureaucracy [. . .] should we are told, facilitate a return to a 'more human' modus operandi, in which people can give full vent to their emotions, intuition and creativity.

(2007: 85, 98)

In some of the texts of Karl E. Weick (1991, 2000; Weick and Westley, 1996), the anti-bureaucratic stance articulated by Argyris and Senge is extended to a general disdain of 'organization' per se. Learning is consistently associated with disorganizing and the flourishing of plurality and diversity. The balancing act between exploitation and exploration is no longer seen as a balancing act at all, but rather as an 'oxymoron'—a self-contradiction. Accordingly, a 'learning organization' is, in Weick's theorization, a paradox: 'to learn is to dis-organize and increase variety. To organize is to forget and reduce variety' (Weick and Westley, 1996: 440). Perhaps, Weick suggests, 'organizations are not built to learn' (Weick, 1991: 119); a thread running throughout his work is that there is a basic conflict between efforts to control and regulate and the ability to stay open and innovative. These anti-bureaucratic, pro-exploration tropes also figure largely in recent work within the sociology of economic life, where 'dissonance', 'search', and 'heterarchy' are also allotted a distinctive moral status and represented as increasingly crucial features of organizational success and flourishing in the present and future (Stark, 2010: 4).

While not everyone has such a low opinion of, or lack of confidence in, the capacities of organizations to engage simultaneously in processes of exploitation and exploration (see, for instance, Raisch et al. (2009) for an assessment of the growing literature on 'organizational ambidexterity'), an increasingly singular concern with exploration is far from unusual within the field of organization studies. Indeed, we might go further and suggest it is in fact part and parcel of an emerging orthodoxy. If, for a moment, we engage in a brief and far from representative examination of the sorts of articles being published in key journals in the field such as *Organization Science* and *Organization Studies*, for instance, we quickly note a concentration of interest in topics that can be classified as relating to 'exploration', and which, relatedly, bring to the surface the idea that bureaucracy and 'old organizational forms' are relics of the past and increasingly irrelevant. A search of the keywords 'change',[3] 'innovation', and 'new organizational forms', for example, shows that these concepts significantly outnumber three classic concepts within OT: 'coordination', 'hierarchy', and 'interdependence'. A simple counting exercise like this does not, of course, constitute any conclusive proof, and it certainly

---

[3] The search for keywords in articles was made in November 2011 in *Organization Science*, *Organizational Studies*, and *Research in the Sociology of Organizations*, using the journal web pages' online search facilities. The following results emerged (the order of digits follows the order of journals): 'Change' (880, 1975, 186), 'Innovation' (691, 1038, 118), and 'New organizational forms' (1132, 1659, 161); in contrast to: 'Hierarchy' (343, 760, 66), 'Coordination' (388, 496, 56), and 'Interdependence' (232, 267, 36). Searches on 'exploration' and 'exploitation' showed the same tendency, of nearly twice as much interest in exploration than exploitation: 'Exploration' (379, 480, 43) and 'Exploitation' (233, 225, 28).

does not tell us how or why these concepts are used more frequently now. One way to proceed is to take a closer look at the scholarly debates as they unfold at conferences, such as the European Group of Organizational Studies (EGOS). Confirming the pattern found in the simple search, only twelve out of fifty-seven subthemes at the 2012 EGOS conference focused on specific issues of 'exploitation' in the sense deployed by March (e.g. 'Trust in crisis: diagnoses and remedies' and 'The governance of effective learning strategies'). Fourteen subthemes focused upon 'other topics' (e.g. 'New forms of organizational ethnography'), and a total of thirty-one subthemes addressed either themes related to 'exploration' (e.g. 'From designing organizational creativity to creativity for organizational design' and 'Luck of the draw—design or serendipity, accident and change?') or critically discussed issues of exploitation in organizations, such as 'power' and 'categorization' in organizational life (e.g. 'Challenging inequality: changing gender and organizations' and 'Reassembling management ethics and CSR'). Here, it seems that the priority accorded to change, creativity, and flexibility and other key tropes of 'exploration' within organization studies comprises two different moves—a double shuffle, as it were. On the one hand, there is an agenda that, by and large, continues and extends the Weickian appraisal of exploration, and, on the other, a critical agenda which is largely suspicious of exploitation efforts whatever form they may take, but which too, in its own distinctive way, is concerned with promoting 'exploration' as a moral ideal.

These two agendas can also be found in the literature focused upon the idea of 'the post-bureaucratic organization' (Heckscher and Donnellon, 1994; Iedema, 2003) and 'post-bureaucracy' (Maravelias, 2003). The first group of authors affirms the proposition that bureaucratic organization has outlived its usefulness and that network-based, flatter, less hierarchical organizational forms—'post-bureaucracies'—are more apt forms for dealing with complex environments in which the capacity for 'exploration' is held to be at a premium. The second group of authors—departing predominantly from critical management studies (CMS)—point to the inconsistencies underlying the rhetoric of 'post-bureaucratic' empowerment, for example—that post-bureaucracies don't deliver on what they promise, not least because they are more bureaucratic or hierarchical in reality, and hence more exploitative, than their advocates can admit (Iedema, 2003: 2). The solution to this presumed 'hypocrisy' is to demand an explicit surfacing of the tensions and contradictions at play in post-bureaucratic organizations:

[O]ur focus of interest has to shift from adopting fixed moral and analytical stances as researchers, to tracing the specifics of how people and organizations wield heteroglossia and monoglossia, and what this does to peoples' work and self, and to the products of their work. (Ibid.: 203)

In this way, the critical agenda does not specifically aim to analyse the realism or one-sidedness of the post-bureaucratic organization, or even how it is put together normatively and technically—as would follow from taking March's maxims seriously. Instead it satisfies itself with a theory programme focused upon analysing organizations and organizing efforts as 'texts', 'discourses', and 'power', repeating many of the (tired) tropes of social explanation (Latour, 2005; du Gay, 2007). A range of 'forces' (let's call them social, for the sake of argument) are interpreted as always already present, and the precise means through which organizations qua organizations are put together and work tend, accordingly, to disappear from the analysis. The organization itself is transmuted into an under-specified arena in which various social forces (power, gender, values, the list can be extremely long and varied) play themselves out, drowning everything organizational and practical in the sea of the social.

Thus, while mainstream management thought has focused on providing the norms and techniques through which organizational success is to be achieved via self-exploration and 'empowerment', its oppositional twin, CMS, has devoted much of its effort to bringing to the surface the human downsides of such norms and techniques, indicating the manner in which 'empowerment', for example, operates as a control mechanism through regulating or disciplining the 'soul' of the employee in an insidious manner (Alvesson and Wilmott, 2002; Fleming, 2005; Fleming and Sturdy, 2009). Here the focus has been on 'self-exploitation'. However, what unites both parties is not only a focus on the mobilization of subjectivity as a key means through which 'post-bureaucratic' organizing is undertaken (whether for or against), but also an enduring attachment to 'exploration' as a normative ideal. Both parties endorse a set of pre-commitments to particular values, including, notably, ideals of 'autonomy', 'liberty', and a romantic conception of 'the full human being'. We suggest that this preference for 'exploration' is also indicative of a (re)turn to metaphysical forms of theorizing within the field of organization studies at the cost of an attachment to what we have termed the 'classical stance'.

'Stances' in Organizational Theorizing

> Work in philosophy, like work in architecture, is very much work on oneself, on one's way of seeing things (and what one asks of it).
>
> Ludwig Wittgenstein

As we indicated in Chapter 2, in *The Empirical Stance*, the philosopher of science, Bas van Fraassen (2002: 3) poses the question: How has so much work in contemporary philosophy reverted to the once moribund *vieux jeux* of metaphysics? It is a question that we now seek to apply to work in contemporary management and organization studies that treats 'exploration' as a normative ideal. In a series of illuminating articles, the historian of ideas, Ian Hunter (2006, 2007, 2008, 2009a) offers some hints as to how this question can be answered by exploring the shared intellectual deportment and attitude that has come to characterize a range of distinctive positions within the humanities and social sciences, again both mainstream and 'critical'. Focusing particular attention on the history of the proliferation of high theory in the post-1960s humanities and social sciences, Hunter (2006: 80) indicates that what has come to be known as the 'moment of theory' began when a certain kind of philosophical interrogation surfaced inside a wide variety of disciplines—linguistics, literary criticism, sociology, organization studies, political economy, the 'psy' disciplines, and jurisprudence—'where it assumed the form of an array of associated but rivalrous theoretical vernaculars'. In other words, the 'moment of theory' cannot be readily identified with a common object or even a shared language. If this is the case, though, what then is it about these manifold forms of theory (which include, inter alia, structuralism, post-structuralism, deconstruction, 'process' ontology, and so forth) that has prompted both exponents and detractors to acquiesce in a single name—'theory'—for them? According to Hunter, the answer to this question resides in the shared intellectual deportment or attitude they exhibit, albeit to differing degrees:

> This attitude is sceptical towards empirical experience (in a more or less Kantian way) [...] which it regards as foreclosing a higher level ('transcendental') experience—and hence cultivates openness to break-through phenomena of various kinds. (Ibid.: 81)

It would seem evident from our discussion that such a comportment precisely characterizes a number of positions within the field of organizational theorizing, broadly conceived, whether they be more popular or populist management thinkers (Peters, Senge), or more mainstream organizational theorists (Weick), keen as they are to cultivate openness to breakthrough phenomena (and thus an antithetical attitude towards entities that are seen as foreclosing such a breakthrough, such as bureaucracy). A leading 'process' scholar, openly acknowledging the influence of Weick, encapsulates the comportment when he writes of the implications of taking a 'processualist' approach to organizational change:

> Relaxing of the artificially-imposed structures of relations, the loosening up of organization. Such a relaxing strategy will allow the intrinsic change forces, always kept in check by the restrictive bonds of organization to express themselves naturally and creatively. (Chia, 1999: 211)

In their suspicion and problematization of 'exploitation', their deployment of social explanation, and their attachment to many of the tenets of post-structuralism, theorists within CMS can also be seen share this intellectual attitude or comportment as well, though, of course, they inflect it rather differently (Alvesson and Wilmott, 2002; Fleming, 2005).

Rather than affirming or denying the truth or falsity of the 'moment of theory', however, Hunter treats its claims as actions or activities (and thus no more capable of being true or false as are swimming, chess, or drawing) that certain individuals perform on themselves as the condition of establishing the inner deportment required to undertake 'theory'. Despite its reliance upon certain kinds of philosophy, he does not approach the 'moment of theory' as a species of philosophy. Rather, he treats it as a 'stance': an ensemble of discourses, a certain kind of intellectual self-stylization arising from the philosophical problematization and reworking of an array of disciplines deemed positivist, empiricist, or representational as a result of this same problematization.

Hunter's approach shares much in common with that of van Fraassen. Neither is interested in equating a distinctive theoretical position with a 'thesis' or 'belief' per se, but rather in exploring it as a 'stance', that is, an attitude or commitment. In other words, the 'sensibility' informing the persona of the theorist is not a belief they choose to hold, but an intellectual comportment forming the register in which beliefs (doctrines, projects, norms, hopes) can be held. In the case of the law, for instance, the crucial thing is not the beliefs held by jurists per se but the existence of a legal profession and a juristic comportment through which juridical norms and doctrines are acceded to. This explains why the central concern of secularizing early modern legal reformers, for example, was not legal doctrine as such—though they were concerned with this too—but the formation of the juristic persona who would accede to such doctrines. Seen in this way, adopting a metaphysical stance, on the one hand, or an empirical stance, on the other, is:

> [A]nalogous to conversion to a cause, a religion, an ideology, to capitalism or socialism, to a worldview such as Dawkins's selfish gene view, or the view Russell expressed in 'Why I Am Not A Christian'. That is so, and not a prospect to every-one's liking. But let us not colour the project with guilt by association . . . all the great philosophical movements have really been of this sort, at heart, even if different in purport. (Van Fraassen, 2002: 61)

Viewed as stances, metaphysical and empirical approaches to organizational analysis are rival attitudes, and should be treated as such. It is not so much that one is 'true' and the other 'false'—they are not reducible to factual theses, so that cannot be the case—but that they are engaged in a battle and there is no position above or below the fray from which to judge them.

While van Fraassen advocates the 'empirical stance' over and against the 'metaphysical stance', he stresses that the former cannot be made consequent with the assertion or belief of a given factual thesis (such as 'experience is the only source of information'). As he puts it, 'there is no factual thesis itself invulnerable to empiricist critique' and which can simultaneously function as 'the basis for the empiricist critique of metaphysics' (ibid.: 46). Any thesis is liable to empirical criticism, and thus none has the capacity to occupy the place from which an empiricist critique of metaphysics can be launched. Rather than a thesis, empiricism is a *stance*, component elements of which include: a dissatisfaction with and devaluing of explanation by postulate, a pragmatist call to experience, a rebellion against high theory, and an admiration for scientific forms and practices of enquiry (in the classic Weberian (Weber, 1989) sense of that term as 'the disciplined pursuit of knowledge', and, as such, not reducible simply to the 'laboratory' sciences, nor to the *content* of the sciences per se). Thus, van Fraassen's 'empirical stance' overlaps considerably with what we have designated as 'the classical stance' in OT.

In the following two sections we present two examples of 'the classical stance' in action in OT, both of which, in effect, address the organization as a practical balancing act between different concerns and criteria of (e)valuation in the manner suggested by March. The first example focuses upon 'bureaucratic organization', and presents a rather different, and, we would suggest, more subtle, description and analysis of bureaucracy than is to be found in the exploration literature. The second, a classic statement of the contingency approach in OT, provides a nuanced analysis of conflicting dimensions of organizing and the different ways in which an empirically specific balance between them is practically undertaken. In outlining these two examples of the 'classical stance', we also have cause to compare their approach and conclusions to the (metaphysical) pre-commitment to 'exploration' characteristic of much contemporary organizational theorizing, whether popular, mainstream, or critical. We suggest that such pre-commitments have the effect of (re)producing a 'one best way' thesis in OT.

Wilfred Brown on Bureaucracy

At the beginning of his classic book, *Complex Organizations*, the sociologist Charles Perrow (1979) notes that the organizational form that has most preoccupied organizational theorizing since the latter's 'disciplinary' inception is, without doubt, 'bureaucracy'. He notes, too, that this organizational form has largely been negatively coded by organizational theorists, and that many of the same criticisms of bureaucracy appear time and time again throughout the history of OT (ibid.: 6). He points, in particular, to two enduring lines of criticism. The first associates bureaucracy with inflexibility, inefficiency, and, at times of rapid environmental change, with a lack of creativity and a pervasive unresponsiveness. The second, which he associates specifically with the humanistic tradition in OT, represents bureaucracy as stifling the spontaneity, freedom, and self-realization of those in its employ. He notes, too, that both lines of criticism are often combined by a single author and 'are echoed by such diverse groups as the radical right, the radical left, the man [sic] in the street, and the counterculture' (ibid.: 6). After many years of studying formal organization, Perrow (1979: 5) concludes that, despite their enduring popularity and reach, these two lines of bureaucracy critique are deeply problematic: 'the sins generally attributed to bureaucracy are either not sins at all or are consequences of the failure to bureaucratise sufficiently'. For Perrow (1979: 200ff) bureaucracy is not an inherently unadaptive organizational form. Indeed, empirically it is a form that has proven capable of undertaking both exploitation and exploration to some effect, creating as well as responding to the environment within which it exists (in Charles Goodsell's (2005) related terms, bureaucracy has proven 'almost uniquely' capable of both 'rule' and 'response').[4]

In making his case for a reconsideration of bureaucracy as a potentially positive, if often fragile, organizational achievement, Perrow (1979: 24–6, 44) had cause to turn at certain points to the work of Wilfred Brown. Brown was an experienced and successful executive and organizational analyst, who rose to prominence in the field of OT, as we indicated in Chapter 3, as a result of his involvement in the first major research project undertaken by the Tavistock Institute of Human Relations in the UK after the Second World War: the Glacier Project. Brown's experience of working within and empirically analysing the operations of bureaucratic hierarchy led him to argue that bureaucracy was neither inherently pathological nor dysfunctional but rather, in contrast, a form that could potentially enable an organization to employ large numbers of people and yet preserve both unambiguous work role boundaries and accountability for work conducted by those occupying those roles. In particular, Brown stressed that the very formalities, or so-called 'rigidities', of bureaucratic hierarchy were not antithetical to flexibility but rather its precondition (see also du Gay, 2000; Stinchcombe, 2001). Instead of being seen as mutually exclusive, as the 'customary view' of bureaucracy within OT would have it, the one is seen as the condition of the other. For Brown, it is the relationship between the two that is important.

Let us then briefly explore in more detail one of the aspects of his approach to OT as a practical science that places Brown at odds with the assumptions about bureaucracy informing 'expressivist' conceptions of exploration in

---

[4] See also the discussion of 'Innovation' in James Q. Wilson (1994).

contemporary organizational theorizing. This relates to the relationship between bureaucracy, flexibility, and creativity. As we have had cause to note, a customary and enduring criticism of bureaucracy as a rule-infused hierarchical form of organization concerns its presumed inability to be adaptive to changes in its environment and thus to be inherently inefficient, unresponsive, inflexible, and uncreative. While the role of rule-bound bureaucratic authority and accountability relations in the reduction of particularism and featherbedding within organizations, and in the protection of individual employees from arbitrary decision-making, is relatively uncontroversial (Perrow, 1979: 23), those very same rules are also the source of considerable unease, not least to those for whom formalization connotes a loss of freedom, flexibility, and creativity, both organizationally and individually. For Brown, such sentiments were both empirically inaccurate and organizationally dangerous: 'There are those who are convinced that formalization means a loss of freedom. Their cry is: "Let's keep it vague so that individuals' creativeness can have a greater chance." But there is plenty of evidence that vague and confused organization is the great enemy of creativeness' (1974: 35).

In Brown's (1965b, 1974) analysis, formalization was viewed as a supple and multifaceted organizational device enabling people and tasks to be deployed at complementary levels, and as a mechanism whereby employees in any given layer were able to add value to the work of those in the layer directly below them. For Brown (ibid.), formal organizations consist of an executive system or employment hierarchy comprising the network of positions to which fulfilment of the organization's work is assigned. This system or hierarchy is made up of a number of roles and consists of all members of the operating organization, a member being in such a role when s/he is carrying out their job responsibilities or tasks. Every role carries with it specified responsibility and authority, which are taken on by the member assuming the role. Work roles themselves here consist of the totality of discretion which an organizational member is expected to exercise, and the prescribed acts s/he must discharge in carrying out the responsibilities of the role to which s/he is attached. The activities constituting a given role are set by the immediate manager and by higher policies and are directed towards an objective set by the higher manager, the whole being carried out within an employment contract. The benefit of such formalization, Brown argues, is that everyone knows their place, and this provides the security required by the individual employee before they can become free fully to develop the discretionary (flexible, creative) component in their own role. Rather than infantilizing employees, by robbing them of liberty or agency, such security fosters their freedom to act in circumstances where ambiguity may exist (where a policy set may leave alternative courses of action from among which the employee has to choose). In other words, and as we indicated earlier in this chapter, rigidity and flexibility are not here seen as inevitably antithetical to one another. Rather, the former can be viewed as the condition of the latter.

The generalized a priori (metaphysical) disdain of bureaucracy (and the equation of bureaucratic rules with the inhibition of liberty, flexibility, and creativity, for example) to be found in expressivist conceptions of exploration as a moral ideal, has its counterpart in the practical world of organizations too. Indeed, it may not be too ingenuous to suggest that the former might conceivably be connected in some 'performative' manner with the latter (du Gay, 2008). It is salutary then, to return to the work of Brown for a more nuanced and subtle formulation of what precisely and specifically is involved in 'executive freedom to act', for instance, once the latter is subject to a pragmatic empirical stance, and not simply to the dictates of a priori expressivist denunciation. In *Exploration in Management*, Brown (1965b: 118) indicates that close empirical examination and detailed description of executive freedom to act or 'the environment which gives a manager freedom to make decisions' can lead to conclusions the very opposite of those assumed by more normative and metaphysical assessments of formalization.

Brown is not naive or romantic about formalization, however. He is more than aware that employers try to take judgement out of work at a number of levels and in a number of ways—by automation, the introduction of prescribed routines, and so forth—in order to increase productivity (1974: 63). Clearly, a fully automated concern would be one with few written rules, the 'rules' being in the machines, as it were. Similarly, it is possible to think of organizations staffed with persons in whom complex rules are 'embodied'—professionals, for instance. Only a small proportion of organizations fit either of these two cases, however. Nor does Brown think it necessary for every organization to start writing up every policy and routine and specifying the work content of every role in Prescribed and Discretionary terms (he was also keen to indicate certain situations under which bureaucratic organization should at all costs be avoided, see Jaques, 1976: 244–7). The work of all organizations changes. Therefore the organization itself has to be dynamic (Brown, 1974: 73). Nonetheless, Brown argues that hierarchy is not an inherent evil, that formalization is not inherently or largely antithetical to creativity and liberty, and that the nature of the work that takes place in different employment hierarchies does need to be made explicit and precisely specified in the manner he proscribes (1974: 33). This is particularly the case, he continues, if we wish to avoid confusion concerning the relationship between persons and organizations.

Some of his fiercest criticisms concerning the dangers of 'personalizing' work concern the normative assumptions relating to 'informal organization', which he views as an aberration rather than as a space in which people exert the agency, intuition, emotion, and creativity of which formality robs them:

There is … a widely held view that formality in organizations deprives people of the right to make decisions and be creative. This theory is false because the raison d'être of formal organization is to use human decision-making ability to its fullest possible extent. Any failure of organization to achieve this situation calls for better organization, not its abolition. The false assumption of the 'informal organization' school of thinking arises from its failure to realize that human work inevitably concerns 'decision-making'. If work does not require decisions to be made there should be no need to employ human beings to do it. The fact is that the informal organization thinkers tend to regard formal organization as a structure of roles down which specific work tasks are delegated. They do not think of roles as containing precisely defined areas over which the occupant has to make all the decisions. As a result, the idea of informality is essential to them, in order to provide the opportunity for somebody to spot the need for a decision to be taken and to have the courage to take it. But if instead the role is defined by delineating an area over which the occupant of the role has, as a duty, to exercise discretion and take the necessary decisions, then there is no need to think in terms of informality as a mechanism for filling the gaps left by inadequate formal organization.   (Brown, 1974: 86–7)

Many years ago, at the high point of the human relations school's dominance in OT, Peter Drucker (quoted in Trist, 1965: 17) noted that 'it has become fashionable of late … to assume that the actual job, its technology and its mechanical and physical requirements are relatively unimportant compared to the social and psychological situation of men at work'. The implication of Drucker's criticism was that, in its singular focus on the 'human factor', OT had lost sight of its own object: the organization. A similar criticism could be directed at contemporary expressivist theorists of exploration, and indeed, their critical counterparts in CMS, for whom such things as the work at hand, and the resources and techniques available to do it, remain strangely absent, and where attention is instead frequently focused upon a set of metaphysical commitments to particular conceptions of the person—the 'full human being'. Meanwhile, the work at hand disappears from view.

The Contingent Stance: Lawrence and Lorsch

For nearly two decades in the mid-twentieth century, the American organizational scholars Paul R. Lawrence and Jay W. Lorsch conducted a series of studies into the appropriate structure and functioning of organizations, formulating and establishing as they did so what became known as the 'contingency' approach within organizational theory (Lawrence and Lorsch, 1967 [1986], 1969). Based on studies of well-performing, middle-performing, and low-performing organizations within three different industrial fields, they argued in their classic text, *Organization and Environment*, that the essential requirements of an organization vary depending on the nature of the task, the environmental characteristics, and the disposition of its members. There is no 'one best way of organizing', they concluded. Rather, an organization should be arranged in a manner that corresponds to the 'situation at hand'. In the following, we suggest that the distinction between exploitation and exploration and, more precisely, the tendency to elevate the latter as particularly desirable to the present and future, illustrates that this once widely recognized maxim appears to have been forgotten (though see Raisch et al., 2009, for a reiteration of its basic premises in relation to debates about 'organizational ambidexterity').

Although it was coined to capture how organizations respectively form or break out of their cognitive code, March's (1991) distinction between exploitation and exploration is not unparalleled in the history of organization theory. In fact, it mirrors a key dichotomy that has pervaded the field of organizational studies and management theory over time and which also formed the point of departure for Lawrence and Lorsch's contingency theory. The dichotomy appears in many intellectual guises: 'order' versus 'openness', 'structure' versus 'process', 'hierarchy' versus 'empowerment', and so forth. Lawrence and Lorsch trace it back to the opposition between 'classical theory' (Fayol, Mooney, Urwick, and Gulick) and 'human relations theory' (Mayo, Rothlisberger, Lewin, and McGregor). They also point to its existence among the wealth of practical managerial tools and techniques that have been developed with the aim of improving organizational functioning. Listing a handful of tools that, at the time when their book was published, were popular in executive life—PERT (programme evaluation and review technique), sensitivity groups, system design techniques, creativity training, cost benefit analysis, motivation laboratories, and so on—Lawrence and Lorsch argue that such techniques tend to fall into one of two categories:

> Each of these techniques seems to carry with it a thrust in one of two directions—either toward greater order, systematization, routinization, and predictability, or towards greater openness, sharing, creativity, and individual initiative. One thrust is to tighten the organization; the other, to loosen it up.
>
> (Lawrence and Lorsch, 1967 [1986]: 61)

Although this characterization may appear somewhat dated, it's not too difficult to apply it to contemporary organizational life. Currently, popular theories, tools, and methods can also be categorized along the tightening/loosening axis: 'balanced scorecards', 'six sigma', and 'key performance indicators', on the one side. 'Storytelling', 'lateral thinking', and 'appreciative inquiry', on the other. Depending on purpose, organizations will employ theories and tools from either, or they will be combined—as they have been practically for some time. As we suggested earlier in this chapter, a rather different situation appears to pertain in the present theoretical landscape, however. At the time of *Organization and Environment*, theories from both sides of the dichotomy were seen as providing an organization with potentially important contributions and choices. Today, we will argue, the scales have definitely tipped towards the 'loosening' side, where the literature emphasizes, for instance, the need for flexible arrangements that foster 'continuous change' (Brown and Eisenhardt, 1997; Weick, 2000), 'improvisation' (Orlikowski and Hofman,1997; Barrett, 1998; Vera and Crossan, 2004), 'entrepreneurship' (Garud, Jain, and Kumaraswamy, 2002; Maguire, Hardy, and Lawrence, 2004; Tolbert, David, and Sine, 2011), and similar capacities. Formerly well-established notions of, for instance, 'organizational design', 'strategy', and 'resource dependency' are, by and large, derided as old-fashioned, or only for the tool-makers that supply the mentioned models and methods for practitioners (Czarniawska, 2013). A central reason for this is the emergence of a distinctive assumption common to many contemporary theoretical streams: that organizations depend for their future upon the softening or transcendence of tight structures. In order to flesh out this conjecture, we will briefly revisit some of the main arguments outlined in *Organization and Environment* to explore the extent to which this assumption is indeed plausible, and, if it is not, what implications this might have for the discussion of exploitation and exploration in the present.

In order to problematize the basic terms in which discussions of effective organizational functioning had been represented within the different wings of organizational theory, Lawrence and Lorsch (1967 [1986]) emphasized the proposition that any organizational system must be adapted to the world outside it and, at the same time, make sure it is internally integrated. In order to cope with the exigencies of the external environment in which they find themselves, organizations, as Lawrence and Lorsch argue, come to develop segmented units, each of which has, as a feature of its function and task, the problem of dealing with some aspect of the conditions outside what it considers to be its own formal boundaries. This *differentiation* of function and task is accompanied by differences in the capacities and dispositions of those charged with fulfilling those functions and tasks, and differences, too, in the formal structure of different departments. As a result of this differentiation, a coordination problem arises, which requires the deployment of appropriate methods of *integration* in order for the organization to function effectively. Integration, too, though, is affected by environmental conditions. The basic necessity for *both* appropriate differentiation and requisite integration to achieve effective organizational performance lies at the heart of Lawrence and Lorsch's hypothesis. To explore this basic proposition, Lawrence and Lorsch (1967 [1986]) decided to seek empirical answers to the question—'What kind of organization does it take to deal with various economic and market conditions?; (ibid.: 1)—through a twofold study. First, they conducted a comparative study of competing organizations in the plastics industry (where the environment was very dynamic and new products had continually to be invented). Second, they compared the findings from the plastics industry with an analysis of high- and low-performing competitors in two other branches of industry: the container industry (which operated in a relatively stable environment) and the food packaging industry (which had a growth rate that was higher than the container industry, but lower than the plastics industry). Two significant findings appeared from these studies: first, the high-performing organizations in all three industries were better at meeting the demands of their environment than their less effective competitors. The high-performing organizations in the plastics industry were more highly differentiated than the high-performing competitors in the food packaging industry, which in turn were more differentiated than the high performers in the container industry. Second, all three high-performing organizations were achieving approximately the same level of integration, but through various means. All of them used, to some extent, the traditional ('classic') methods of paper systems, formal managerial hierarchy, and direct managerial contact between members of different departments. However, the repertoire of integrating mechanisms included integrative departments, permanent or temporary cross-functional teams, and the deployment of individual integrators. The appropriateness of each device or mechanism seemed to vary with the environment:

> The more differentiated an organization, the more difficult it is to achieve integration. To overcome this problem, the effective organization has integrating devices consistent with the diversity of the environment. The more diverse the environment, and the more differentiated the organization, the more elaborate the integrating devices. (ibid.: 157)

The ability to resolve conflicts arising between different parts of the organization proved to be central to the degree of integration obtained within an organization. Based on their findings, Lawrence and Lorsch argued that the effective organizations developed conflict-resolving practices consistent with their environment. Thus, in the plastics industry, conflicts tended to be resolved by the integrating department, both at high and low levels of the organizational hierarchy, because no single part of the organization possessed all the necessary, requisite knowledge. In contrast, the container organization tended to solve its inter-unit conflicts either through the sales department or at the upper management levels, since the information required for appropriate decision-making tended to be located there as a direct effect of the way the organization related to its environment.

Lawrence and Lorsch's conclusion was decisive: no one best way of organizing suitable to all circumstances could be reasonably identified. Neither one particular organizational form (e.g. a bureaucracy) nor one particular motivational approach (e.g. 'Theory Y') was always and everywhere 'the best'. Rather, organizations must arrange themselves in ways that correspond to the specific environment in which they operate. It is impossible to decide once and for all whether a strict hierarchy or a flat structure is relevant, or whether an organization should try and solve conflicts through formal means and executive intervention or through 'democratic' negotiations at all levels. The first type of arrangement tends to be more relevant or appropriate in situations where the basic task is well defined because of a stable environment. The latter form tends to correlate with more uncertain and changing environments where many types of input are needed. And yet this does not mean that an organization located near one of the ends in the stability–change continuum requires either 'more' or 'less' organization. To organize for a dynamic environment does not necessitate a 'freeing' up of the organization in the way that many contemporary anti-bureaucratic approaches suggest (Keller and Price, 2011). The picture painted by Lawrence and Lorsch is much subtler. The more varied and turbulent the environment, the more internal differentiation is needed, and the more diverse and manifold the integrating devices and conflict-resolving mechanisms will be. Nor does their work suggest the organizational necessity of fostering or developing only certain personal dispositions and capacities at the expense of others. There is no sense here of the need to cultivate 'the whole human being' as a basic principle of organizational flourishing in the manner suggested by expressivist advocates of 'exploration' as a moral and organizational ideal, quite the contrary in fact. The differentiation of function and task is necessarily accompanied by differences in the personal capacities and dispositions of those required to fulfil them. The roles have to be coordinated to ensure effective performance, but the latter requires the development and deployment of requisite integrating mechanisms, *not* the development of integrated persons; a point that is sometimes missed by advocates of 'organizational ambidexterity', where the latter begin to foreground 'ambidexterity' as a personal capacity to be encouraged and fostered (see, for instance, Smith and Tushman, 2005). Thus, Lawrence and Lorsch's text contains none of the romanticism regarding either organizational arrangements or human flourishing that has come to characterize expressivist conceptions of 'exploration' as an ideal to be fostered per se. In so far as they have anything to say about the way organizations and persons working within them might develop in the future in order to operate effectively in potentially more turbulent and fast-changing environments, they stay resolutely pragmatic, indicating that, under such circumstances, organizations might:

> [N]eed to establish and integrate the work of organization units that can cope with even more varied sub-environments. The differentiation of these units will be more extreme. Concurrently, the problems of integration will be more complex. Great ingenuity will be needed to evolve new kind of integrative methods.
>
> (Lawrence and Lorsch, 1967 [1986]: 238)

This possible 'multiorganization' organization of the future may need more leaders, because there are many more subtasks to be achieved, each of which requires different forms of management. The parts of the organization that focus upon the development of new solutions may well be led by managers with a capacity for innovation and the ability to take risks. The parts of the organization that perform more routine tasks, in contrast, are likely to be led by managers that 'fit more closely our traditional...models' (ibid.: 244). However, in supplementing these two types of leadership, the multiorganization is likely, to a higher degree than before, to require 'integrators', that is, managers who actively coordinate and integrate all the specialized functions of the organization. The authors also suggest that top management would increasingly need to attend to the integration of the entire organization and 'formulate a general framework of purpose to guide the efforts of the parts' (ibid.: 245).

At the time *Organization and Environment* was published, the concept of 'organizational learning' had not acquired the degree of fashionability it later obtained. Lawrence and Lorsch only refer to the work of James March a few times in the book. However, they do credit March and Simon with being among the first in the field of OT to fully recognize 'the importance of differentiation and integration' (ibid.: 270) and there seems to be a distinctive family resemblance between this pair of concepts and that of 'exploration' and 'exploitation'. Both sets of authors highlight the dynamic relationship between, on the one hand, the processes through which an organization relates to an environment to gain knowledge about demands and possibilities and, on the other, the mechanisms by which this insight is brought together and practically coordinated. The important lesson from Lawrence and Lorsch's study, however, is that it is very unlikely, in fact something of a fundamental error, to assume that organizations face situations where they can rely on just one of these dynamics. What kind of organization can survive if it abstains from relating in some or the other way to its environment—if it does not bother to explore it just slightly? Likewise, is it not rather romantic to think of an organization that can do away with all of its integrating mechanisms—where its members simply do whatever they themselves find relevant? Any organization must find a balance between those two dimensions in relation to 'the situation at hand', a point forcibly made by Simon

(1946), to which will return in our concluding comments. In fact, like Simon (1946) and Parker Follett (1982), for instance, Lawrence and Lorsch stress that their main point is the need for a detailed understanding of these situational demands rather than a call for developing organizational typologies:

> First, we believe that the major contribution of this study is not the identification of any 'type' of organization that seems to be effective under a particular set of conditions. Rather, it is the increased understanding of a complex set of interrelations among internal organizational states and processes and external environmental demands.   (Lawrence and Lorsch, 1967 [1986]: 133)

It is precisely this focus on the 'situation at hand', and the pragmatic lash up of the devices and dispositions deemed necessary to dealing with its contingencies, that differentiates Lawrence and Lorsch's approach not only from expressivist conceptions of 'exploration' as a moral ideal or overriding principle of organization and human conduct, but also from certain contemporary conceptualizations of *the* 'ambidextrous organization' as a form in and of itself (Tushman and O'Reilly, 1996). Somewhat strangely, this warning seems to have been lost in discussions of today's organizational challenges and possibilities. It is now widely agreed that 'bureaucratic' forms of organizing are relics of the past: increasingly irrelevant and problematic types of organization. In contrast, 'flexible', 'entrepreneurial', or 'ambidextrous' forms of organizing are almost unanimously portrayed as aptly suited to what is conceived of as a generalized state of fast and omnipresent change and, in addition, that they are also more desirable for 'humanistic' reasons. From such a perspective, the two hypothetical questions just posed are no longer understood as equally hypothetical.

While it is certainly recognized as an absurd proposition that organizations can afford to ignore exploration of their environment—most texts call for embracing diversity and letting a thousand flowers bloom—it is now a collectively shared assumption that organizations are better served by reducing their integrating efforts to a minimum. 'Rules', 'orders', 'authority', and 'coordination' are designations that no longer have the legitimate ring they possessed at the time *Organization and Environment* was published. Likewise, 'exploitation' and 'integration' have come to acquire connotations of rigid forms of organizing that are no longer relevant because the demands of the environment (a meta-environment, in effect) have so fundamentally changed. In fact, we would like to suggest that a peculiar (metaphysical) exaltation appears to have replaced Lawrence and Lorsch's pragmatic concern with a specific assessment of the fit between an organization's inner arrangements, its core tasks, the differentiated personal capacities and dispositions necessary for the fulfilment of those tasks, and the environment in which it operates. If organizations are arranged in ways that allow its members to creatively explore the environment, start innovative processes, and transgress structures, a democratic, open, trustful, and effective atmosphere will ensue. Despite the tempting and optimistic outlook of this vision, it must be characterized as something of a contemporary metaphysical riff on a very old theme: the belief in a 'one best way of organizing' that had appeared a number of times throughout the history of OT up to the moment of Lawrence and Lorsch's study and the programme of contingency theory it inaugurated.

Concluding Comments

In this chapter we have argued that, in much contemporary organizational theorizing, popular, mainstream, and critical, there is a pronounced tendency to treat 'exploration' as something approximating to an 'expressivist' ideal, by which we mean that the capacities, dispositions, and 'values' routinely huddled together under this heading—innovation, play, dissonance, disruption, risk taking, improvisation, and so forth—have been allotted a *moral* primacy over and above, and indeed, in basic opposition to, those capacities and dispositions March labelled 'exploitation'.

We suggested that the manner in which 'exploration' functions as an expressivist ideal in contemporary organizational analysis is related to the 'metaphysical stance' characteristic of certain sorts of theory—such as process ontology (as deployed in Weick's work, for instance), or various forms of post-structuralism (as deployed by various critical management scholars, for instance). This 'metaphysical stance', we argued, is, amongst other things, characterized by a scepticism towards empirical experience, which it implicitly or explicitly regards as foreclosing a 'higher'-level ('transcendental') experience, and thus seeks to cultivate openness to breakthrough phenomena of various kinds. The remarkable powers and possibilities allotted to 'exploration' as a cluster of attributes which can enable organizations and individuals to 'break through' to the sunny uplands of empowerment, innovation, and human flourishing, is one aspect of this; the other is, of course, the scorn and disdain heaped upon organizational forms and practices which are deemed to precisely foreclose or negate the appearance of these 'higher'-level experiences—namely bureaucracy and those other dull and 'instrumental' organizational practices gathered under the mantle of 'exploitation'. Here, we would suggest, following Weber (quoted in Bourke, 2009: 106), 'theorie' transmutes into 'theodizee'.

The battle against metaphysics and its 'theological aura' in organization studies is best joined, we argued, via adoption of what we have termed the 'classical stance'. In contrast to its metaphysical twin, the 'classical stance' consists of a radically different attitude, sensibility, and comportment, characterized, inter alia, by a pragmatist call to experience, and a rebellion against high theory. In elaborating the difference between adoption of a 'metaphysical' and the 'classical stance' within OT, we had recourse to two important interventions within the field, both of which offered clear and present challenges to the a priori assumptions about the negativities of bureaucracy and the positivities of exploration pervading much contemporary organizational theorizing. The work of Wilfred Brown offered a descriptive analysis of bureaucracy, viewing the latter less as an inherent barrier to, but rather as a precondition of, the capacity to 'explore'. Rather than assuming the superiority of 'exploration' over and above other considerations, Lawrence and Lorsch's analysis exhibited a pragmatic concern with the specific assessment of the degrees of fit between an organization's design and coordination arrangements, its core tasks, the differentiated personal capacities necessary to their fulfilment, and the environment in which it undertakes its work. As we have stressed, their analysis is very much focused upon the exigencies of 'the situation at hand'.

Like March, both Brown and Lawrence and Lorsch point to the problems of espousing and promoting, implicitly or explicitly, 'a one best way' of organizing, whether that 'one best' is associated with a particular motivational theory, a set of value commitments, or a particular organizational form deemed suitable to all 'situations at hand'. For them all, justifying a reconfiguration of organizational arrangements on the presumed superiority of a speculative norm or 'principle' is the business of a metaphysics of morals, as opposed to a prudent and pragmatic organizational analysis. As we have already had cause to note, this is not a novel conclusion in OT, as elsewhere (in political theory, for instance: see Bourke, 2009). In 1946, Herbert Simon made an important intervention in OT along precisely these lines. In his paper, 'The proverbs of administration', March's erstwhile collaborator offered a detailed argument against the tendency within the OT of his time to elevate one principle of organizing over and above all others on the basis of unwarranted assumptions or pre-commitments.

He went on to argue that the administrative theory of his time suffered from lack of precise description and thus from a degree of 'superficiality, oversimplification [and] . . . lack of realism' (Simon, 1946: 63), and that this had some unfortunate consequences, since decisions about how to organize and which principles to follow must depart from a clear understanding of the 'content' of the organization's purposes: the situation at hand. Heralding the proposition of contingency theory, Simon drew attention to the need for studying carefully the 'conditions under which competing principles are respectively applicable' (ibid.). As a first step, he proposed the development of a vocabulary for a precise description of administrative organization. The 'first task of administrative theory', Simon continued, 'is to develop a set of concepts that will permit the description in terms relevant to the theory of administrative situations. These concepts, to be ... useful, must be operational; that is, their meanings must correspond to empirically observable ... situations' (ibid.: 62). Echoing, Mary Parker Follett's (1982) notion of the 'law of the situation', and indeed, the approach espoused by the tradition of casuistry or case-based reasoning (Jonsen and Toulmin, 1988), Simon suggested that it was not 'sufficient merely to identify' principles, axioms and adages of organization:

> Merely to know, for example, that a specified change in organization will reduce the span of control is not enough to justify the change. The gain must be balanced against the resulting loss of contact between the higher and lower ranks of the hierarchy ... Hence administrative theory must also be concerned with the question of the weights that are to be applied to these criteria—to the problem of their relative importance in any concrete situation. This is not a question that can be solved in a vacuum. Arm-chair philosophising about administration ... has gone about as far as it can profitably go in this particular direction.   (1946: 66)

Simon's analysis offers many parallels to our own. Like Simon, we do, of course, acknowledge that concepts are necessary to assist in empirical specification, but not just any sort of concepts. The work of Brown, and Lawrence and Lorsch, is important in this respect, we suggest, as both offer precise formulations of 'empirical concepts' that have a clear and pragmatic reference to organizational reality, and which assist in specifying this reality in order to analyse and assess the type of arrangements and balances between contradictory criteria of (e)valuation that are appropriate. Their conceptual work stands in stark contrast to that which has flourished during 'the moment of theory', and which we suggest still pervades all sorts of organizational theorizing in the present: process, power, dissonance, disruption, heteroglossia, and so on. Perhaps even 'exploitation' and 'exploration', in the manner elaborated by March, can be seen, in the light of Simon's comments, to be a little too generalized and not specific enough for the task at hand (the same can be said about the concept of 'ambidexterity', which tends to take on a theoreticist life of its own: see, for instance, Cao, Gedajlovic, and Zhang, 2009; Raisch et al., 2009). Overall, as Wilfred Brown put it: 'the price of a realistic perception of this dynamic thing called organization is constant exploration and adjustment of attitude in the face of the facts as they emerge' (1965: 37). Exploration, indeed, but from the position of the classical, not the metaphysical, stance in OT.

5

Task and Purpose as (Continuing) Core Concerns

Do Organizations Need to Know What They Are Doing?

When, in 2014, the British retailer Tesco announced a £250 million accounting error, concern was raised about the company's trading model, which built upon what appeared to be unsustainable operating margins, and likewise about Tesco's auditor PwC, who had failed to uncover this gross accounting irregularity. The Tesco scandal, however, was also seen as an example of board incompetence. As one commentator put it:

> I am not surprised the board missed the signs. Among the 10 main board directors, there is currently only one executive director, Dave Lewis, the new chief executive. He joined a few weeks ago from Unilever. Like every single other director on the main board, he has no executive experience as a retailer whatsoever. The nearest the board gets is experience from the consumer goods industry—from a former CEO of Unilever and a former CFO of Cadbury. Elsewhere, the board boasts three non-executives who have worked at banks—Schroders, Standard Chartered and Barclays, to be precise. Another non-executive has worked in the telecommunications industry, another in glass manufacturing. And it has two non-executives who have worked in government—here and, bizarrely, the Netherlands (where Tesco has no operations at all). Tesco's recruitment policy for directors clearly doesn't include the requirement for them to have any hands-on background in their specific industry at all.
>
> (Luke Johnson, *Financial Times*, 23 September 2014)

The case of Tesco is not unique. It is a recurrent complaint that corporate boards increasingly consist of members without 'domain knowledge', that is, expertise and experience within the company or organization's key areas of business. In 2002, the Sarbanes–Oxley Act was enacted in the USA as a response to corporate failures such as the Enron scandal. Among other things, the Act required corporate auditors and board members to be 'independent' from the interests of the company. However, the financial meltdown in 2008 made it clear that this rule does not ensure that board members are also competent. As with Tesco, the board of Citigroup—a US banking and financial services corporation facing insolvency in 2008 and receiving a $306 billion rescue package from the US government—consisted at the time of the financial crisis of sixteen independent members, of which only one had ever worked at a financial services firm (Pozen, 2010). This is not only a characteristic of many corporate boards: executive directors and other top management positions are also often recruited from outside the organization's business domain. One of the reasons for this development may be the prevailing influence of agency theory (see Chapter 2) and the belief that, by simply providing the right incentives, the best executive people will be attracted (Feldman and Montgomery, 2015). However, the disregard of the value of domain knowledge and experience is also legitimized and even advanced by developments in intellectual thought and ideas within contemporary organization theory (OT) and organization studies. In particular, we will argue that the lack of appreciation of domain knowledge may be coupled to the widespread scepticism here towards classic concepts such as 'task' and 'purpose' as central for the understanding of organization and management. We suggest that the contemporary agreement that management and board governance does not require domain-specific knowledge is a symptom of a wider forgetting or rejection of the idea that organization is a purposeful and content-specific activity.

In the classic formulations, it was repeatedly emphasized that to think of management, administration, and organization crucially implied an idea and knowledge of something—a task or a purpose—from which management, administration, and organization have to depart, around which they must revolve, and which form the raison d'être and the key determinant for any type of organizational arrangement. Consider, for example, the following quote from Chester Barnard's *The Functions of the Executive*: 'An organization comes into being when (1) there are persons able to communicate with each other (2) who are willing to contribute action (3) to *accomplish a common purpose*' (Barnard, [1938] 1968: 82; emphasis added). This common purpose, or primary objective, is something that is crucial to understand, even if it also comes with its own difficulties, as Lyndall Urwick argued in *The Elements of Administration* (1943: 27):

> [T]he true objective of any business undertaking must be to make or to distribute some product or service which the community needs. The proof that it is doing so is that in exchange the community will give rather more of other products and/or services than, in terms of the medium, money, have gone into producing it. But while 'the proof of the pudding is in the eating', the pudding must first be made. And it is this primary objective, the exact nature of the product or service which

the business exists to make or render, which is very often most imperfectly apprehended, still less defined.

Task and purpose were the sometimes implicit, but nevertheless crucial, points of departure for questions of administrative organization and coordination. This emphasis was continued in two significant streams of thought— contingency theory and socio-technical systems theory—that, in some respects, can be represented as the last cries of OT as a coherent discipline before it proliferated and fragmented into multiple subdisciplines (sometimes gathered under the heading of organization studies). In different ways, these two schools advanced the principle that there is no 'one best way of organizing', but that organizations must structurally and practically be arranged— divided and coordinated—according to the specific practical tasks they are to accomplish, and with a due understanding of their particular purpose and the environment in which they are operating.

Today, the notions of purpose and the practical task organization are almost absent from the vocabulary of OT and organization studies.[1] The academic literature has cultivated a high level of scepticism towards the idea that these notions and the focus they entail are particularly relevant for the understanding of organization and management. The concepts of purpose and task are considered as relics from the organization theoretical past and largely out of sync with the rapidly changing and globalized conditions besetting modern organizations. Actually, the seeds of this sort of scepticism were sowed shortly after the classic writers published their ideas. Beginning, perhaps, with Herbert Simon's critique of classic administrative theory for being based on 'proverbs' (Simon, 1946), Simon and March later advanced the perspective that, while 'goals' were certainly an aspect of organization, goal-setting and satisficing were pervaded with a 'bounded rationality', which undermined their practical relevance. They criticized the classic theorists for treating purpose and associated sets of tasks as 'given in advance' (March and Simon, 1958: 41) and for not paying sufficient attention to the rise of new goals and activities. As we will show, even though Simon did not reject the role of goals and tasks in organizational or 'administrative behaviour', his and March's approach to understanding organizations took a path that eschewed empirical specificity and emphasized theoretical and mathematical reasoning. They explicitly rejected the idea that 'organization' can usefully be defined and classified as a particular activity or entity, for example, that an organization has a formal

---

[1] As we shall explain in this chapter, this is true even if there are subfields of contemporary organization theory—e.g. strategic management—that use a vocabulary of 'objectives', 'business model', 'portfolio', and 'core competence'. While the focus of proponents of such subfields may appear in line with the classic organization scholars, their interpretation cultivates a strong preference for a very general, and, in fact, metaphysical, approach to practical organization.

purpose—often given in organizations' contractual relations—which is of importance to its nature and functioning:

> It is easier, and probably more useful to give examples of formal organizations than to define the term. The United States Steel Corporation is a formal organization; so is the Red Cross, the corner grocery store, the New York State Highway Department [...]. We are dealing with empirical phenomena, and the world has an uncomfortable way of not permitting itself to be fitted into clean classifications.
> (March and Simon, 1993: 20)

Thus, although it is often exactly the differences in purpose and task that formally differentiate organizations from each other, March and Simon doubted such 'clean classifications'.

Another critique of purpose or task as a relevant concern came from Philip Selznick in his 1948 article 'Foundations of the theory of organization':

> Organization, we are told, 'is the arrangement of personnel for facilitating the accomplishment of some agreed purpose through the allocation of functions and responsibilities' [...]. Viewed in this light, formal organization is the structural expression of rational action [...]. But as we inspect these formal structures we begin to see that they never succeed in conquering the non-rational dimensions of organizational behaviour. (Selznick, 1948: 25)

What seemed obvious for many practising managers and for the classic writers—that it is crucial to understand a given organization's purpose and tasks in order to practically organize and manage it—was thus problematized in a way that would continually be repeated—with subtle and not-so-subtle changes of emphasis—by subsequent generations of organization scholars.

In portraying the classic organization and management theorists as operating with 'given' entities, and by equating notions such as 'purposeful arrangement' with 'structural expression of rational action', the door was opened for a broad rejection of task and purpose as useful notions on the ground that they expressed a (naive) belief in 'rational action' and 'technical rationality'. As the years passed and fewer and fewer organization scholars appeared to have read the classic texts, but rather seem to have relied on secondary sources which routinely presented the classic organization and management theorists as 'rationalist' (see, for instance, Wren, 1994: 313), the latter's ideas about purpose and task gradually appeared more and more dubious or were simply forgotten. Today, OT and organization studies seldom focus upon the concrete tasks of a given organization (and its way of accomplishing or not accomplishing them), but nurture instead a set of broader topics such as 'change', 'learning', 'institutions', and 'identity', and comparison of organizations along these dimensions. In this chapter, we will investigate this development by identifying first the field's different types of hesitation against 'task' as a relevant focus.

We do so by locating certain common tropes and assumptions across otherwise disparate communities of thought. We then revisit the classical stance on task and show that the arguments and ideas articulated by its practitioners are quite different from the stereotyped rendering that their critics put forward. Rather than viewing tasks as 'given' and 'uniform' entities—as is routinely claimed by contemporary scholars—the classic organization theorists advocated a situated and dynamic understanding of task, work, and organization. Moreover, they pointed to the dangers associated with losing sense of these concrete couplings. Finally, we return to the problem opening the chapter, about the lack of domain knowledge among corporate directors and others. Giving an example from contemporary school organization and management, where big reforms are made without clear discussion of the school's purpose and tasks, we argue that the public sector also suffers from lack of domain knowledge. Even if it is not intellectually *à la mode*, there is every reason to reintroduce and redeploy the classic concern for organization as a purposeful and task-specific activity.

Contemporary Doubts about 'Task' as a Core Concern

During the 1980s, it was clear that OT was developing into an increasingly amorphous discipline. Bifurcating into the 'harder', more economically oriented, 'organization science', and the less nomothetic and more open-ended 'organization studies', meant that new sets of concepts began to displace those characterizing classic OT and the schools following in its wake. Among the core concepts that fell out of favour, 'task' and 'purpose' are particularly noteworthy. They used to be considered crucial for what defines organizations vis-à-vis other social groupings such as friends, mobs, and movements. Moreover, specifying a given organization's particular task was the starting point for determining how, practically, it should be organized and managed (Barnard 1938; Simon, 1947; Rice, 1963). However, task shifted from being a key concern for practising managers and organizational analysts, and the premise for other organization theoretical concepts such as 'differentiation' and 'coordination' (Lawrence and Lorsch, [1967] 1986; Mintzberg, 1979) developed, to become the epitome of the sort of concept organization studies was deemed not to need. Looking across the diverse field of contemporary organization studies, the arguments for abandoning a preoccupation with task and purpose can be sorted into five types of problematization, which frequently relate to or overlap with each other.

The World Has Changed

The notion of change has gained a firm foothold across organization theoretical communities and studies of organizations (see Chapter 3), both as a generalized epochal condition and in relation to particular diagnostics of a world increasingly 'globalized', 'networked', 'digital', and thus constitutively 'uncertain'. We are continually told that we have entered an era characterized by flux and turbulence, where organizations are operating on premises and in markets that constantly evolve and change (Wren, 1994; Bartlett and Ghoshal, 2002). The pervasiveness of information technologies creates whole new types of social relations and business areas, completely changing the communication and production relations of modern organizations (Castells, 1996; Tapscott, 1997). Here, modern organizations cannot depend upon 'the stable infrastructure of the twentieth century', it is argued, since the world has changed beyond recognition (Thomas and Seely Brown, 2011: 17). In the old economy, the world was interpretable and tasks were demarcated and tangible, whereas in the new they are emergent, intangible, and bound up with impression management and image-making: 'The successes of many corporations are, to an increasing degree, affected by how they manage their images. Doing a good job in a narrow technical and functional sense is not enough' (Alvesson, 1990: 388). In fact, to approach tasks as discreet and enduring phenomena may be detrimental to long-term organizational success. Thus, it is generally agreed across much of the literature, that, in this ever-changing world, it is a key competence to stay flexible and avoid becoming preoccupied with the fulfilment of particular objectives that may soon turn out to be too narrowly defined. In this general diagnosis, 'task management' must yield to 'strategizing'. Where it would earlier suffice for managers to focus on the effectiveness of the organization's task accomplishment, it is assumed that their focus must today be directed towards the future through 'strategic management', that is, through positioning the organization vis-à-vis 'competitors' (Porter, 1985), allocating resources to areas of 'competitive advantage' (Grant, 1991), 'enacting the environment' (Smircich and Stubbart, 1985), and 'managing stakeholder relations' (Freeman, 2010). Only in combination with a constant scanning and positioning of the organization does it makes sense to manage the internal resources and activities and 'strategically align' the two dimensions. Thus, it is a key competence to learn from and respond to change 'as it happens' (Senge, 1990; Kanter, Stein, and Jick, 1992; Stacey, 1993; Weick and Sutcliffe, 2007), and organizations should no longer be assessed simply on their ability to accomplish particular tasks. What matters is their ability to strategically and continuously choose the right tasks in different situations of change and crisis (Hirschhorn, 1999), to constantly renew themselves and stay 'self-perpetuating' (Pfeffer, 1997) and to make sure internal and external dimensions are 'strategically aligned' (Henderson and Venkatraman, 1993) and have a 'dynamic fit' (Zajac, Kraatz, and Bresser, 2000). In sum, the true indicator of an organization's succes is no longer its task accomplishment, but its self-renewing capacity on a metalevel, e.g. its ability to manage its 'change readiness' (Armenakis, Harris, and Mossholder, 1993), its 'ambidexterity' (Tushman and O'Reilly, 1996), and its 'dynamic capabilities' (Teece, Pisano, and Shuen, 1997).

Task Orientation Hampers Innovation

A related argument is that a strong focus on task militates against key facets of organizational survival and flourishing, such as 'creativity', 'playfulness', and 'innovation'. The underlying assumption is that the association of organizational intelligence with 'well-defined objectives' and a 'calculative rationality' (Levinthal and March, 1993) runs a double risk. First, systematic accentuation of tasks may lead to an obsession with objectives and plans and reformulation of these that, by and large, become rituals with no true significance for the actions and engagement of employees, or, alternatively, leads to distrust and hostility between managers and employees. Second, the goals and challenges of today are seldom given and stable, but complex, multiple, and conflicting (Eisenhardt and Westcott, 1988). Rather than technical skills and task orientation, these require 'paradox management', with organizations and their employees needing to be equipped with a 'much greater sense of the holistic and harmonious interrelationships among people inside and outside of the organization' (ibid.: 189). Paradox management strengthens the ability to reframe apparent tensions by 'fostering conditions that facilitate freedom in and support the reframing process' (Bartunek, 1988: 155) and also stimulates a relevant shift of focus from 'primary tasks' to 'primary dilemmas' (Hoggett, 2006). At the same time, it is deemed crucial for organizations to constantly innovate, and this necessitates 'leadership' that sets direction and inspires action, rather than bureaucratic 'management' of plans and procedures (Bennis, 1989; Kotter, 1996). Building upon the distinction of Burns and Stalker between 'organic', flexible organizations versus 'mechanistic', bureaucratic forms of organization (Burns and Stalker, 1961), it is argued that innovative organizations are associated with the former type's informal atmosphere of 'freedom, looseness, creativity' (Kanter, 1983: 30), whereas organizations that stay content with the latter's restricted task definitions and continue previously successful ways of accomplishing such tasks might be prone to 'competency traps' (Levitt and March, 1988), and thus come to prevent themselves and their members from developing 'double-loop learning' (Argyris and Schön, 1996), that is, modifying tasks in the light of experience and possibly rejecting them to the benefit of more appropriate goals and behaviours. Rather than a narrow focus on 'task', organizations must cultivate 'equivocal visions' to facilitate awareness of the field of possibilities and openness to 'serendipity' (Nonaka, 1991).

Task Offers Too Simplistic an Understanding of Organizing Processes

A third popular argument is that 'organization', 'management', 'task', and so on are practically and theoretically not conceivable as distinct entities and are better approached as a mutable effect of 'fields', 'networks', 'discourses', 'flows', and 'processes'. The foundation for this argument was, among other things, laid by the introduction of the system metaphor in OT. Systems theory was introduced into organization and management theory in order to convey two points—that an organization is a whole (system) defined for a particular purpose (or 'function' as it was often termed) and made up of cooperating parts; and that changes in some elements will affect the entire system (Barnard, [1938] 1968). However, it was soon argued that these points carried an understanding of organizations as 'closed systems' and an fixation upon the system's inner workings, as if it was a closed circuit with no input from the outside. It thus became widely accepted that it is just as important—and some schools of thought such as new institutional theory argued that it was even more important—to focus upon the relationships between an organization and its surroundings. Allegedly, in contrast to the classic organization theorists' view, organizations should be conceived of as 'open systems' (Scott, 1981) (see Chapter 2). Accompanied by a general turn towards social embeddedness and social constructionism across the human and social sciences—for example, the impact of Peter L. Berger and Thomas Luckmann's *The Social Construction of Reality* (1966)—the system metaphor itself began to be displaced by broader notions such as 'institutional fields' (Powell and DiMaggio, 1991), 'networks' (Powell, 1990; Nohria and Eccles, 1992; Salancik, 1995), and 'relations' (Granovetter, 1985; Dyer and Singh, 1998). Another attack on the organization as task system was coupled to a growing scepticism regarding 'a single-minded preoccupation with structure' (Tsoukas, 2003: 609) and the call to abandon the organization as a 'noun' and study instead the processes through which organization 'emerges' (Tsoukas and Chia, 2002; Hernes, 2008). In this view, to think about organizations as delimited entities (or, for that matter, as specific activities) related to designated tasks that must be formally coordinated, misses all the ways in which decisions and actions are increasingly distributed across levels of analysis—individuals, governments, corporations, non-government organizations (NGOs), and so on. Even more importantly, it also falsely assumes that there is a stable point or purpose in time where an organizing process starts and ends or from which it can be evaluated. Rather, organization happens in 'a world on the move . . . where connectedness prevails over size, flow prevails over stability, and temporality prevails over spatiality' (Helin et al., 2014: 268), and where organizing is a process through which signification emerges rather than the other way round: 'The organizing process is precisely made of the "shuttle which weaves together the woof and the warp of the fabric under construction in the semiosis"' (ibid.: 155). In order to capture this fluid 'becoming' reality of organization, one must leave a narrow understanding of organizations as 'authoritatively coordinated interaction' (Tsoukas, 2003: 618) and see them as part of 'patterned interaction' in an extensive and complex 'chaosmos' (ibid.).

Task is Power in Disguise

In line with this 'expanded' view of organizations and organizing processes, it has also been emphasized that organizations are inevitably arenas for social and political struggles. Accordingly, attempts to define the primary or core task of an organization are not neutral acts, but expressive of particular ideological beliefs and vested interests. The steps towards this perspective were many, beginning, perhaps with the argument that even if organizations appear as formal systems, 'unwritten laws' and 'cliques' are at work below the surface of this formality (Selznick, 1948, 1949; Gouldner, 1957)—a point that was soon backed up by research in organizational decision-making, showing, for instance, that decision processes were led by coalitions (Cyert and March, 1963). Although the 'garbage can model' of organizational decision-making also emphasized the randomness of con-nections between problems, solutions, interests, and concerns (Cohen, March, and Olsen, 1972), many scholars continued to address the role of 'power' (e.g. Pfeffer, 1981) and 'ideology' in organizational action and decision-making (e.g. Brunsson, 1982; Starbuck, 1982). This focus was fur-ther strengthened throughout the 1980s. Many organizational scholars engaged in 'critical' analyses of the 'rational' management and design of organizations, and sought to expose what Perrow had termed the 'underlife' of organization (Perrow, 1972). An example is the studies of French com-panies carried out by Michel Crozier (Crozier, 1964; Crozier and Friedberg, 1980), which emphasized the 'strategic games' and 'power struggles' at play there. In numerous analyses, 'political' or 'unjust' dimensions of organiza-tions and organizational goals were disclosed. Together with inspiration from Marxism, critical theory, and post-structuralism, they laid the ground for critical-theoretical traditions such as 'labour process theory' (Braverman, 1974; Burawoy, 1979), 'radical humanism' (Burrell and Morgan, 1979), 'critical management studies' (Alvesson and Willmott, 1992), 'feminist organization studies' (Calás and Smircich, 2006), and studies of 'power and organizations' (Clegg, Courpasson, and Phillips, 2006). Here, 'task' and 'purpose' were rejected as legitimate, self-evident matters and analysed as effects of power plays that can and should be exposed, problematized, and critiqued.

Humans before Tasks

Finally, the focus on task has been questioned because it is considered to 'instrumentalize' organizational life, thus suppressing its moral and affective dimensions through reducing the 'whole human being' to a cog in an impersonal machine or 'cold monster'. This argument has often been raised in relation to bureaucracy and its asserted 'depersonalization of relationships' and 'displacement of goals whereby "an instrumental value becomes a terminal value"' (Merton, 1940: 563). The bureaucratic preoccupation with ends and rules (or purpose and procedures) is viewed as a key driver of an increasingly rationalistic instrumentalization of more and more aspects of human activity (Ritzer, 2004). Bureaucracy and technical-rational forms of organizing are not necessary for organizational thriving and operation, it is argued, but are products of superimposed theoretical 'perspectives' or 'images', which illuminate only some aspects of organization and organizational life (Morgan, 1980). In this view, a focus upon goals and ends reflects an underlying 'machine metaphor' (as mentioned in Chapter 1) with which organizations are conceived as instrumental structures made up of intricate, yet logically connected parts and elements, and where 'the human beings expected to work within such mechanical structures are to be valued for their instrumental abilities' (ibid.: 614). However, organizations are so much more, it is held, than this metaphor allows. They are multifarious, 'heterogeneous' entities, in which people live, dream, relate, and interact, and where many types of phenomena make up a motley and vibrant whole that cannot and should not be reduced to the imagery of a cold engine devised for a specific end. As such, there is every reason to look beyond or beneath the standard parlance of classic OT and its narrow emphasis of 'task', 'span of control', and so on. If this technical-rational language game is suspended, it becomes possible to investigate and appreciate the many 'excluded' or 'silenced', yet 'immanent', aspects of organizational life and organizational beings, which contribute to making organizations the rich and surprising landscapes they are: 'friendship' (Krackhardt, 1992), 'bodies' (Hassard, Holliday, and Willmott, 2000), 'aesthetics' (Linstead and Höpfl, 2000), 'emotions' (Fineman, 2008), and so forth. All these dimensions emerge when the narrow instrumentalist narrative is transgressed, and organization can be rendered in all the colours of the human spectrum.

Revisiting the Classical Stance on Task

If the arguments against 'task' differ in their emphasis and conclusions, they generally share the belief that a practical understanding of organization as task system is both simplistic and dangerous. They encourage instead a shift to concepts and methodologies focused upon broader and often metaphysical themes in the social sciences ('change', 'networks', 'power', 'openness', etc.). Paradoxically, however, this shift, in many ways, forms a return to what originally motivated many of the classic scholars to put forward a strong emphasis on 'task' and 'purpose'. Let us present some of the most important arguments of these scholars in order to understand their concerns and their proposal to think of and practically work with 'task' as a core object. Despite a certain dispersion of interests and vocabulary, a clear line of thought runs through these classic texts on organizations and management. It coheres around the idea that an organization is an entity that should not be confused with other types of human assemblages (see the Introduction, Chapter 1, and Chapter 2). What distinguishes an organization is the existence of a collective 'task' or 'purpose'; something that unites its members in concerted action for a shorter or longer period and which can be explained to and by them. Once a purpose is agreed upon, much can be decided and arranged, whereas its absence will change the dynamics of the group entirely and potentially lead to a disintegration of the organization.

As we have already indicated in Chapter 1, one of the earliest and clearest voices expressing these arguments was the American organization and management theorist Chester Barnard, who was also a practising business executive and public administrator. Drawing on his extensive experience of managing organizations, he stated that:

> The necessity of having a purpose is axiomatic, implicit in the words 'system', 'coordination', 'cooperation'. It is something that is clearly evident in many observed systems of cooperation, although it is often not formulated in words, and sometimes cannot be so formulated. In such cases what is observed is the direction or effect of activities, from which purpose may be inferred.
>
> (Barnard, [1938] 1968: 86)

For the executive function, the purpose of the organization is a crucial concern. It brings together the members of the organization into a 'cooperative system', Barnard argued, which the executive must systematically address, monitor, and intervene in if necessary. Even though the purpose may be difficult to delimit and express (and often individual motives and goals may be mistaken for it), the activities and elements of an enterprise should be understood as parts of a whole arising around a common purpose: 'the inculcation of belief in the real existence of a common purpose is an essential executive function' (ibid.: 87). A 'common purpose' is what establishes the organizational or 'cooperative reality' as a distinct entity in its own right in contrast to an incidental collection of individuals.

Barnard's writings became central to a number of theoretical understandings of organization, not least the work of Herbert Simon, who was later awarded the Nobel Prize for his theory of 'bounded rationality'. In his influential book *Administrative Behaviour* (1947), Simon continued Barnard's work and focus upon organizational purpose as a key feature of the executive function, and in particular of 'administrative decision-making'. Whereas Barnard emphasized that the executive's 'inculcation of belief' in a collective purpose is essentially a moral endeavour (O'Connor, 2012), Simon put weight on the way organizational 'goals' and 'objectives' are cognitively important in stimulating certain types of action, and 'administrative behaviour': 'Organizations and institutions provide the general stimuli and attention-directors that channel the behaviours of the members of the group, and that provide those members with the intermediate objectives that stimulate action' (Simon, 1947: 100). He recognized that organizations often find themselves facing more than one goal or objective, and introduced the notion of decision-making, not as a linear, rational activity, but one of 'satisficing' and finding 'good enough' solutions: 'Decision making processes are aimed at finding courses of action that are feasible or satisfactory in the light of multiple goals and constraints' (ibid.: 274).[2]

The role of task as a pivotal concern for organization was further elaborated in two subsequent schools (they preferred the notion of 'task' rather than that of 'purpose'). The first was the contingency school, which primarily emerged as an American research tradition, but also had key British contributors. Departing from a situation where OT seemed stuck in an irreconcilable disagreement between 'classic organization theory' and the human relations tradition, contingency theory emerged as a way to transgress this polarized debate between what was presented as a 'rationalistic and universalistic approach' to organization versus a human relations approach, which generally advocated low-structure organizations and widely shared influence. One of the central contributions came from Paul R. Lawrence and Jay W. Lorsch, who conducted a series of studies into the appropriate structure and functioning of organizations (Lawrence and Lorsch, [1967] 1986, 1969. See Chapter 4, this book). They argued that the essential requirements of an organizational arrangement vary depending on the nature of the task, the environmental characteristics, and the disposition of its members. There is no 'one best way of organizing', Lawrence and Lorsch argued: any organizational system must be adapted to the world outside it and, at the same time, make sure it is internally differentiated and integrated to solve its task. Accordingly, the organization must develop segmented units, each of which has the task of

---

[2] Despite the centrality of the term 'objective' in Herbert Simon's theory on organizations, he gradually downplayed its significance and became more interested in the cognitive aspects—the 'bounded rationality'—of decision-making. Thus, in his subsequent writings with James March, he problematized the classic preoccupation with task and advocated a focus upon uncertainty and ambiguity as a premise for organizational decision-making.

dealing with some aspect of the conditions outside the organization. This differentiation of function and task is accompanied by specializations of the capacities and dispositions of those charged with fulfilling those functions and tasks, and differences, too, in the formal structure of departments. As a result of this differentiation, coordination problems arise, which require the deployment of appropriate methods of integration so that the organization can function effectively. The basic necessity of both appropriate differentiation and requisite integration to effective organizational performance lies at the heart of Lawrence and Lorsch's hypothesis, and the central question they pose for an organization to find its appropriate structure is this:

> The environment with which a major department engages is decided by the key strategic choice, 'What business are we in?' Once that decision is made, whether explicitly or implicitly, the attributes of the chosen environment can be analysed [...]. Internal attributes of the organization, in terms of structure and orientation, can be tested for goodness of fit with the various environmental variables and the predispositions of members. (Lawrence and Lorsch, 1967: 209)[3]

In this quote, we can note that the authors use the notion of 'business' rather than 'purpose' or 'task'. However, these concepts must be seen as naturally related in that a choice of 'business' entails one or more particular 'task(s)' that the organization then must perform as 'a system of interrelated behaviours' (Lawrence and Lorsch, [1967] 1986: 3).

Numerous studies elaborated and developed this empirical and conceptual understanding of relationships between task, environment, and organizational arrangement. Some of the key contributions were the work of James D. Thompson on different types of 'task interdependence' (Thompson, 1967), and of Charles Perrow on 'task variability' and 'task analysability' (Perrow, 1970). The studies and conceptualizations connected to the 'contingency hypothesis' was subsequently combined and theorized by, among others, Henry Mintzberg. Synthesizing findings from the many empirical studies carried out in relation to the contingency hypothesis, he presented a 'configuration framework' comprising five ideal types of organizational arrangements, each emphasizing different design elements and coordinating mechanisms and making up a particular 'configuration' (Mintzberg, 1979). Task was regarded as one of the key contingency factors for the

---

[3] The notion of 'strategic choice' here may be interpreted as foreshadowing the strategic management school's emphasis on the significance of strategic analyses and fit. However, one notable difference between the contingency approach of Lawrence and Lorsch and this later school is the awareness in the former of the organizational arrangement as an intricate and constantly developing interactional system in relation to a concrete task. The latter tends to emphasize the games and competences of strategic positioning in a competitive market, while paying less attention to the 'inner workings' and delicate balancing acts of the concrete organizational arrangement. Also, as mentioned, it tends to carry a general hesitation against the importance of 'task'.

appropriateness and efficiency of each configuration. A hospital, for example, where tasks are characterized by relatively high uncertainty (what does the patient suffer from?) and ambiguity (is this the only possible disease they may have?), and therefore require considerable coordination between nurses, doctors, administrators, and so on, work must be organized differently. Staff must, for example, have more discretionary power than at a radio factory producing low-end, mass-market radios, where the tasks are relatively standardized and can be automated to a large degree. At the same time, however, an organizational arrangement is never completely configured, but always subject to 'pushes' and 'pulls' in different directions, which is why the process of fitting an organization to its tasks is an ongoing accomplishment. Likewise, different configurations present different types of strengths and weaknesses, and thus different challenges and risks for management and staff.

Contemporaneous with the emergence of the contingency approach was the development of the 'socio-technical school' at the Tavistock Institute of Human Relations. Its core interest was the challenge of organizing 'technical' and 'social' elements in task-solving systems in order to balance well-being and emotional life against practical and efficient task performance. The Tavistock research set out to experiment with and understand how organizations, as 'socio-technical systems', should and could be arranged around a fundamental basic task: a 'primary task'. This primary task is not to be understood as a once-and-for-all designation that the organization is 'created' to fulfil and from which it must not depart, since the primary task may change over time as a result of internal modifications and/or external dynamics (Rice, 1963; Miller and Rice, 1967). Furthermore, just as Simon had emphasized, organizations may have more than one primary task (Rice, 1963: 189). Nevertheless, it is around the primary task(s) that the 'technical' and 'social' parts of the organizational system must be arranged, in a way that minimizes the constraints of one part on the other. It is a key concern for managers as well as organizational analysts, to enquire into the relationship between the organization's primary task, its internal and external environments, and its technical and social dimensions, and to 'fit the organization to its task' (a formulation that bears strong resemblance to the vocabulary of the contingency school without being directly related to it). Exactly what constitutes a good fit cannot be determined once and for all. Tasks, environment, and technical and social systems develop over time, which is why a requisite organizational arrangement at one point in time may begin to present a number of dysfunctions later on. Ultimately, 'the function of leadership must be located on the boundary between the enterprise and the external environment', so that the relationship between them is managed in a way 'that will allow [...] followers to perform their primary task' (ibid.: 209–10). This implies constantly asserting 'rational, mature aspects' of individuality (i.e. a realistic understanding of the task, the conditions for solving it, and one's role in this) against a potential alliance between primitive emotions within oneself and external group pressure towards ideas or stances that are ultimately irreconcilable with the task situation: 'By organization is meant a set of administrative arrangements to cope with a given task. In this sense, individuals and groups [may also] have "organisations" which may be more or less disorganised' (Rice, 1965: 15).

While it is crucial to know one's task in order to organize in a requisite manner, it is also difficult because the task may elicit unpleasant emotions, which can be avoided by downplaying or displacing the task. A number of Tavistock scholars related the notion of a primary task to what they termed 'organizational defence mechanisms', that is, organizational routines and responses serving to protect members from negative or frightening emotions associated with the task (Jaques, 1953; Menzies, [1979] 1988). They emphasized that organizational structure must facilitate task accomplishment, but that, in so doing, it may be influenced by other factors such as personal needs, covert tasks, and group needs, for example, the task itself may give rise to strong feelings which need to be contained (Lawrence, 1986; Obholzer and Zagier Roberts, 1994). It is a balancing act to simultaneously serve the primary task and meet such needs and covert tasks: 'Appropriately harnessed, covert tasks and needs may enhance a group's capacity to work effectively and creatively, by providing vitality as well as material which can be used in its work. When undetected or ignored, however, they may provide major constraints on task accomplishment' (Singer et al., [1979] 1999: 23). It is therefore crucial for an organization to realistically define its primary task and the associated constraints, and explore the appropriateness of its current ways of working (Miller, 1976; Obholzer and Zagier Roberts, 1994). This is not an easy balance to strike as the primary task is often an elusive phenomenon (Dartington, 1998; Willshire, 1999), is multifaceted and holds inner tensions. It is also crucial to understand that a task focus does not imply rigidity:

> [W]e must have a degree of formal organization to coordinate the activity of the business. Nevertheless, if the resultant delineation of task and activity are regarded as limits to activity, then we clog up the whole organization ... organization must be regarded as something that sets up 'soft' boundaries to activity; guidelines to be crossed as necessary rather than rigid fences.   (Brown, 1963: 3)

Although the contingency and Tavistock programmes emphasized, respectively, the situational characteristics of the organization and its environment, and the relationship between psychological and organizational processes, they bore remarkable similarities regarding the intimate, foundational relationship between 'organization' and 'task'. Both departed from the basic premise that organizations are systems of concerted effort, which must be arranged to 'fit' the requirements stemming from the task and the environment in which the task is to be accomplished. In this sense, organization is always, or should strive to be, requisite to its core task, even if management orthodoxy or group sentiments would like to have it otherwise. Organizations that forget their task, allow other ideas to substitute for it, or ignore the situation they exist in, will be organizations that function less well and eventually come to undermine their own existence.

Organizational Reforms without a Compass

Today, almost fifty years after the height of 'task' as a concept in OT, the classic literature on task and organization is seldom read and, at best, allotted just a brief description in standard textbooks on OT. In fact, OT is itself seldom taught as a discrete topic. Instead, organization and management is usually covered by courses in any number of different areas, such as 'organizational behaviour' or 'strategy', for instance, thereby breaking the understanding of organizational arrangements as purposeful wholes into a 'micro view' and 'macro view', respectively. Very few students finish their business or management education with more than a second- or third-hand understanding of classic OT, and often with little training in analysing task and requisite organization. In the following, we will discuss the absence of a classic organization theoretical perspective in one current public debate about organization and its functioning. Using a brief example—the organizational reforms of primary schools in Denmark—we will show that the absence of an open and clear discussion about the purpose and organization of schools has resulted in a bewildering situation where 'change' is cherished as a self-evident good and where multiple, and often mutually conflicting, programmatic ideas are implemented with little concern for the overall effect.

The Bewilderment of Public School Reform—an example

From the 1980s onwards, public organizations have been increasingly problematized and subjected to reforms of different kinds. As part of the 'modernization' of the welfare state, reform attempts have been inspired by the promises and principles of new public management (NPM), but also by broader theories and discourses about, for instance, the 'information society', 'globalization', 'innovation', and 'reflexivity'. Since 1937, the law describing the purpose of the Danish schools has been subject to a series of revisions. In 1937, the law was changed so that its dual purpose—to 'further and develop the children's dispositions and competences' and 'strengthen their character'—was no longer directly tied to the state and to Christianity. In

1975, the purpose was elaborated to include the task of collaborating with parents, developing the child's 'fantasy and wish to learn', and 'preparing pupils to live and participate in a democratic society'. This version was altered again in 1993, so that it also came to include the task of 'familiarizing pupils with Danish culture' and 'enhancing their understanding for other cultures and for the human interaction with nature'. In 2006, this was once more revised to include, for the first time, the formulation that the purpose of the school is to 'prepare children for further education'. This development has been viewed as indicative of a general movement from a welfare state model to a competitive state model in which a concern for the social and cultural coherence of the state has been replaced with a focus upon the economic performance of the state (Pedersen, 2008). However, some of the old expectations of the school are still present, complicating the overall picture. The school has become a hybrid of 'liberal freedom', 'conservative ideas of community', 'neo-liberal ideas of opportunistic personhood', and 'social-democratic ideals of a welfare society' (ibid.: 43, translated from Danish).

At the same time, schools have been exposed to numerous and often conflicting task demands and management principles, often with no clear connection to the revised formal description of a school's purpose. On the one hand, schools and school administrators have been prompted to focus upon 'strategy, evaluation, organization and documentation', on the other, they have been encouraged to emphasize 'innovation, flow and recognition' in teaching and management (Juelskjær et al., 2011). A broad and mixed battery of governance instruments has been introduced, consisting of NPM tools such as contract steering and documentation, standardization of delivery, and merging of schools into larger units, but also less specific models and projects aimed at cultivating 'innovation', 'child-friendly environments', and 'network relations'. This stream of new models and instruments is far from exhausted: some recent introductions include the principle of 'team organization' of teachers, mandatory 'pupil-plans', and a break with the right of teachers to organize their working hours themselves. Thus, schools and school managers find themselves in a complicated and paradoxical situation: being repeatedly urged to innovate, be flexible and inclusive, and engage in stronger collaboration with parents and local communities, while also having to comply with contracts, key performance indicators, a top-down-imposed standard curriculum, and mandatory tests, little of which is clearly coupled to the formal—and in itself very broad—description of the school's purpose. Although these paradoxical demands might have particular Danish dimensions, it is a general experience across many Western countries, not least the USA (Adams and Ginsberg, n.d.) and Great Britain. Here, additional challenges are faced regarding the relationship between public and private schools (an issue that is not quite as present in Denmark, where all types of primary schools must follow national regulations). Like their Danish counterparts, primary schools in these two countries have experienced a series of education reform movements that laud standardized tests and interest in quasi-market approaches, with non-union teachers and private management as the solution to the problems of public education (cf. Denvir, 2011; Vasgar, 2011).

Despite persistent public debate about the school's purpose and organization, and despite the issue's broad societal relevance, however, school organization and management has been a rather neglected topic in organization studies. Only a few articles can be found in key journals such as *Organization Science, Organization Studies, Academy of Management Review*, and *Academy of Management Journal*, and they primarily use the school as a case, or simply as a brief example, in relation to generic themes such as job enrichment (Umstot, Mitchell, and Bell, 1978), institutionalization processes (Casile and Davis-Blake, 2002; Segal and Lehrer, 2012; Quirke, 2013), social capital (Pil and Leana, 2009), rule-breaking (Martin et al., 2013), public sector reforms (Bejerot and Hasselbladh, 2013), and organizational identity (King, Clemens, and Konty, 2011). Only two articles and three short comments (Hambrick, 2005; Ouchi et al., 2005; Rynes et al., 2005; Weick, 2005; Ouchi, 2006) directly address the management and organization of schools. They all revolve around William Ouchi's book *Making Schools Work* (2003):

> When state and national legislators, regulatory bodies, and stock exchanges deliberate on policies that affect business and their stakeholders, they routinely invite economists and legal scholars to weigh in. But it is very rare for management scholars—who of course know quite a lot about the functioning of firms—to have a say. (Hambrick, 2005: 961)

'[I]f only we could successfully influence managers to use our research, organizations might avoid counterproductive investments in ineffective fads and fashions' (Rynes et al., 2005: 925). In fact, Ouchi's book is not even directed towards fellow organization theorists, but towards parents. In a subsequent book, Ouchi (2009) further elaborates what he finds is a crucial problem of modern school organization: the creation of large centralized schools and the matrix organization of teaching, where each teacher is assigned a large number of pupils and must follow a standard curriculum. This reduces one-on-one teacher–pupil contact and makes it very difficult for the teacher to teach in a way that fits the individual pupil's needs. A basic point of Ouchi's study is that schools must be organized and managed in a way that understands the task of teaching in a nuanced manner and builds on key insights about work organization and management practice from other organizational studies.

Ouchi's analysis was criticized in several book reviews (e.g. for not clarifying to what degree success is due to organizational principles or to gifted managers

(Hanushek, 2010)). However, there are no other recent studies of schools within OT with which to compare it. The literature on school management is typically written by scholars within education science, and addresses predominantly either the level of concrete didactic practice or the level of broader school–society relations.[4] When it cursorily touches upon the school as a practical organizational entity, the literature tends to draw on the same common tropes and broad recommendations that pervade contemporary organization studies. Schools are portrayed as petrified institutions that need to reform themselves and develop new ways of organizing in 'times of unprecedented change'. A consistent theme is the need for more creativity and flexibility. Schools must strive to become 'learning organizations' and engage in 'organization development' characterized by open-ended search processes: 'The road takes shape as we walk it [. . .] never being completely sure about the goals or the plan, and never being sure whether the goal has been reached' (Dalin, 1998: 189). Schools and teachers are advised to engage in 'change management', and school managers are encouraged to 'create conditions for reflection, open dialogue, mutual respect for ideas and for both professional and institutional growth' (Moos and MacBeath, 2000: 64; our translation). In order to navigate between the many concerns and constantly changing conditions facing them, school managers are advised to adopt a 'reflective' and 'integrative' style of management. By and large, they are told to leave an understanding of management 'anchored in power and control' and act as leaders of a group rather than of a hierarchy: 'Managers must manage not from the top of the pyramid, but from the centre of the tissue of human relations' (Murphy, 1994: 26; our translation). More effective schools are schools with leadership at all levels and with 'clear, simple, flatter structures' and, for example, 'an uplifting ethos: visually and aurally positive' (Brighouse and Tomlinson, 1991: 5). Other analyses highlight simply the values of exploration and reflexivity: 'throwing new light upon the taken-for-granted routines of everyday life' (Juelskjær et al., 2011: 14; our translation). However, through investigations of, for instance, the 'power forms' at play and the way managers 'translate' and 'are translated' in attempts to introduce new ideas and steering principles, this literature also relays a deep scepticism of planned organization: 'By understanding management as translation we break with an understanding of management as implementation, i.e. as something that happens top-down in a managerial hierarchy. Instead [we shall] study management as formative and transformative translations' (ibid.: 17; our translation).

---

[4] An exception is the work of Richard D. Elmore on school organization and accountability. He addresses the overall problem of pressing through top-down reforms without involving teachers directly in the organization redesign and change processes. This results, he argues, in a decoupling of reforms from the 'technical core' of teaching, and allows teaching to continue as a practice largely outside managerial reach (Elmore, 2000).

Across the texts, the school is cast as an organization in need of reinvention in a heterogeneous, changing, and globalized world. The encouraging and democratic tone which accompanies the message passes lightly over concrete organizational issues and challenges such as those taken up by classical OT: What is the primary task or purpose of the school? (And is it reflected properly in the formal description of purpose?) Are there disagreements or conflicting tasks? How to practically accomplish them, and coordinate across them? How to balance 'social' and 'technical' elements? To what degree is team organization or discretion regarding work relevant? What should be accounted for, by whom, and how often? What should be the specific authority structure between teacher and head of school? And so forth. The task and organization of teaching is left unspecified and replaced by a broad call for experimentation and change readiness. How specific reform elements fit or clash with the tasks or with each other are, by and large, bypassed; so are analyses and discussions about defensive versus relevant organization. The analyses prefer instead to move 'up' at the level of societal diagnosis, discussing the school as expressive of, for instance, 'neoliberalism' or 'a learning society'; or 'down' to the level of interpersonal relations, advocating for trust, collaboration, and abandoning the 'false security' of plans and managerial objectives. Rather than assisting a precise delineation of the school's tasks and its appropriate organization (e.g. on what specific terms and for what practical reasons shall schools adopt or discard this or that principle?) the school management literature adds new layers of general, abstract—sometimes even romantic—principles on top of those already circulating in and perplexing the field. It is an open question what the effect of all this is.

Task as a 'Core Object' in Organization Theory

In OT, it used to be unthinkable to discuss organization without addressing task. Task was a core object—practically and theoretically—without which a given phenomenon could be analysed and discussed, although, as a result, it would not be an organizational analysis. Organizations were understood as complex or simple wholes of concerted efforts arranged in relation to specific tasks; these arrangements would naturally differ when their task altered. Accordingly, the starting point for an organizational analysis was the identification and investigation of its concrete task(s). Over time, however, core concepts like task have virtually disappeared from organization studies and a particular stance has been cultivated across the different approaches and traditions, which deems such core concepts problematic for epistemic, ontological, and political reasons.

One effect of the lost focus on core objects seems to be a tendency to prefer general to specific discussions and conclusions. OT has, for instance, become less interested in particular organizations such as schools and favours instead more general or generic themes such as 'network organization' and 'innovation', which means that school organization is more or less ignored as a relevant issue in itself. School management is discussed by other disciplines such as education, but not with a clear focus upon 'task' and practical organization. In fact, the texts in that field often convey the same scepticism about 'task' (and, for that matter, about 'organization' and 'management'), and the same general and metaphysical recommendations that characterize contemporary organization studies. In this manner, the organization of schools is treated academically in a way that glosses over a detailed analysis of its task organization and leaves it vulnerable to detached programmatic ideas and models from above and beyond. Although it was once a core axiom in OT that organizations should not be managed as if they are essentially alike— what supports task accomplishment in one type of organization can be quite dysfunctional in another (Mintzberg, 1979)—the battery of new management tools and reform ideas is typically discussed in terms of 'power' or 'resistance' and not in terms of their (lack of) appropriateness for an organization's core tasks. This does not make such analyses irrelevant per se, but it gives them a distant and general, rather than a practical and precise, character. Schools, of course, are just one example; the same goes for hospitals, universities, prisons, banks, retail companies, and so on. It has become unfashionable to enquire into the task differences between organizations and to hesitate when organizational principles from one sector are transposed onto another (not least if it is 'soft' principles like team organization).

What, then, might it mean to approach organizational issues not with a 'metaphysical' stance, a 'critical' one, or, for that matter, an 'engaged' one, but, in the words of Mary Parker Follett, with 'a conscious and responsible attitude' (Follett, 1982: 21)? The key argument of this chapter has been that the concepts of task and purpose with which OT once created its relevance and distinctiveness are crucial; in fact, they are key to what distinguish organizations and organizing. Taking 'task' as a starting point in the analysis of the school, for instance, may look intellectually unambitious when set against the spirit pervading the engaged suggestions of new forms of management or the 'exposé' of critical sociological analyses. As such, the whole idea of approaching a phenomenon in a practical and concrete manner through the use of core concepts may easily be ridiculed. However, working from an empirical investigation of task and purpose does not suggest a 'simple' analysis, as it is often posited—or, for that matter, a 'functionalist' one—but one originating from the principle that 'organization' is something that emerges in relation to a task or purpose (which is not given once and for all, but must be revised and recalibrated time and again). As Bruno Latour has argued—addressing what distinguishes 'the organizational' from, for instance, the political—'organization' is not a thing in which some action or another happens. It is a particular 'mode of existence', which can only be grasped if one shifts from speaking *about* organizations to talking and acting *organizationally* (Latour, 2011: 171).

Latour uses the notion of 'script', whereas we, in line with the tradition of organizational and management writers, use the concepts of task and purpose. What unites them is the point that 'organization' cannot be meaningfully discussed and evaluated in isolation from what is being 'organized'. This implies that organizations differ from each another, depending on this 'what' and on the situations in which this 'what' is to be realized. An organization's task cannot be determined from a distance and with a vague idea of its concrete situation.

What is a given organization's task and how—though what coordinated arrangement of means—is it to be fulfilled under given circumstances? Pursuing this question will not lead us away from, but closer to, an organization's reality—its organizational reality—we suggest. Task and purpose are conceptual devices for unfolding and exploring this reality and determining the organizational arrangement's relevance, effectiveness, and sustainability. Without them, the organizational reality become opaque and even grossly distorted, as in the cases of Tesco and Citigroup outlined at the beginning of this chapter. It is a paradox, however, that the disciplines of OT and organization studies have contributed significantly to downplaying, even ridiculing, these devices and the classical stance with which they are associated. Since about the 1980s, the idea that task is a relevant concern has been slowly but surely dismantled, and scholarly work has instead latched onto general themes in the social sciences (e.g. 'power' and 'network'), metaphysics (e.g. 'inescapable change' and 'transgressive learning'), and a broad, unspecific discussion of how 'things could be otherwise'.[5] When the ability to sort out important differences between organizations as task arrangements is lost—and organizations are treated as mere containers for processes going on outside them—there are few effective arguments against the spread of detached 'best practice' principles (such as that of 'team organization' or 'lean management'). To lose sight of task is to become utterly out of touch with the idea of specific sorts of organizations as practical realities. That was a key point made by practitioners of the classical stance.

---

[5] As Charles Turner (1992: 3) put it in another context: 'the declaration that a particular mode of human connection is not natural is no longer made to contrast it with the truly natural mode, nor out of a conviction that the achievement of the truly natural mode is the task of politics. Now, politics is that declaration, that predicative activity, the assertion that a state of affairs could have been and can be otherwise.'

But is 'task'—in the case of OT—really the right core object? Why not other classical notions such as 'system' or 'decision'? On what terms shall its value as a practical-epistemic artefact be assessed? Importantly, core objects should neither be understood as 'absolutes' in a metaphysical sense, nor 'true' in a positivist sense, but as concepts that are practically useful for a discipline by articulating those aspects of its phenomena that allows the discipline to 'intervene' in them (Hacking, 1983). Accordingly, whether a discipline has the right core objects should be judged on its ability to relate practically to its phenomena. In this light, the changed vocabulary and knowledge interests of organization studies and its declining practical relevance are intimately related, as we argue at greater length in the Conclusion to the book. By gradually dissociating itself from its core objects, OT has weakened its ability to explore organizations in a way that informs their practical management and helps sort out appropriate interventions from inappropriate ones.

Disciplines evolve through experimentation—theoretically and empirically—but, as we suggested in Chapter 2, conceptual innovation may lead a discipline so far away from a practically useful understanding of its objects of study—for example, by making it indiscernible from this or that other phenomenon—that it loses its relevance. Our proposition is that OT will gain renewed and much needed relevance to the degree it succeeds in rediscovering its core objects, among which 'task' seems to be particularly central, rather than, as some have suggested, bringing yet more arcane theoretical fireworks to the party (Lounsbury and Beckman, 2015). Today, the research tradition associated with the classical stance—detailed empirical studies of organizations and their ways of accomplishing core tasks (or failing to do so) and, taking from such close descriptions, a number of principles and situational caveats which appropriate practical organization must take into account—has fallen out of favour. Maybe this is a fate befalling not only organization studies, but other areas of the human and social sciences too? Could it be that, in letting of the idea of themselves as 'practical sciences' and embracing the 'moment of theory', these disciplines have come to dispense with the core objects that afford them their practical relevance? Maybe, in the pursuit of new theoretical horizons, much work in the human and social sciences has reached an impasse in which a certain isomorphism has begun to develop; where the points and recommendations sound remarkably alike across fields? If this is the case, and we have tried to illustrate its plausibility, the way forward may indeed be to revisit the core objects of each discipline. This might in turn also lead to the discovery that practical relevance is not a matter of choosing between 'theory' and 'practice', but of studying a phenomenon as a particular instance of a core object.

6

Authority and Authorization

If the concept of 'task' has fallen into abeyance within the field of organization studies and yet organizations nonetheless continue to exist in large part for the coordinated performance of particular tasks (and the properties of those tasks continue to have certain basic effects upon organizational structures, processes, and outputs), then it seems plausible to claim that 'task' should not be designated as an anachronism, but rather considered a cornerstone concept within organizational analysis as a practical science. Like 'task', the once central concept of authority is similarly deemed out of kilter with both the empirical reality of contemporary organizational life and the norms animating current organizational analysis; 'authorisation and authorising relationships' are widely represented as 'hierarchical and bureaucratic and by implication old-fashioned. Metaphors and analogies abound about organic, flexible, liberated organizations that are unrestricted by rules and therefore more creative; leaderless teams and unclear authority abound' (Macdonald, Burke, and Stewart, 2006: 34). In this chapter, we seek to rehabilitate the concept of 'authority' within organization studies, indicating, in much the same way as we did in relation to 'task', the centrality of the concept to organizational analysis as a practical science. After all, within organizations of all descriptions, authority and authorizing relationships continue to be of the utmost practical importance. Indeed, it is difficult to think of a system of effective coordination where authority is absent. An employment contract, for instance, gives the organization or its agents the sanctioned right, within certain limits, to determine the work of an individual occupying a particular role. This right, also sanctioned by the individual through the acceptance of the contract and defined by its limits, comprises the *authority* available to the organization vis-à-vis the individual as a role holder or 'employee' (meaning any member of the organization) (See especially Newman & Rowbottom, 1968). Moreover, when taking up a role within an organization, an individual will need the organization's agreement to or sanctioning of her or his use of various resources to undertake and complete the tasks that together constitute that role. This sanctioned right to deploy resources at their discretion comprises the *authority* of an individual as an employee in their organizational role (and only in that role). The individual employee may need to spend money, use equipment, or direct the work of other employees, for example (Newman & Rowbottom, 1968). In each case, while the authority is a positive grant to action, its extent can only be defined in terms of limits: 'X may spend up to $500 on entertaining clients' is in effect a definition of the extent of authority; 'X may not employ more than the current number of staff unless sanctioned by Head Office so to do' is a definition of the extent of authority. The test of authority, then, is by way of a sanction—that is to say, as Parker Follett (1940) and Barnard (1968) specified, agreement explicit or implicit by the people (as role holders in an organization) affected. Thus, if an individual employee says to their superior in an organization, 'You have no authority to instruct me to undertake this task', the rights and wrongs of the case can only be settled by reference to the limits of *authority* stated or implied in the original or amended contract of employment. Similarly, if a superior says to their subordinate, 'You have no authority to undertake that work', reference must be made to the limits of *authority* stated or implied in the work instructions given at some earlier point to the individual role holder (Newman & Rowbottom, 1968:30ff). In both cases, authority and authorization are to be specified, formally, and thus 'de-personalised' in relation to the organizational 'law of the situation' (Parker Follett, 1940: 29–35), which is only 'comprehended in coordination' (Barnard, 1968: 184).

This exercise in recovery is necessary, in no small part because the contemporary disavowal of the importance of authority, both as a key concept within organization studies and, more significantly, as a constitutive element of formal organization per se, has some clear and present dangers. We shall have cause to specify these throughout the chapter, when we discuss particular cases where organizing without authority is attempted or encouraged, or where clear lines of authority are absent or such lines are tangled or blurred. In specifying the importance of authority along both intellectual and practical axes, we will stress once again the significance of *formality*. As we have indicated at various points throughout this book, for many scholars of organization formality is a dirty word or a fraud. For us, though, as for the practitioners of the 'classical stance' we refer to, formality and formalization is central to understanding and performing organization. If that centrality is denied, and, as a result, there are no written or otherwise explicitly recognized or prescribed limits to work roles in organizations (i.e. no duly constituted *authority*), for instance, then clearly no one will really know what decisions they are authorized to make. Such a condition is unlikely to approximate to a sunny upland of enhanced freedom, creativity, innovation, and performance, but rather to a stressful and anarchic 'state of nature' (Brown, 1965a; Stinchcombe, 2001). More significantly, perhaps, the purposes for which the organization is instituted are unlikely to be met. Organization, in a very real sense, will not exist without duly constituted, and thus clearly defined, authority.

In seeking to rehabilitate 'authority' in organization, conceptually and practically, we focus in particular on the work of three key practitioners of the 'classical stance'—Wilfred Brown, Mary Parker Follett, and Chester Barnard—indicating the centrality of authority and authorizing relationships to their analysis of what makes up good organization, operationally as well as morally. In so doing, we seek to contrast their attitude and approach towards 'authority' and 'authorization' with the 'anti-authorizing' tenets of practitioners of the metaphysical stance in contemporary organization studies.

Authority as a Cornerstone of Organization

> Making decisions is always difficult because there is always a lapse of time before we know whether we acted wisely. But if we are to be judged on every occasion not only on the wisdom of our decisions themselves, but also on whether we were correct in assuming that the responsibility was or was not within our authority, then our work lives will be intolerable... Thus, there is a minimal degree of formalization which must exist if we are individually to possess explicit knowledge of the discretion which we are authorized to use, *and will be held responsible* for using. Formalization of organization delineates roles and role relationships; formalization of policies makes clear to people the area in which they have freedom to act. Without a clearly defined area of freedom there is no freedom. This, in fact, is a very old story... *there is no real freedom without law.*
>
> Wilfred Brown, 'Informal organization?', 1965

In his discussion of authority and authorization as a crucial constitutive element of organization, the organizational theorist and practising executive (minister of state and university pro-chancellor) Wilfred Brown had recourse to tropes and images derived from the work of Thomas Hobbes. For Brown, as for Hobbes, liberty and authority were not antithetical to one another, but, to the contrary, the latter was the condition of the former. Like his predecessors, Mary Parker Follett and Chester Barnard, whom, as we shall see, he drew upon extensively, Brown deploys a range of sources, historical, sociological, political, and psychological, for instance, in seeking to articulate the distinctiveness of organization as an object of analysis and practice—of organizational theory (OT) as a practical science. More often than not, though, it is history, and especially the history of political thought and constitution building, that informs his analysis (Mant, 2007: 421). For Brown, the Glacier project, as it came to be known, was, in no small part, a political experiment designed to give members of that organization the same opportunities for political representation as employees that they enjoyed in their role as citizens within the body politic. This meant that, for Brown, Glacier needed to develop a structure of organization and a constitution that would replicate the organs of government outside it—a representative system to make the laws (the works council), an executive system to put these into practice (management), and an independent judiciary to adjudicate on cases of conflict (the appeals procedure). It was in seeking to institute this vision that Brown came to focus so intently on the matter of authority and its centrality to 'what makes up good organization' (Brown, 1965a: 32) and, in so doing, to rely on the work of Thomas Hobbes. After all, perhaps more than any other so-called 'political theorist', for Hobbes everything hung on understanding authority aright and the language appropriate to it (Oakeshott, 1975; Skinner, 2002; Condren, 2006). His conception of liberty revolves around the compatibility of freedom and necessity, such that freedom presupposes the presence of authority, not its absence. Hobbes's enduring image of 'the natural condition' or 'state of nature' was intended to explain the necessity of authority: the horrors of that condition are threatened by people not accepting the reciprocities attendant upon there being a ruling authority. Hobbes's elegant solution for escaping from the 'state or nature' into a 'civil state' revolves around the establishment of an absolute authority—the sovereign—an artificial, unitary 'person' whose judgements are binding on all. The consequences of refusing allegiance to the only body capable of protecting them from external threats and indeed from each other, Hobbes argued, will always be worse for people, individually and collectively, namely 'miseries and horrible calamities' that accompany 'Warre' (Hobbes, 1996: 128). 'Where there is no common power, there is no Law; where no law, no Injustice' (ibid.: 90), from which it follows that:

> [T]he civil Lawes are to all subjects the measures of their Actions, whereby to determine, whether they be right or wronge, profitable or unprofitable, virtuous or vitious, and by from them the use, and definition of all names not agreed upon, and tending to Controversie, shall be established. (Hobbes, 1969: 188–9)

The securing of liberty then, individually and collectively, is dependent upon an established authority and settled and known rules of conduct, embodied in laws. The 'civil state' furnishes individuals with a secure and consistent basis in which to enjoy freedom in a way that the 'natural condition', where everyone is potentially free to do anything and hence free to be enslaved, cannot. Therefore, to demand a right to 'natural liberty' (or spontaneous order) independent of established authority, is, for Hobbes, to invite a sort of anarchy: the appeal to natural liberty being, in effect, a mechanism for returning people to 'a state of nature' or condition of 'perpetual Warre' (Condren, 2002: 72). The images and tropes deployed by Hobbes surface regularly in the work of Brown, as we shall now see. They are also not unconnected to the sorts of claims regularly expressed by practitioners of a metaphysical stance within organization studies. As we will have cause to note, though, here the idea of a 'natural condition' loses the negative connotations bestowed upon it by Hobbes.

The significance of Hobbes's approach to authority and authorization for Brown's analysis of organization becomes clear when we consider the reasons the latter gave for his break with the 'human relations' and 'group relations' schools in the late 1940s. As he indicated with characteristic frankness in the *Glacier Project Papers*,

> some of the current theories about organization ... seek to explain the impact of people on the policies which govern the operation of the company in terms of theories about the psychological interaction of groups and of the degree of identification of the individual with the company. Formal organization is thus seen as something that may disrupt these informal mechanisms of association.
>
> (Brown, 1965b: 158)

For Brown, such suspicion or overt denigration of formality and formalization 'distorts the whole frame of reference within which organization as a subject is considered' (ibid.). Between 1939 and 1947, as chief executive at Glacier, Brown admitted he followed both human relations and group relations orthodoxies, with the effect that the structure of roles and their relation one to another within the Glacier organization became 'hopelessly confused. The result was a dangerous weakening of the authority of managers and no consequential feelings of freedom or satisfaction on the part of the members of the company' (ibid.). This confusion, and the consequent negative impact upon organization, he indicated, was, in no small part, due to the unorganizational nature of much human relations and group relations thinking. For Brown, the latter schools often assumed that the actual job, its technology, and its mental and physical requirements were relatively unimportant compared to the social and psychological situation of people at work: 'Organizations exist to co-ordinate the ... work of ... people towards a common series of tasks. If we are to establish sound, viable organization, then we must understand the nature of work. We must be able to talk about its content in explicit terms' (Brown, 1965a: 72–3)—that is, formally. In *Exploration in Management*, he succinctly sets out this credo:

> Effective organization is a function of the work to be done and the resources and techniques available to do it. Thus changes in methods of production bring about changes in the number of work roles, in the distribution of work between roles and in their relationship to one another. Failure to make explicit acknowledgement of this relationship between work and organization gives rise to non-valid assumptions, e.g. that optimum organization is a function of the personalities involved,

that it is a matter connected to personal style and arbitrary decision of the chief executive, that there are choices between centralised and types of de-centralised organization etc. Our observations lead us to accept that ... organization must be derived from an analysis of the work to be done and the techniques and resources available.   (Brown, 1965a: 42; italics in original)

For Brown (1965a: 64–5), it was clear that, unless prescribed boundaries were set on the decision-making work that employees undertook within an organization, it would be impossible to coordinate their work 'towards a common end'. If top management did not set coordinating policies which prescribed the discretion of managers throughout the organization, individual managers would be 'entitled to make decisions that could create chaos'. This is because, without prescribed boundaries to their discretion, managers would not know where their 'authority and responsibility to make decisions starts or finishes'. They could not then be held accountable 'either for failure to make necessary decisions or for making decisions which, in fact, usurp the authority' of their own managers. As a result, work, and thus 'organizing', would be conducted in 'a twilight of continuous uncertainty' (ibid.: 63):

> If the need for formal organization is denied and as a result there are no written or explicitly recognised prescribed bounds to the work roles, then, clearly, no one really knows what decisions he or anybody else is authorised to make. Every time an individual in the company faces a problem, his first thought would have to be: 'Is it my responsibility to deal with this or not?' In the absence of prescribed bounds he does not and cannot know. Therefore he will have to decide first whether or not to act. Then, if he decides to do so, he will have to make decisions on what action to take. But, once he has made his decision, others may question his right to do so. His manager may 'bawl him out' or may praise him for 'showing initiative'; the individual does not know in advance which response he will get ... Neither criticism can be valid unless the discretion in the role has been made explicit. There is need to avoid situations in which the use of personal networks, manipulation of other people, lobbying of support 'etc.', is required by the individual to discharge the work of his role. The absence of clear-cut statements about authority, responsibility and task, create such situations (Brown, 1965a: 69) ... The degree of formal organization required is that which will ensure that all necessary decisions are made which will keep at a low level inter-personal jealousy and confusions about authority; which will avoid leaving people in a continual state of uncertainty as to how far they can go in making decisions, and which will prevent individuals assuming personal positions of power and influence which have no connection with the degree of authority required by them to perform the tasks allotted to them.   (Brown, 1965b: 154–5)

For Brown (1965b: 153), morally expressivist appeals to 'informality' as the bedrock of organizational creativity, innovation, freedom, and flexibility were 'the converse of my business experience'. They were, rather, appeals to disorganize; to return to 'a natural condition' in the Hobbesian sense. As Brown (ibid.: 153–4) put it, 'a deliberate policy of leaving organization unformulated is tantamount to the deliberate setting up of a situation of anarchy. I use the word "anarchy" in its original sense, i.e. "the want of government in a state".' Echoing Hobbes's statements about law and injustice, Brown argues:

> It is not absence of law, which allows creative use of discretion, but an explicit area of freedom bounded by the law which reduces anarchy and allows the individual to make his [sic] contribution... A little reflection will surely enable each of us to see that we want a system of law, despite the fact that at times we find it irksome, first, because we desire to be protected from the effect of the unlimited decisions of our fellows and, secondly, because without limitations on our freedom of decision, we must carry unlimited responsibility. (Brown, 1965b: 153–4)

Brown (1976: 289) stressed the need for an explicit acknowledgement that what he called the 'executive system'[1] was 'brought into being to perform the work of the company, that its structure must be a function of such work, that it must be capable of constant adaptation to match the changes in the work, and that the total work must be divided between all the roles in the Executive System'. He then posed the rhetorical question: To 'what extent is this to be done with deliberation and in a statable manner', in other words, 'formally', and, to what extent is it 'to be left to be decided by the pressure generated by group and individual interaction', in other words, informally? (ibid.). His answer is clear and precise:

> the salient result of the latter process is that the people involved in the situation lack full and consistent knowledge of who does what. The assumption made by some is that this is a situation of liberty for the individual, but is it not more accurate to say that such a situation is one where the right to do certain types of work is decided by the competitive ambitions and power positions of the individual concerned? Jones may well feel a need to carry a certain area of responsibility but, supposing that Smith equally feels that his needs can be met only by carrying that same responsibility, what then? If they are left to fight it out, that can scarcely be called a situation of freedom for either of them. (Ibid.)

Nor would it be a situation in which the efficiency of, or indeed prospects of survival for, the enterprise (and thus the securing of the purposes for which it was instantiated) were enhanced. No doubt informal groups are capable of improvising a kind of order, but what the latter is and how it contributes to the securing of an overall organizational purpose can only be known after the

---

[1] Brown (1965b) defined an 'Executive System' as comprising the network of positions to which the company's work is assigned. It is made up of positions which he called 'Executive Roles'. The executive system included all members of the operating organizations, a member being in their role while they are carrying out their job responsibilities.

event, as a historical fact; there will be no prior, logistical guarantees. The latter, after all, is the provenance of 'formality' (Stinchcombe, 2001).

Even at the time of its development, much of what Brown articulated about the relationship between authority, formality, and organization appeared counterintuitive, and, as a result, out of step with contemporary organizational opinion (Gray, 1976; Mant, 2007). This is even more so nowadays, when, as we have noted throughout this book, so much work in OT has adopted a metaphysical stance towards its core object, with the result that once key concepts in the field, including 'authority', 'formality', and even 'organization' are deemed anachronistic and largely irrelevant to contemporary concerns. To continue to utilize such terms meaningfully is to leave oneself open to the sorts of criticism regularly levelled at generals: that they prepare for the last war, rather than the next. However, to continue the analogy, no matter how strange and altered contemporary conditions of warfare—or ('disruptive') organizing—might at first appear, generals and political leaders—or managers and organizational analysts—may find that there is much to be learned from the past that can be applied to the present and future (Slim, [1956] 2009: 612). That, of course, is a key contention of this book. Anachronism in organization studies may well reside less with the classical theorists than with their contemporary heirs, for whom the classical conceptual repertoire is deemed largely redundant, unless it can be somehow interpreted into their own favoured idioms. In this manner, Parker Follett, and Barnard, for instance, are given contemporary standing, but only in so far as they are turned into, respectively, an anti-bureaucrat (Nohria, 1995; Child, 2013), and a corporate culturalist and open-systems theorist manqué (Scott, 1992). Brown's work has escaped this fate, but at the cost of being 'disappeared' from the canon of OT altogether. Indeed, it is difficult to imagine how his work could be mobilized to endorse contemporary enthusiasms without extraordinary sophistry being deployed. The effort involved would hardly be worth it. As Mant (2007: 426), puts it, 'Brown was about clarity, precision of concept, formality, and the centrality of authority as liberating factors.' For many contemporary organizational analysts, as we have indicated, formality and authority are the antithesis of flexibility and liberty, not their concomitants. It is unsurprising, then, that Brown is no longer a household name in the field. That does not mean, though, that his formulations possess no traction. Significantly, Brown's own formulations are indebted to those of Parker Follett and Barnard, whose work he drew on extensively, if not always in an openly acknowledged fashion. The 'Parker Follett' and 'Barnard' that Brown deploys in his texts, though, are a long way from being the archetypal anti-bureaucrat or corporate culturalist conjured up by some contemporary writers. Indeed, the contextualist readings of Parker Follett and Barnard provided by O'Connor (2012), for instance, in no sense paint a picture of these two classicists as the progenitors of contemporary metaphysical enthusiasms, but rather signal them as practitioners of organizational theorizing as a practical science.

The Law of the Situation

Much of Parker Follett's work deals with authority, the giving of orders, leadership, coordination, and control. With the exception of leadership (and to some extent 'control', or rather its ever-present critical twin, 'resistance'), to which we will return in due course, the other topics that preoccupied her have received little attention within organization studies in recent years. While her work mixes normative prescriptions with maxims drawn from her own personal experience, it is important to remember that she was far from being an 'armchair theorist' of the sort derided by Simon (1946) in 'The proverbs of administration'; rather, she had considerably more familiarity with practice than could be claimed by most academics working in business schools today (O'Connor, 2012). Like Barnard and Brown, Parker Follett is clearly preoccupied with matters of form and system and, like them, she is not at all interested in developing a conceptual edifice as an end in itself. Metaphysics and ontology are almost completely absent from her work. She is not simply seeking to 'inform', but equally to persuade, transform, or produce a 'formative effect' for a specific audience—most notably managers (du Gay, 2015). In so doing, she shares with Barnard and Brown a fundamental recognition that 'theory' can only take you so far, and that principles underdetermine conduct. This helps explain her concern with 'casuistry' (not a term she uses, but something she practises and encourages others involved in organizing so to do too (hence her singular focus on the 'law of the situation')): 'I have often been interested to watch how often disagreement disappears when theorizing ends and the question is of some definite activity to be undertaken'[2] (Parker Follett, 1982: 17). While much is made of Parker Follett as a 'prophet' of contemporary enthusiasms in the field of management and organization studies, such as 'networks', 'empowerment', 'teams', 'ambidexterity', 'anti-hierarchy', or 'dissonance' (Kanter, 1995; Nohria, 1995; Child, 2013), such framing occludes as much as it enlightens, not least by appearing somewhat at odds with core elements of her work, such as the abiding respect for and promotion of scientific management, the significance accorded to 'depersonalization' in organizational relations, and the central belief in authority and its relation

---

[2] It is interesting to compare this quote with the opening sentences of Jonsen and Toulmin's (1988) classic *The Abuse of Casuistry*, where the same disposition is evident. Parker Follett's work thus indicates quite precisely the problems attendant upon the sort of 'theoreticist' approach to practical problems of organizational design advocated by Greenwood and Miller (2010) for instance. See Chapter 2 this volume.

to task coordination. It is these latter elements of Parker Follett's work that we find echoed in Brown's (and indeed Barnard's) work on organization as a practical science. Indeed, the appropriation of elements of Parker Follett's *oeuvre* to further the cause of contemporary expressivist ideals such as 'anti-bureaucracy' or 'empowerment' is dependent upon a considerable degree of semantic and pragmatic decontextualization for its effectivity. Because Parker Follett talks about the importance of 'process' or 'horizontal relations', for instance, it is easy enough to assume she must comply with contemporary conceptual formulations, although these sometimes only approximate to the language she used.

It can appear intuitively plausible for critics of bureaucratic organization, for example, to point to elements of Parker Follett's work that give succour to their own normative enthusiasms (Kanter, 1995; Nohria, 1995; Child, 2013). Sure enough, there are many instances where 'hierarchy' as a principle of organization is questioned or criticized by Parker Follett, but rarely is it dismissed *tout court* as always and everywhere a fundamental problem, or as 'inherently dysfunctional' (Child, 2013: 90). Rather, the practices of coordination, which Parker Follett (1982: 131) calls 'the most important point in organization', are continually related to the nature of the task or function being undertaken: '*Authority must be Functional and Functional Authority Carries with it Functional Responsibility*' (ibid.: 117; emphasis in original). In other words, the most effective way to exercise authority is to depersonalize the giving of orders and emphasize the requirements of the task to be undertaken and not the rights of one individual over another (ibid.: 21–41). This formulation precisely echoes Weber's description of the proper functioning of bureaucratic organization. As he put it:

> Legally and actually, (bureaucratic) office holding is not considered ownership of a source of income, to be exploited for rents or emoluments in exchange for the rendering of certain services, as was normally the case during the Middle Ages ... nor is office holding considered a common exchange of services, as in the case of free employment contracts. Rather entrance into an office ... is considered an acceptance of a specific duty of fealty to the purpose of the office (*Amstreue*) in return for the grant of a secure existence. It is decisive for the modern loyalty to an office that, in the pure type, it does not establish a relationship to a *person*, like the vassal's or disciple's faith under feudal or patrimonial authority, but rather is devoted to impersonal and functional purposes ... The political official—at least in the fully developed modern state—is not considered the personal servant of a ruler. (Weber, 1978: 959)

It is not therefore bureaucratic hierarchy that Parker Follett sets her sights against, but rather the leftovers or residue of feudalism and patrimonialism—what she often terms 'Bossism'—that plagued the organizational landscape she surveyed. Hence her strong advocacy of 'depersonalization', another key component of the ethos of bureaucratic office outlined by Weber.[3]

If orders are interpreted by those receiving them as evidence of the exercise of personal power rather than of legitimate functional authority, she writes, then employees will seek to evade or resist them. Similarly, those with legitimate functional authority should not be afraid to issue orders simply because they might be seen as 'bossing'. As Parker Follett (1982: 30) puts it, if orders are depersonalized 'then there would be no overbearing authority on the one hand, nor on the other that dangerous *laisser aller* which comes from the fear of exercising authority. Of course, we should exercise authority, but always the authority of the situation', which, as she continues, can only be comprehended in coordination. Thus, just as with Brown, Parker Follett (1982: 118, 121) insists that an employee 'should have just as much, no more and no less, authority as goes with his [*sic*] function or task... Legitimate authority flows from coordination.' And, like Brown, she believes the scientific study (in the Weberian sense of the disciplined pursuit of knowledge) of management and organization is crucial to this development. 'Scientific Management', she suggests,

> tends to depersonalize orders... one might call the essence of scientific management the attempt to find the law of the situation. With scientific management the managers are as much under orders as the workers, for both obey the law of the situation. Our job is not how to get people to obey orders, but how to devise methods by which we can best *discover* the order integral to a particular situation.
>
> (Ibid.: 30)[4]

That leads her to highlight the 'essential nature of coordination' to such an endeavour. 'A genuine coordination or integration gives you control. That is why coordination is the most important point in organization' (ibid.: 131).

Like Brown, Parker Follett believes obedience and liberty are perfectly compatible and that those who suggest otherwise are often indulging in wishful thinking. Taking issue with the norms animating the stance of the associationalists and guild socialists of her time, Parker Follett (1982: 35) argues that: '[T]hat group of political scientists... who are denying the power of the state, say that we cannot have obedience *and* liberty. I think they are wholly wrong,

---

[3] '[T]he more you are "bossed" the more your activity of thought will take place within the bossing-pattern, and your part in the pattern seems usually to be opposition to the bossing' (Parker Follett, 1982: 28).

[4] Parker Follett's assessment of scientific management is echoed by Brown. Indeed, it is interesting to note that a number of organizational analysts highlight the similarity between the Glacier project and scientific management (Kelly, 1968; Gray, 1976). The entirely negative representation of scientific management that developed in the wake of Braverman's (1974) *Labour and Monopoly Capital* has gradually given way to a more nuanced assessment. For an interesting pre-Braverman discussion of the 'failure' of the scientific management movement, see Ernest Dale (1969: 42–6) *Management Theory and Practice*.

but I think we should ask ourselves to what we owe obedience. Surely only to a functional unity of which we are a part, to which we are contributing': in other words, to the organization and the purposes for which it is formed and maintained. For Parker Follett (1982: 42), the first test of 'business organization and administration' as an activity is precisely 'whether you have a business with all its parts so co-ordinated, so moving together in their closely knit and adjusting activities...that they make a working *unit*...a functional whole or integrative unity'. In other words, organizations exist to coordinate the work of people towards a common purpose, an integrative unity. A formal organization, therefore, is one in which the various functions or series of tasks are explicitly related to one another such that they make up a working unit. In such a situation—where authority relates to function and function carries with it consequent responsibilities—liberty and obedience are reconciled. Because orders are not arbitrary, personal, or otherwise 'bossed', but rather relate to the 'law of the situation', obedience to them is not evidence of a lack of freedom for employees, but rather of a clearly defined area of freedom within which they can exercise discretion, which in turn they will be held responsible for using. In words that could have easily been written by Brown, Parker Follett (1982: 42) concludes:

> A young trade unionist said to me, 'How much dignity can I have as a mere employee?' He can have all the dignity in the world if he is allowed to make his fullest contribution to the plant and to assume definitely the responsibility *therefor*.

Authority and Formal Organization: Chester Barnard

> 'I know nothing that that I actually regard as more "real" than "authority".'
>
> —Chester Barnard

As we indicated in Chapter 1, Wilfred Brown has often been represented as the 'British Barnard', not only because he was both a successful practitioner of organization and a renowned 'organizational theorist', but also because his practical stance towards matters organizational shared more than a family resemblance to Barnard's. This is particularly evident when it comes to the question of authority.

As Gray (1976: 424), among others, has indicated, Brown made 'full use of Barnard's "acceptance theory of authority"' in both his executive practice and his writings on organization. This is evident, for example, in Brown's approach to employee ('worker') participation in organizational decision-making. While he did not think that employees should have a say in decision-making within an executive system—this was the province of management, and he believed that most employees wished managers would get on

161

with it and competently so—he did believe that employees should have some form of representation in organizational policy formation in so far as the latter affected them as members of the organization (his vehicle of choice for this was a constitutional one, a unanimous voting works council). He believed this form of representative participation in policy decisions would enhance the legitimate authority of management. He did so because, à la Barnard, he maintained that, unless employees accepted managerial decisions and acted upon instructions issued, then no authority had actually been exercised. Through the mechanism of constitutional representation in policy formulation, Brown sought to induce that acceptance whilst simultaneously enhancing what Barnard (1968: 172ff) described as 'the system of objective authority', and thus both the efficiency and effectiveness of formal organization. Indeed, like Barnard, Brown argued that organization as a practical science is fundamentally focused on the system of objective authority. Without it, 'a cooperative personal attitude' among individual employees could not be maintained, because no one would know if orders issued were legitimate or not, nor where their own responsibility and accountability for task performance began or ended, 'so that they cannot know who is who, what is what, or have the sense of effective coordination' (ibid.: 175). The system of objective authority, or what Brown calls 'the executive system', is, for Barnard, the 'primary or essential continuing problem of a formal organization. Every other practical question of effectiveness or efficiency...depends upon it' (ibid.: 175). This is why, for Barnard, as for Brown, when it comes to organization there is nothing 'more real than authority'.

The constituent elements of Barnard's system of objective authority also bear remarkable resemblance to many of the key facets of Weber's bureaucratic administration as well as echoing central features of Parker Follett's axioms and adages on authority and organization that have been outlined. In turn, as we have indicated, they are taken up and elaborated by Brown, without, it must be said, any major alteration in their basic precepts.

Barnard (1968: 172–3) begins his elaboration by indicating, as did Weber, Parker Follett, and Brown, the singular importance of *formality*. Authority, he states, 'is always related to something in a *definitely* organized system'. 'Definitely' here means 'formally': 'The word "authority" is seldom employed except where formal organization connection is stated or implied.' Because all 'authoritative communication in organization' is formal, it means, for instance, that orders can only be issued by those with requisite 'official' standing—those with an official role or persona, and only sent to those who are likewise members of the organization in specified positions:

> This is what we mean when we say that individuals are able to exercise authority only when they are acting 'officially', a principle well established in law and

secular and religious practice.[5] Hence the importance ascribed to time, place dress, ceremony, and authentication of communication to establish its official character. These practices confirm the statement that authority relates to communication 'in a formal organization'.   (Ibid.: 173)

An order therefore has the presumption of authority when it issues from a requisite position within the formal organization. It loses such a presumption if, for instance, it is does not fall within the orbit or competence of such a position—what Barnard terms 'a communications center'—or if the order, à la Parker Follett, 'shows an absence of adjustment to the actual situation which confronts the recipient of it' (ibid.: 173).

The system of objective authority must therefore 'be definitely established' through devices such as making official appointments known within the organization, assigning each individual to an official position, and by 'general announcements, by organization charts, by educational effort, and most of all by habituation, that is by securing as much permanence of system as is practicable' (ibid.: 176; see also Chapter 1, this volume). The fixing of objective authority is therefore undertaken through the creation and maintenance of a formal executive system made up of fixed positions occupied by individuals acting in an official capacity as an organizational persona (du Gay, 2007).[6] An objective system of authority therefore presupposes the establishment of a formal organization in which every employee must occupy an official position and that the tasks related to such positions must be so coordinated as to fulfil the purpose for which formal organization is instituted: 'In ordinary language this means "everyone must report to someone" (communication in one direction) and "everyone must be subordinate to someone" (communication in the other direction). In other words, in formal organizations, everyone must have a definite formal relationship to the organization' (Barnard, 1968: 176). The system of objective authority should not therefore be susceptible to vagueness, ambiguity, or incoherence; it must be followed all the way up and all the way down, otherwise the formal organization could quickly disintegrate. As Barnard (1968: 177–8) puts it:

[A] communication should pass through every stage of the line of authority. This is due to the necessity of avoiding conflicting communications (in either direction) which might (and would) occur if there were any 'jumping of the line' of organization. It is also necessary because of the need of interpretation, and to maintain responsibility.[7]

[5] See the discussion of the immanent rationality of law and organization in Chapter 2.

[6] Again, with this formulation Barnard's work points backwards to Weber and forwards to Brown.

[7] Barnard's adherence to casuistry is evident here. As he suggests, 'a considerable part of administrative work consists in the interpretation and reinterpretation of orders in their

In a talk to the Committee on Work in Industry of the National Research Council, Barnard illustrated this precept from his experience as director of emergency relief in the state of New Jersey:

> One of the rules pretty generally followed in organizations of large size is not to 'jump' the line of organization in passing out orders or getting information. If you have an order from the top you give it through the line, and information from the bottom comes through the line. You avoid this sometimes skilfully and artistically, but as a rule it is necessary to follow the line. I thought in the particular instance of the relief organization that I was dealing with people who had not been inoculated with high organization practice. I suspected that the reactions we had to take into account in established organizations were artificial, and when I found it convenient to do so with the relief organization I went directly to the local man, and thus attempted to save trouble for everybody. Nevertheless, I found that what happened was exactly what would have happened in the telephone organization if I had done it there—personalities, emotion, diffusion of responsibility etc.
>
> (quoted in Wolf, 1974: 88–9)

In addition to 'no jumping the line', Barnard similarly stresses that the system of authority should never be interrupted in operation, as similar problems to those articulated will quickly arise, namely the sorts of dysfunctions put forward by Brown—individuals assuming personal positions of power and influence which bear no realistic connection to the proper authority required by them to do the work allotted to them by the executive system:

> During the times when organizations are at work, in principle the line of authority must never be broken; and practically this is almost . . . literally true in many cases; this is one of the reasons which may be given . . . for the elaborate provision made in most organizations . . . for the temporary filling of offices automatically during incapacity or absence of incumbents. These provisions emphasize the non-personal . . . character of organization authority, as does the persistent emphasis on the *office* rather than the *man* that is the matter of indoctrination of many organizations, especially those in which 'discipline' is an important feature.
>
> (Barnard, 1968: 179–80)[8]

For Barnard (1968: 181), 'the only lines of authority are complete lines'; the executive system which, if functional for the achievement of organizational purposes, is a 'total' structure of authority and responsibility, where everyone knows their place (to whom they report and for what they are accountable): 'if the formal line of authority is interrupted . . . "politics" runs riot' (ibid.: 180).

---

application to concrete circumstances that were not or could not be taken into account initially' (1968: 165).

[8] The separation of 'Office' and 'Person' is, of course a key element in Weber's discussion of the ethos of bureaucratic administration. As we have already seen in this chapter, it is also allotted a crucial place in Parker Follett and Brown's discussions of authority in formal organization.

In addition, and as importantly, these lines should be as direct and as short as practically possible to avoid confusion, ambiguity, and uncertainty. In general, Barnard (1968: 177) states, 'the shorter the line the greater the speed and the less the error'.[9]

The final factor in the system of objective authority that Barnard focuses upon is the importance of what he terms 'authentication'. In brief, this means that a particular member of the organization issuing an order must be known to occupy 'the position of authority' requisite to the domain covered by the order; in other words, 'that the position includes the type of communication concerned—that is, it is "within its authority"; and that it actually is an authorised communication from the office' (ibid.: 180). Barnard says that such practices of authentication often differ within and between organizations, but that the basic structure and purpose of these practices remains remarkably consistent:

> Ceremonials of investiture, inaugurations, swearing-in, general orders of appointment, induction, and introduction, are all essentially appropriate methods of making known who actually fills a position and what the position includes as authority. In order that these positions may function it is often necessary that the filling of them should be dramatized, an essential process to the creation of authority ... that it, it is essential to inculcate 'the sense of organization'. This is merely stating that it is essential to 'organization loyalty and solidarity' as it may be otherwise expressed. Dignifying the superior position is an important method of dignifying all connection with organization, a fact which has been well learned in political and religious organizations. (Ibid.: 181)

According to Barnard (1968: 230), as for Parker Follett and Brown, for 'every organization to survive', it 'must deliberately attend to the maintenance and growth of its authority'. This is not a statement that appears to have had much traction within many areas of organizational life, nor within the field of organizational theorizing in recent years. Indeed, quite the contrary appears to be the case. As we suggested earlier in this chapter, authority and authorizing relations are regularly represented as old-fashioned and unsuited to a world of incessant change and the proliferation of 'disruptive micropowers' (Naim, 2014). In such a world, 'Objective Authority' and its semantic twin, 'formality', are seen to be 'decaying' because they are deemed unsuited to contemporary 'social' (cultural, political, economic, etc.) realities (Beck, 2005).

---

[9] In his introduction to Wilfred Brown's *Exploration in Management*, Eric Trist (1965: 20–1) writes that Brown's experience led him to express a 'strong preference ... for keeping the number of essential steps in the hierarchy as few as possible', and for similar reasons to those articulated by Barnard.

From Authority to the 'State of Nature' in Organizational Analysis and Practice

The extent to which hostility to authority and authorizing relations within contemporary organizational discourse constitutes, on the one hand, a pragmatic response to changed realities or, on the other, represents, to paraphrase Carl Schmitt (1986), 'an artful system of norms and methods' for weakening organization is something of a moot point within the field of organizational studies, broadly conceived. Clearly, a cursory genealogy of many fashionable ideas in the field of organizational studies that claim to describe, chart, and/or offer a response to new realities—'change', 'learning', 'post-bureaucracy', 'disruptive innovation', and so forth—quite quickly establishes their metaphysical pedigree. Indeed, as we have already indicated in Chapters 2, 3, and 4 of this book, near-identical ideas are constantly trotted out without the slightest notion that, in the words of Albert Hirschman (1977: 133), these 'had already had ... an encounter with reality ... that was seldom wholly satisfactory'. The opposite sort of forgetfulness is also in evidence, however—one which sees in determinate organization only impediment, oppression, and anachronism, for instance, and which fails to register that, despite their historical contingency, certain organizational concepts and devices—'task', 'coordination', and 'authority'—are important because they meet specific organizational needs and fulfil particular purposes. They cannot therefore easily be dispensed with without risking the dissolution of that which they help to constitute: formal organization. As we have seen, Parker Follett, Barnard, and Brown all uniformly affirmed that authority was organizationally indispensable and that the only real lines of organizational authority were 'complete lines'.[10] The desire to dispense with, to jump over, or otherwise avoid clear and unambiguous lines of authority has been a consistent trope since the mid-1980s, not only within the world of organizational analysis but also in the worlds of government and commerce; furthermore, such ambitions are mooted without any sense of the often less than savoury outcomes that their previous encounters with reality had produced. An example or two should prove useful.

'Sofa-Style' Government: Against 'the System of Objective Authority'

The controversies surrounding the decision to go to war in Iraq as a result of the attacks in the USA on 11 September 2001 are still very much alive. Many of

---

[10] In the language deployed by Pufendorf (quoted in Hunter, 2009a) to describe political authority in a civil state, 'incomplete lines of authority' were indicative of an 'irregular' as opposed to a 'regular' state, and thus denoted a 'defective sovereignty'.

these revolved around questions of authority and authorization. In the USA, considerable concern has been voiced over the manner in which the threat posed by international jihadist terrorism was invoked by the George W. Bush presidency to bypass established lines of authority in various areas of government, not least in intelligence gathering and appraisal, and military interrogation, for example, in the pursuit of greater speed, flexibility, adaptation, and innovation in countering what was represented as an entirely unprecedented terrorist threat. The assumption here was that 'security' could only be assured if existing lines of authority were bypassed to accord with the urgency, novelty, complexity, and so forth of the perceived terrorist threat. The aim of the measures advocated and enacted was to 'end business as usual, to cut through red tape, and give people the authority to do things they might not ordinarily be allowed to do . . . If there is some bureaucratic hurdle, leap it' (Tenet, quoted in Betts, 2007: 142). In the UK, the Hutton and Butler reports shed considerable light into the organization of government under the premiership of Tony Blair, indicating, in so doing, how constitutionally surprising and administratively disabling the Blair regime's informal 'style of organizing' and specific approaches to authority and authorization had proven to be (Hennessy,2004; Quinlan, 2004; du Gay, 2006). We will focus on each of these in turn.

In one way, the often rather unedifying picture of a far from 'joined-up' administration in action that both the Hutton and Butler reports provided was neither that surprising nor particularly disturbing. Rather, insiders considered it indicative of the 'fog of government' with which anyone who had any intimate knowledge of the workings of Westminster and Whitehall for any length of time would be familiar. As Quinlan (2004: 125) has pointed out, though, there were significant exceptions to that relaxed recognition. Of crucial import here was the evidence elicited by Hutton of the 'remarkable informality (to use no sharper term)' of how the business of government was transacted under the Blair premiership, which, as Quinlan indicates, 'was surely an uncomfortable surprise, even to cognoscenti' (2004: 125). The Butler report also made much of what it described as the informal 'sofa style' of government operating in and around No. 10 Downing Street, and voiced some remarkably adverse comment upon how the relationship between career civil servants, most especially those working in the intelligence services, and figures in the prime minister's inner circle, functioned. That report ended with what was, in its context, a dramatically critical six-paragraph conclusion about the general way in which the prime minister had organized and conducted his administration.

One key facet of this, as a number of commentators pointed out, was a suspicious and hostile attitude towards traditional relations of authority and formality within governmental administration; this attitude derived in no small part from what Peter Hennessy has termed the particular 'pair of spectacles' through which the governing party viewed the purposes of governmental administration. Interestingly, the entire Labour shadow cabinet had been given 'pre-office' training in contemporary management and organizational thinking at Templeton College, Oxford, in 1996, and the attempts to operationalize the norms and techniques introduced to them at this time—on 'change', 'culture', 'innovation', 'leadership', 'performance', and 'delivery', for instance—were core elements of the Blair 'style of organizing'. Hence the importance attached to cultivating an informal 'all on one team mentality' that overrode established distinctions of office, function, and authority, along with inculcating a 'just do it' ethic among public servants, and with the unprecedented deployment of partisan appointments—special advisers and other 'irregulars'—in key positions in governmental administration, some vested with constitutionally anomalous powers to issue orders to civil servants (thus accentuating the problem of authentication outlined by Barnard).

A cocktail of inexperience in government, suspicion of official machineries of administration, and a remarkably uncritical belief in the powers of their own favoured forms of managerial 'modernization' proved lethal to established conventions framing the conduct of Labour governmental business, as the scene disclosed by Hutton and Butler made only too clear. Changes in the machinery of government, often, it seemed, reflective of a marked impatience with due process and collective, deliberative decision-making, appeared to have had some serious downsides, though, ones that could have been predicted in advance if due consideration had been applied. As Quinlan (2004: 127) argued, it was not at all clear that the changes initiated always rested upon 'sufficient understanding that existing patterns had not been developed without practical reason'. In that context, the revelations elicited by Hutton of the extent to which, under the Blair administration, the traditional bureaucratic practices of careful and precise note-talking and writing of minutes had fallen into abeyance were both striking and worrying. It was seen most vividly, perhaps, when Jonathan Powell, the prime minister's (partisan and thus constitutionally and organizationally 'unauthenticated') chief of staff, disclosed to Hutton that, of an average seventeen meetings a day in Downing Street, only three were minuted. What Butler famously described as 'the informality and circumscribed character of the Government's procedures' seriously risked 'reducing the scope for informed collective political judgement'. As another former cabinet secretary, (Lord) Richard Wilson (2004: 85) commented in relation to this point, formal meetings and minute-taking, for instance, might seem overly 'bureaucratic' and thus very unmodern technologies, yet they play a crucial practical role in ensuring good government, and provide a necessary underpinning for the realization of constitutionally sanctioned authority and accountability requirements by ensuring that a proper record of governmental decision-making existed and that agreed actions are clearly delineated. Linked to this, both Quinlan and Wilson indicated concern with the government's near exclusive focus on 'delivery' at the expense of attention to due process. As Quinlan (2004: 128) put it, a singular focus on delivery can easily:

> [S]lide into a sense that outcome is the only true reality and that process is flummery. But the two are not antithetical, still less inimical to one another. Process is care and thoroughness; it is consultation, involvement...legitimacy and acceptance; it is also record, auditability and clear accountability. It is often accordingly a significant component of outcome itself; and the more awkward and demanding the issue—especially amid the gravity of peace and war—the more it may come to matter.

The informal and personalized ways of doing business established at No.10 also had serious repercussions for the possibility of the Cabinet exercising the constitutionally important role of 'collective responsibility' on what Butler described as the 'vital matter of war and peace'. As Hennessy (2004: 73) argued:

> [T]he Butler Report suggests that the reliance on 'unscripted' oral presentations from Mr. Blair and the ministers in his inner group on Iraq, without supporting papers ('excellent quality papers were written by officials but these were not discussed in Cabinet or Cabinet committee') meant that it was...'obviously much more difficult' for Cabinet ministers on the outer rim to test out the evidence and arguments of the inner circle even though the discussion ranged over 24 meetings of the full cabinet.

Wilson (2004: 85) agreed, adding that the danger of 'informality' is that it can 'slide into something more fluid and unstructured, where advice and dissent may either not always be offered or else may not be heard. This is certainly a matter which engages collective responsibility.'

The demands of the 'just do it' ethic and the absence of thorough analysis, and of the bureaucratic system for conducting it, was conspicuously displayed in a number of other governmental farragoes. What Hutton and Butler suggested, though, was that this was not simply a reflection of the 'normal' complexities of governing, but rather a widespread feature of the 'New' Labour 'style' of government; a product, in large part, of the government's attempts to bypass established machinery, and the rules and procedures they gave effect to, in the pursuit of its own form of what Jane Caplan (1988), in another context, described as 'government without administration'. In Quinlan's (2004: 127–8) words, as a result of the Hutton and Butler enquiries it looked increasingly like the Labour government had little interest in or tolerance for distinctions of function, authority, and responsibility 'between different categories of actor within the Government machine (except perhaps when political defences needed to be erected, as over the purported "ownership" of the September 2002 dossier)'. Rather, 'there was a sense of all participants—ministers, civil servants, special policy advisers, public relations handlers—being treated as part of an undifferentiated resource for the support of the central executive'. In attempting to bypass established lines of authority—to 'jump the line' in Barnard's words—politics literally ran riot.

The manner in which the Blair administration's 'managerialist pair of spectacles' led to tangled or blurred lines of authority and accountability in governmental administration is also powerfully evidenced by the confused nature of the organizational status attributed to the government's weapons expert, Dr David Kelly, whose suicide after being publically named as a source for BBC reports critical of claims concerning the existence of weapons of mass destruction (WMD) in Iraq led to the establishment of the Hutton Inquiry.

As the Hutton report put it, David Kelly's employment within the civil service was 'somewhat complex'. It was in fact quite far removed from a conventional civil service appointment, to the point, once again, of being considered 'irregular' and 'unauthenticated' in terms of traditional lines of authority and accountability within governmental administration. There are a number of aspects to this, but we will focus only on the organizational dimension here. Dr Kelly worked for an agency organization within government. The latter originated in recommendations from the 1988 report to the prime minister from the Efficiency Unit: *Improving Management in Government: The Next Steps* (Efficiency Unity, 1988). Although the report was commissioned by and made to a Conservative government, there was enthusiastic and bipartisan support for the reforms it mooted. Key here was the idea that 'agencies' should be established to carry out the executive functions of government within a policy and resources framework set by a department. The purpose of creating such agencies was to achieve 'better value for money and steadily improving services'. A novel view of the comportment of civil servants was also stressed; one in which all officials were expected to 'show real qualities of leadership', not least because responsibility for the day-to-day operations of each agency was to be effectively delegated from the relevant minister to the relevant agency chief executive. While some very clear and pressing constitutional and organizational problems arose as a result of the practical operation of the policy/operations split that the agency system effected, which had, at their heart, issues concerning the location and practice of authority between ministers and agency heads, for instance, when the Blair government was sworn in in 1997 it was nonetheless determined to extend and enhance the approach to public administration developed by its Conservative forebears.[11] This was illustrated in a speech given by Prime Minister

---

[11] The literature on the constitutional, ethical, and organizational problems of the agency model is now quite vast. For early and still largely prescient accounts, see for instance, Chapman, 1992; O'Toole and Jordan, 1995; du Gay, 2000; Suleiman, 2001.

Blair in February 2004, when he emphasized the conduct he expected of civil servants: innovation, leadership, adventurousness, and openness to the public. He proposed to end tenure for senior posts (they were to become four-year placements) and to recruit extensively from outside for senior civil service posts. He believed that such shifts would create 'a Civil Service equipped to lead', with 'people willing to take responsibility for a challenge' (Blair, 2004, quoted in Chapman, 2006: 59). This is a brief organizational background to the 'next steps agencies' David Kelly worked for. Indeed, his employment had shifted from an agency, DERA (the Defence Evaluation and Research Agency) to the DSTL (the Defence Science and Technology Laboratory), whose organizational status was what is known as a 'Trading Fund', a device for making public administrative bodies more business-like, and often, over time, a step on the way to their eventual privatization. In the context of governmental administration, these organizations have a somewhat ambiguous status and standing, being, on the one hand, subject to traditional rules and procedures in the context of existing constitutional authority and accountability arrangements, and, on the other, operating in a less regulated environment with more opportunity for independent decision-making and flexibility of working, and with implications for individuals working on their own. The lack of clear, formally instituted and stated authority relations pertaining to such entities was reflected in the confusion and ambiguity surrounding Dr Kelly's employment status and the authority associated with it. Was he a civil servant? Was he a special adviser? Was he of junior or senior standing? Did he have authority to speak to the media, or did he not? And so on and so forth. The confusion was expressed in evidence to the Hutton Inquiry where Dr Kelly was represented, inter alia, as 'an adviser', 'a consultant', 'not a full-time Ministry of Defence official', and 'a respected technical source' (Hutton, 2004: paras 305, 353, 375–6, 383). Indeed, Kelly's wife, in evidence to Hutton, said of her husband's employment that 'it seemed to have been a very loose arrangement with the Ministry of Defence' (ibid.: para. 435). The point we wish to emphasize here is that the 'managerialist pair of spectacles' through which the Blair government, like its immediate Conservative predecessors, viewed the public administration as an institution of government, led to the creation of tangled, blurred, and defective lines of authority, where, in the words of Barnard and Brown, no-one knew their place exactly, to whom they reported, and for what they were accountable. In such a situation, politics did indeed run riot, and Dr David Kelly found himself, unwittingly, at the centre of a political storm that ultimately consumed him. In effect, the lack of clear lines of authority and hence a lack of precision regarding his own organizational status and role, meant that Dr Kelly was caught firmly in the intolerable dilemma outlined by Wilfred Brown (1965a: 69–70), whereby not only was he judged on the wisdom of the decisions he took, but also on whether he was correct in assuming that the responsibility for making those decisions in the first place was within his authority. Not only this, the self-same lack of formality and clear lines of authority enabled the government of the day to decide what it was and was not prepared to accept responsibility for, including Dr Kelly's fate. As a former head of the British civil service indicated in relation to this very point, holding onto formal procedures not only allows for decisions to be made with requisite authority and for accountability to be assured, it also 'provides fairness for the individual, and, by precluding prejudicial comment, some protection from the sort of political maelstrom into which Dr. Kelly was drawn' (Wilson, 2004: 84). In other words, the lack of such formal lines of authority and accountability and the freedoms they establish and express led to Dr Kelly being allotted an extraordinary role that he was in no way prepared for or should have been expected to fulfil: he became politically accountable to parliament in the place of his direct political superiors and largely at their behest. One could suggest he became a scapegoat because normally, under established conventions, known collectively as the Osmotherly Rules, a civil servant appearing before a parliamentary select committee, as Dr Kelly was forced to do in front of the Foreign Affairs Committee, does so as a persona, that of his or her minister, as not as an individual self, expressing personal views and opinions and being held individually politically accountable for these. Dr Kelly's appearance was not represented or conducted in this spirit, and thus not only were the seeds of injustice sown for Dr Kelly, the lack of clear lines of authority, formality, and due process also put paid to 'the practice of orderly collective government' (ibid.: 84–5).

Concluding Comments

> Formalities and procedures were the wisdom of human organization and were in themselves civilizing instruments…a way of causing a pause in the impatience of things, so that everything could be properly checked and considered.
>
> Frank Moorhouse, *Grand Days*, 1993

Given the prevalence of assumptions about the negative relations between authority and organizational, and personal freedom, innovation, and flexibility, within contemporary organization studies, as elsewhere, it is hardly surprising that the importance ascribed to 'authority' and associated terms such as 'formality', 'constraint', and 'prescribed boundaries' by practitioners of the classical stance is regarded with at best suspicion and at worst outright hostility by many of those eager to promote the radical reform of organizations and organizational life—whether they be critical intellectuals, management consultants, or policy wonks of varying political hues. For these personas, authority and authorizing relations suggest limits to the scope for spontaneous action and possibilities of transformation, as was clearly evidenced in our discussion of the Iraq farrago. Worse, they can imply a degree of conservatism (we prefer the term conservation)[12] and the legitimacy of certain forms of subordination. These are not qualities that naturally appeal to those persons seeking to advocate radical transformation; those whom we may regard as embodying what Moorhouse terms 'the impatience of things' or what Kronman (1993: 161) describes as manifesting 'that passion for purity which motivates the adherents of every great... simplification'. Despite the opprobrium heaped upon authority and authorizing relationships, though, it remains the case that they are inescapable elements of organization as a distinctive endeavour and object. There can be no organization without authority, just as there can be no organization without task. There can, of course, be lots of other things without authority, but organization is not one of them. Authority is not some by-product that can be removed at will to produce more innovative, flexible, faster, freer organizing. The work of Brown, Parker Follett, and Barnard makes this evident enough and, for that reason, as for many others, is worthy of revisiting by anyone interested or involved in thinking and undertaking 'formal' organization. Exposure to the work of these and other practitioners of the classical stance in OT might also help dampen the desire to accede to a metaphysical comportment amongst those claiming to be students of formal organization. Adopting the classical stance would necessarily be something of a conversion experience in this instance, as van Fraassen argues: one involving the development of a habitus or disposition, including both the abandonment 'of a certain combination of words as senseless', as Wittgenstein (2005: 300) put it, and a certain resignation, 'but one of feeling, not of intellect'. This is where the challenge lies, for 'it can be difficult not to use an expression'—'learning organization', 'ambidextrous', 'institutional logic', 'agencement', 'governmentality'—'just as it is difficult to hold back tears, or an outburst of rage' (ibid.). The classical stance is thus of much more than arcane academic interest. Acceding to it places one in a particular disposition towards 'formal organization', very different from the metaphysical stance currently so powerful an attractor in this disciplinary field, but to which we welcome newcomers.

---

[12] The sort of distinction is also deployed by Kaufman (1995) in his classic, *The Limits of Organizational Change*.

Conclusion

Comportment and Character in Formal Organization and Its Analysis

A key argument of this book has been that organizational theory (OT) has dispensed or lost touch with the 'classical stance', has increasingly adopted a 'metaphysical stance', and, in so doing, has come gradually and sometimes suddenly to lose its own core object—'formal organization'. We have suggested that this development has little to commend it. The book has attempted not only to show what is at stake in the battle between the classical and metaphysical stances in OT, but also to indicate as clearly as possible why practising the former is preferable to cultivating the latter. As we have sought to show, adopting a metaphysical disposition towards matters of formal organization is like attempting to undo a knot wearing boxing gloves. It simply isn't up to the task, nor is it worth the effort. Our central contention has been that there is much to be gained for OT in reconceiving of itself as a practical science of organizing in the manner of its classical antecedents, and in reviving and readopting the classical stance and thus the sort of persona associated with it.

The 'classical stance', we have suggested, approaches formal organization (and its analysis) as a way of life. Adopting it involves not simply the disciplined pursuit of formal organizational knowledge in the Weberian sense, but also the cultivation of a distinctive persona, the formation of an organizational 'character'. As we have sought to indicate throughout the book, 'the classical stance' does not seek to provide a systematic or totalizing theory of organizing, as the latter, should it be claimed to exist, would be too general and loose—too metaphysical—to possess any explanatory reach or practical utility; however, it does seek to furnish those who adopt it with a method and a purpose with which to orient themselves both in formal organizational thought and in formal organizational life. Indeed, the absence of a clear divide between organizational thought and organizational life is one of the notable aspects of the 'classical stance' that is worth reviving.

The classical stance can also be seen to embody an *ethos*: it has what Weber termed 'characterological' effects, as it seeks to prepare individuals to think clearly and practically about matters of formal organization *and* at the same time also assists in preparing them to responsibly take up a place within a formal organization (without a crisis of conscience, for instance). An ethos, as Hadot's work shows, is something we live, and, as Stuart Hampshire remarked, 'a way of life is a complicated thing' (quoted in Lilla, 1981: 14). It is not primarily a set of (theoretical) propositions to be applied with more or less precision to cases that arise in (organizational) life; rather, as van Fraassen indicates, it is an attitude, comportment, outlook, a set of virtues and habits which we learn, sometimes rationally, but often through other means, such as training, indoctrination, example, and prestigious imitation. Michael Oakeshott's (1962: 62) quaint but still insightful analogy between moral habits and grammar captures a certain aspect of the latter well:

> We acquire habits of conduct, not by constructing a way of living upon rules or precepts learned by heart and subsequently practised, but by living with people who habitually behave in a certain manner: we acquire habits of conduct in the same way we as we acquire our native language.

Barnard and Brown, for instance, were exemplars in this Oakeshottian 'characterological' sense, in the manner in which they approached matters of formal organization and the way they practised formal organizing. Regretfully, as we have seen, much contemporary OT lacks an *ethos* in this sense. Rather, theory construction, theory application, and metaphysical speculation are its prestigious practices, whether they be analytical or critical in orientation. Students preparing for a life in formal organizations are therefore unlikely to receive much in the way of practical guidance from contemporary OT—what we might term an organizational education, something akin to a moral education which inculcates virtuous habits as well as formal organizational knowledge; rather, they are more likely to be exposed to all sorts of discourse which can provide them with assistance in, for instance, finding 'power' or 'contracting relationships', on the one hand, or 'logics' and 'materialities', on the other, in every facet, nook, and cranny of organizational life. No doubt this is all very interesting, but in what way does it approximate to an education, a way of forming what Parker Follett termed a 'conscious and responsible', as well as a practical attitude and comportment towards formal organization? And if the idea of 'forming' smacks too much of 'indoctrination' or 'manipulation', is not the attempt to 'influence behaviour', as Barnard put it, 'the purpose of education'?

As we indicated in the Introduction to this book, Hadot made the same point in relation to philosophy when he wrote:

> What is ultimately the most useful...? Is it discourse on language or on being and non-being? Isn't it rather, to learn how to live...?
>
> (Quoted in Davidson, 2009: x)

In this spirit, we can suggest that the 'classical stance' in OT provides an education in formal organization as a way of life in a manner that the metaphysical stance does not. Indeed, the latter cannot do so because it is resolutely antithetical to formal organization. Adopting the metaphysical stance leads one away from, not further towards, formal organization. It therefore turns out to be a less than optimal stance to adopt in a field ostensibly devoted to organizational education because, as we have stressed throughout this text, it dissolves the field's core object—'formal organization'. And because it lacks an 'organizational' ethos, the persona associated with it appears unfit for purpose. And yet, metaphysical personas have had, and continue to be accorded, remarkable standing and prestige within the field. Deploying Weber's terminology, we might well argue that if one wishes to evaluate contemporary organization studies characterologically, then the human type for which it, by way of external and internal (motivational) selection, optimizes the chances of becoming the dominant type, is in fact a resolutely anti-organizational persona. This doesn't seem a very useful state of affairs. It appears even less so when one considers that currently such anti-organizational personas also garner remarkable prestige and standing in the practical worlds of organizing in the public, private, and so-called third sectors. How then to reassert the prestige and standing of an alternative disposition, comportment, and ethos within these worlds, one which does combine practical rationality with ethical seriousness?

Character and Conduct in Organization Theory and Formal Organization

> Every order of social relations, without exception and however constituted is, if one wishes to evaluate it, ultimately to be examined with respect to the human type for which it, by way of external and internal (motivational) selection, optimises the chances of becoming the dominant type.
>
> Max Weber (1917 [1988]), *Gesammelte Aufsätze zur Wissenschafstlehre*

> True heroism is minutes, hours, weeks, year upon year, of the quiet, precise, judicious exercise of probity and care—with no one there to see or cheer. This is the world.
>
> David Foster Wallace (2012), *The Pale King*

In a series of detailed studies, Wilhelm Hennis (1988, 2000) has convincingly argued that the work of Max Weber should be viewed as fundamentally concerned with questions of *character* and *conduct*, and that the work itself expresses a particular stance, attitude, or comportment towards these questions. Hennis (ibid.) indicates that, at the heart of Weber's work lies a moral anthropology at profound variance with both a positivistic and high theoretical social science, one which, in Weber's own words, had sought to 'shift its location and change its conceptual apparatus so that it might regard the stream of events from the heights of reflective thought' (Weber, 1949, quoted in Hennis 1988: 104). In such a social science, the central problems preoccupying Weber, questions of *lebensführung* (the conduct of life), of 'personality', and of 'life orders' (*lebensordnungen*), would hold little interest. However, if we managed to descend from such heights, Hennis suggested they might once again become very important indeed. For Hennis (1988: 104), Max Weber's work finds a place in the prehistory of this sort of abstracted or otherwise highfalutin social science only once his central problems, questions, and stance are neglected. In Hennis's view, Weber's work belongs, rather, to the late history of a rather different *practical science* and embodies a distinctive *ethos*. In *Science as a Vocation*, Weber asks: How are individuals to develop 'character' or 'personality' (*Persönlichkeit*) in institutional and organizational life? His answer is clear and direct: individuals with 'personality' are those willing and able to live up to the ethical demands placed upon them by their location within particular life orders; individuals whose life conduct within those distinctive orders and powers—the university, the bureau, the firm, the parliament—can combine *practical rationality with ethical seriousness*. As Weber puts it in *Science as a Vocation*, 'Ladies and gentlemen: Personality is possessed in science by the man [sic] who serves only the needs of his subject, and this is true not only in science' (1989: 11). The individual with 'personality' is one who is capable of personal dedication to the instituted purposes of a given life order in a manner that 'transcends individuality' (Hennis, 1988: 88).[1] It is in this sense that it is possible, for example, for bureaucrats to be 'personally' committed to the ethos and purposes of their distinctive office even though that ethos lies outside of their own personal (i.e. individual) moral predilections or principles.

In his recent book, *The Road to Character*, David Brooks (2015: 71) consciously picks up on Weber's characterological concerns and locates them in the context of what he describes as 'an age of institutional anxiety', one where 'people are prone to distrust large organizations'. Paralleling certain of the themes of the present book, as well as of Weber's work, Brooks (ibid.) argues that little to no standing attaches to the idea or practice of submerging 'our

---

[1] Hadot (2011: 66–7) makes the same point, 'one must get rid of the partiality of the individual and impassioned self...Self-detachment is a moral attitude that should be demanded of both the politician and the scholar.'

own individual identities in conformity to' the instituted purposes of 'some bureaucracy or organization'.[2] Or, as Weber put it, to living up to the characterological demands of the given life order in which we find ourselves:

> No one wants to be an Organization Man. We like start-ups, disruptors, and rebels. There's less prestige accorded to those who tend to the perpetual reform and repair of institutions. Young people are raised to think that big problems can be solved by a swarm of small, networked NGOs and social entrepreneurs. Big hierarchical organizations are dinosaurs...This mentality has contributed to institutional decay...if everybody is told to think outside the box, you've got to expect that the boxes themselves will begin to deteriorate.   (Ibid.: 71)

Institutional decay in both the world of formal organization and in that ostensibly devoted to its analysis, OT, and the increasing dominance of a particular stance towards matters organizational—one we have designated 'metaphysical'—are not perhaps unconnected. Indeed, the metaphysical stance, we suggest, has contributed precisely to the decay described by Brooks, not simply by advocating the imperative to 'think outside' of, but by actively seeking to dissolve 'the box'—that core object of OT, formal organization—altogether.

Brooks's own challenge to the prevalence of an anti-formal organizational 'mindset' is pursued via 'exemplary' case studies of those deemed to exhibit (organizational) 'character', such as George Marshall, chief of staff of the US Army during the Second World War, and perhaps the main 'organizational architect' of the Allied victory (ibid.: 105–29) and post-war European reconstruction (the 'Marshall Plan').

Brook's discussion of Marshall's conduct as 'organizational statesmanship' parallels Barnard's analysis of 'the conduct of those...adept in executive practice' in terms of statesmanship (Barnard, 1968: xxviii, 235; O'Connor, 2012). For Barnard, as we have seen, the development of executives—those whose fate it is to try to live up to the ideal of organizational statesmanship—involves de-emphasizing 'theoretical' intellectual ability in favour of the intuition, know-how, and similar characteristics that are related to extensive and intensive training, practice, and experience. That is why—à la casuistry—he emphasized the use of maxims and examples in preparing executives for the reality they would face in their roles, as well as the inculcation—through training, practice, indoctrination, and so forth—of attitudes within organizations. According to Wolf (1974: 51), it was Barnard's practical realism and his ethical intent—the stance he adopted—that led to his significant and lasting contribution to understanding, inter alia, the importance of formality in

---

[2] This is a point made in one of the best novels focused upon the mundane routines and tasks of formal organization published in recent years, David Foster Wallace's (2012) *The Pale King*.

organization, the necessity of authority, the role of non-logical thought processes, of complex causality, and thus the need for developed capacities for judgement in organizations, and of the limits and distortions of material incentives, for example. As Wolf (1974: 52) puts it, '[T]hese were relatively startling concepts when he first presented them and many still find them difficult to accept. They are, however, concepts which describe reality . . . concepts which practitioners' once upon a time, at least, "knew to be sound"' (Wolf, 1974: 51). For Barnard, undertaking executive work and learning to exhibit 'organizational statesmanship' involves cultivating a sense of formal organization as a whole as well of the total situation relevant to it. This 'sense' is developed by 'book-learning', to an extent, but 'working in organizations' and 'working with people who are adept at handling' organizational matters is crucial (Barnard, 1942, quoted in Wolf, 1974: 52). Here, Barnard echoes, *avant la lettre*, Oakeshott's comments about acquiring habits through practice and prestigious imitation. This is how 'organizational statesmanship' is made.

Barnard's comments and approach find contemporary resonance in Jean-Philippe Robé's (2011) interrogation of the dire consequences for formal organization of the adoption and operation of the norms of agency theory:

> We need statesmen at the helm of large firms. To enable them to fulfil their role, it is necessary to loosen the leash subjecting them to the shareholders by a mistaken agency theory.   (Ibid.: 78)

The attitude and comportment towards organizational reality favoured by Robé bears a striking resemblance to that animating the 'classical stance' in OT, one which precisely combines *practical rationality and ethical seriousness*. However, for such a stance to flourish, the leash not only of 'agency theory' but of the metaphysical stance more generally needs to be broken. Only then can the sort of organizational statesmanship described and advocated by Barnard, for instance, have any chance of (re)establishing itself. As Robé (2011: 78–9) makes clear, the statesmanship he has in mind effectively involves, *à la* Barnard, cultivating a sense of formal organization as a whole, including, of course, its instituted purposes, as well of the total situation relevant to it. Cultivation of such a 'sense' is impossible in an environment where the norms and techniques flowing from the adoption of agency theory hold sway. They are equally difficult to establish and foster in domains in the grip of other managerial and organizing vernaculars similarly in thrall to the metaphysical stance.[3]

In institutions of state, civil, and military, for example, the introduction and establishment of those norms and techniques commonly referred to under the

---

[3] See, for instance, Anthony Kronman's (1993) discussion of the fate of 'the lawyer statesman' in *The Lost Lawyer: Failing Ideals of the Legal Profession*.

umbrella heading of the new public management (NPM) has been widely criticized, not least for undermining the ability of these institutions to exercise their proper roles by redefining their purpose and modus operandi (Schaefer and Schaefer, 1992; Rohr, 1998; Chapman, 2000; du Gay, 2009; Bailey, 2013; Strachan, 2013a; Goodsell, 2014). The 'leash' of the NPM and its privileging of 'responsiveness', often framed in narrow principal/agent terms, is widely regarded as having restricted the capacity of the public administration to fulfil its (constitutionally sanctioned) purpose as an institution of government, and for senior civil servants to learn and practise their core task, 'administrative statesmanship' (Uhr, 1993; Lawler, Schaefer, and Schaefer, 1998; Rohr, 1998; du Gay, 2009). As Herbert Storing (1998), Richard Chapman (2000), and John Rohr (1998), among other scholars, have pointed out, several features of formally organized civil service systems—their members' comparatively long tenure in office, their accumulated knowledge, and their relative independence from direct popular control—make them repositories of statesmanship. In urging that higher-level civil servants and the bureaucracy as a whole be understood as practising 'administrative statesmanship', these authors are not—contra Jensen and Meckling (1976), for instance—*inventing* something that didn't actually exist and then demanding that an existing entity conform to it; rather, they are specifying a role that was already being performed, but rarely acknowledged, and seeking to clarify its nature so as to encourage those undertaking it to perform it better. Storing (1998), for instance, borrowed heavily from Sir Henry Taylor's [1836] 1992) classic 'handbook' for senior civil servants, *The Statesman*, to stress the unique *political* role that the public administrative apparatus plays, in the sense of promoting the fundamental ends of the state it serves, and not in terms of being tied to the partisan programme of any one political party (which would undermine its capacity to serve other parties). Storing argued that the very qualities that distinguished the professional career public administrator from the elected politician, for instance, such as relatively long tenure in office and unparalleled professional expertise in practically 'running the country', enabled that category of organizational persona to serve a unique kind of political role, one which could complement the skills and capacities required by the professional politician, while having its own distinctive and legitimate statist raison d'être. As Taylor ([1836] 1992) indicated, the essentially political role of the senior civil servant necessitates a particular education and training so that this category of person develops the sort of character and capacity for judgement appropriate to the office—of 'administrative statesman'—that s/he effectively occupies. An education in 'administrative statesmanship' would place considerable emphasis on political history, the ethics of office, and the interpretation of constitutional convention and statute, for instance, as well as a thorough immersion in the 'classical stance' in organizational analysis and conduct

(Schaefer and Schaefer 1992; Rohr, 1998; Chapman, 2000). For the senior civil servant, dealing with the comprehensiveness of the ends of government is concerned with making decisions about what the 'public interest' or 'common good' of their country requires at particular points and in relation to specific issues, within the limits of the office they occupy, and subject to the established constitution or laws. In this sense, the office of the senior civil servant is not best considered or understood, as advocates of the NPM have had it, as a 'field of business', narrowly understood. Rather, as Wilfred Brown (1974: 71–2) indicated, from his position as a government minister:

> There is a strong case for suggesting that if, as a civil servant, you are advising on policy or legislation, you may, in deciding on what exploration of the facts to carry out, whom to consult, whether to risk putting in your minute now or to wait for further facts, and what advice to give, be taking decisions which are going to affect society more seriously than what look like more important decisions in other types of work.

As Brown (1974: 73) indicated on numerous occasions, it is pointless only to discuss organization in the abstract; rather, one must be able to discuss, in explicit terms, the work that particular sorts of organization are set up to perform, and thus the sorts of personal capacities and dispositions one needs to cultivate in those undertaking that work in order that they can perform it efficiently, in Barnard's sense of that term.[4] Upon taking up his position as a minister of state, Brown admitted that he initially approached his new position with a mindset formed and framed in a different organizational context. This led him to misconstrue the nature of the work being undertaken by civil servants in his department and thus to misunderstand the standards by which it should be judged. In a critical engagement with a well-known businessman who had publically demanded, as many did in the 1960s and 1970s and continue to do so today, that the civil service become more 'business-like', Brown (1974: 71–2) admitted that he was:

> [O]ften frustrated when I first joined the Board of Trade by the length of time it took for officials to react to some suggestion I wanted to pursue, or to give me advice for which I had asked. The subject-matter frequently seemed fairly trivial to me and I felt it ought to be possible to investigate it rapidly. Later I began to realize that any decision had to be put into its proper context. In business a decision might affect some thousands of people; in Government a decision that looked of the same order of importance on the basis of content might affect up to fifty million people... Because it is so difficult and so upsetting to the public for

---

[4] It is interesting to note in this regard that around a third or so of the chapters in March's (1965) canonic *Handbook of Organizations* focus on different sorts of formal organization instituted to pursue particular purposes—organizations such as prisons, hospitals, public bureaucracies, military organizations, and schools, among others.

Government to retrace its steps decisions must, therefore, be taken with the greatest possible care. This is the burden of officials in the Civil Service.

That burden is fundamentally a political as well as an administrative one, and handling it prudently necessitates the cultivation of 'administrative statesmanship'.

Brown's comments were echoed *avant la lettre* by the public administration scholar H. E. Dale (1943) when he sought to highlight the nature of the work undertaken by senior officials in the British civil service in contrast to that undertaken by senior executives in other areas of formally organized activity. In particular, he too indicated the limited usefulness of the 'business' analogy to those effectively engaged in 'administrative statesmanship', by applying that analogy mercilessly (and humorously) to the Westminster parliamentary system. The British civil service, Dale pointed out, works under the supreme control of a committee accountable to over six hundred elected 'shareholders', of whom up to half are likely at any given time to be less than favourably inclined to the current policies advocated by the committee. Any fairly large section of this body of six hundred is able to raise a set debate on any part of the organization's business or on any transaction they may select at almost any time. The leaders of the opposition group are at liberty to propose that the committee, or at least 'the director' responsible for a mistake, should be publically reprimanded, and if a proposal is carried, 'the director', and possibly even the whole committee, will have to resign at once. Not only this, any of 'the shareholders' is entitled at any time to ask any question s/he chooses about any matter of business, from issues of broad policy down to the level of precise detail, and to expect a full and accurate response within two to three days. Furthermore, 'the shareholders' with these rights and powers sit at the organization's headquarters for several hours per day, on five days per week, for around eight months of the year.

As Dale pointed out, an important consequence of this form of organization is that the work of the 'senior managers' is not, in practice, primarily concerned with 'business management' (in the manner commended by the NPM, for instance), as it is focused on *politics* in the most comprehensive and non-partisan sense of that word. Hence, to repeat, the role of senior civil servants in this parliamentary system approximates to and requires the practise of 'administrative statesmanship'. Given this, it is important therefore to highlight the consequences of operationalizing the norms and devices of management and organization that deny the reality or necessity of 'administrative statesmanship' in this situation and/or actively occlude its cultivation, such as those associated with the NPM. At the same time, it is salutary to foster and promote the rather different stance articulated by Chapman, Rohr, Storing, and their fellow travellers: one that both acknowledges (not least through detailed description) the specific nature of the work undertaken by senior members of governmental bureaus and also articulates ways of assisting them in understanding their role and performing it better—thus combining, in Weber's terms, 'practical rationality with ethical seriousness'.[5]

Similar concerns about the decline or occlusion of a distinctive kind of (organizational) 'statesmanship' can be found in another, very different, public institutional context: the military. Over the course of the last decade and a half, the armed forces of a number of Western states, most especially those of the United States and Great Britain, have been involved in waging a war that has been robbed of scale and definition by the imprecision of the language used to describe its goals, and an absence of organizational means to prosecute these. The designation 'global war on terror' (which morphed into 'the long war') was always more metaphysical than pragmatic, and many organizational dysfunctions flowed from this (Bailey, 2013). Both designations approached the conflicts in Iraq and Afghanistan as elements of a grand design. So grand was the design, though, that, where the global war on terror began and where it ended was never clear, and how its success was to be judged even less so. As Hew Strachan (2013b: 11–12) has argued, the 'global war on terror' was a policy that was not actionable. It aimed to erase a means of fighting— 'terrorism'—not to achieve a practical, political goal. It lacked a clear geographical focus, was uncertain about the space in which it was set, or, rather, 'it was clear, but the notion that it embraced the whole world was not particularly helpful'. It created a field of operations too extensive and vaguely defined, such that even the scale and reach of the world's only superpower 'could not be sensibly applied within such a framework' (Strachan, 2013b: 12). Tellingly, neither the 'global war on terror' nor 'the long war' (how long is long?) had clearly and precisely defined enemies. Wars are framed by the hostility which underpins them: the participants need to know who the enemy is, not least so that they can practically engage with and defeat them, and indeed know they are so doing: 'The enemy in the "global war on terror" ranged from evil individuals, notably Osama bin Laden and Saddam Hussein, to entire ethnic and religious groups' (Strachan, 2013b: 12). Overall, specific threats were made bigger and less manageable by the use of a (metaphysical) vocabulary—the 'global war on terror'—that was imprecise. And, as with our discussion of the metaphysics of 'change' in organization studies (Chapter 4), it is specificity that begets the (appropriate) calibration of means to ends. Or, as Strachan (2013b: 45) puts it in the military context, 'awesome military power requires concepts for the application of force that are robust because

---

[5] As Michel Debré, the founder of the École Nationale d'Administration in France put it, that prestigious institution was designed first and foremost to instil in its students *le sens de l'Etat* ('a sense of the state').

they are precise'. One of the most important of these in the military lexicon is the concept of 'strategy', what Clauzewitz (1975) considered the 'art of the commander' and a branch of statesmanship.

As Strachan (2013a) indicates, while Bush and Blair continually talked of having strategies for the prosecution of the global war on terror, and, indeed, that the war was itself part of a grander strategy—the equally metaphysical 'forward strategy of freedom', as Bush coined it—their use of the term 'strategy' was fundamentally meaningless. In this, they were in good company. In context after context, from sociology to OT, from cookery to fishing, strategy has been appropriated to explain just about anything, being something that 'individual actors' and 'social actors', such as organizations, have or deploy, or something they do (the dire term 'strategizing' indicating that the 'doing' of 'strategy' is a process of becoming and, of course, a multiplicity). No wonder then that, as Strachan argues, the term strategy confronted an existential crisis—the universality of the term robbing it of any specificity and leaving it only with banalities (2013b: 27). The fact that so many parties, to debates about the global war on terror, for instance, liberally used the term strategy would suggest that they knew what strategy was. However, nothing was farther from the truth:

> Clausewitz defined strategy as the use of the battle for the purposes of the war. For him ... strategy was the art of the commander. Today, strategy is too often employed simply as a synonym for policy. Bush and Blair said they had strategies when they did not. They had ... idealized visions of a post-war order, but these ... were not linked to regional realities or military capabilities. The circumstances prevailing in Iraq were different from those in Afghanistan, and they in turn were unlike those on the borders of Israel or in Indonesia. What gave each of these conflicts homogeneity was less their underlying natures than the 'war on terror' itself, a phrase which created the very unity of effects which waging that war in the first place had sought to deny.   (Strachan, 2013b: 11)

Being a metaphysical designation, the global war on terror was 'astrategic' and this had serious consequences for those charged with prosecuting it. The absence of strategy, in effect, robbed senior commanders of the possibility of doing the job they were uniquely formed to undertake, and thus, in so doing, exercising their own particular brand of organizational statesmanship.

Strategy is, of course, about war and its conduct. It is a profoundly pragmatic endeavour, concerning the application of means to ends. It is 'an attempt to make concrete a set of objectives through the application of military force to a particular case' (Strachan, 2013b: 12). It is thus the glue that binds policy to operations and has to rest, fundamentally, on an understanding of war and war's nature, because the latter will affect policy and operations in turn. And war is the vocation of the military. Prosecuting a global war on terror allowed no place for strategy as a viable concept and tool for the shaping and understanding of war, even though the word kept being bandied about by almost everyone involved (much as 'organization' is a term used by practitioners of the metaphysical stance in OT, even though they have robbed it of any specific meaning). In the war of terror, means could not be related to aims (in a military sense) or to objectives (in a political sense). Strategy had no place. It was abandoned. That a key concept and object of military *lebensführung* could be dispensed with in an ostensible 'war' perhaps tells us something about how events can proceed when metaphysical speculation enters this particular domain of organized existence.

If strategy lost its coherence as a key concept and object of military organization and practice at the hands of the 'war on terror', it was also left institutionally homeless as well. At the beginning of the twenty-first century, strategy predominantly had a formal organizational home in the military in both Britain and the USA. This is hardly surprising given that strategy, as the art of the commander statesman, is the province of generalship. As we indicated in Chapter 6, however, the Bush and Blair administrations were both suspicious of formal organization and established (bureaucratic) mechanisms of government, and shared a preference for informal networks ('sofa-style government') that sidestepped established procedures. This led them to forfeit formal organizational instruments for the development of strategy. In the planning of both the wars undertaken by the USA in Afghanistan and Iraq, for example, professional military opinion seemed at best marginal and at worst derided by the Bush administration. Both the joint chiefs of staff and the National Security Council were sidelined. Meanwhile, in London, a small team within No. 10 Downing Street gave 'broad policy direction but all too often based, it seemed, on inadequate study of the consequences' (Sir Hilary Synnott, quoted in Strachan, 2013b: 80. See also Chapter 6, this volume). This sidelining of strategy, of formal organizational fora for its development, and of those for whom its formulation is a profession—military commanders—was never destined to lead to a virtuous relationship of means, ways, and ends— and thus to a successful political or military outcome. Waging war has its own formal organizational requirements, not least those which can both enable and encourage politicians to 'get real' and listen to military professionals concerning what can be done in practice, as opposed to what politicians might like to happen in theory, and thus those where military professionals themselves feel able to speak realistically about military matters and about the nature of war. The global war on terror proceeded without such formal organizational means in place to enable this to happen, or such formal organizational means as did exist were sidelined. In Britain, in true NPM fashion, the main department of state concerned with military matters and thus ostensibly the 'strategic headquarters', the Ministry of Defence, elevated financial management over the direction of strategy and military thought (Strachan, 2013b: 24, 74–5). The result has been a lack of practical rationality and ethical seriousness in the organization of the state for war. As Strachan (2013b: 43, 25) puts it, '[T]he state...has an interest in re-appropriating the control and direction of war. That is the purpose of strategy. Strategy is designed to make war useable by the state, so that it can, if need be, use force to fulfill its political objectives....The first step in this process is a clear articulation of what strategy is; the second is its application in the machinery of state.' Military professionals can only live up to the obligations of their office, and exercise the instructions of the commander statesman, if the formal organizational means exist for them to do so.[6]

Hennis proposed to place Max Weber in the lineage of those thinkers, starting with Thucydides, who sought practical knowledge of the world as it 'is', and engaged in a quest for the cultivation of judgement and a prudential wisdom that comes from an understanding of contextual specificity and the contingency of circumstance. The crucial turns in Weber's language all point in this direction, Hennis argues—the call for a 'science of reality' or 'the actual', a *wirklichkeitswissenschaft* (see Scaff, 2014: 70). This is the language of knowledge of human affairs as a 'practical science', and not of abstract theorizing and metaphysical speculation or longing. This is also the language of the classical stance in OT, as we have tried to show, and it has much to commend it.

---

[6] In 2011, the professional head of Britain's Royal Navy, Admiral Sir Mark Stanhope, stated that, in his opinion, the British fleet 'could not continue the Libya campaign without harming other naval operations'. In so doing, he was living up to the obligations of the office of state he occupied. His reward for this was to be summoned to No. 10 Downing Street at the behest of the prime minister, and the next day a statement was issued by the government stating that Admiral Stanhope 'agreed that we can sustain the mission as long as we need to'.

References

Adams, J. E. and Ginsberg, R. n.d. *Education Reform: Overview, Reports of Historical Significance* <http://education.stateuniversity.com/pages/1944/Education-Reform.html> (accessed 23 January 2016).

Adler, P. ed. 2009. *The Oxford Handbook of Sociology and Organization Studies: Classical Foundations.* Oxford: Oxford University Press.

Alvesson, M. 1990. Organization: from substance to image? *Organisation Studies* 11(3): 373–94.

Alvesson, M. 2013. *The Triumph of Emptiness.* London: SAGE.

Alvesson, M. and Sandberg, J. 2013. Has management studies lost its way? Ideas for more imaginative and innovative research. *Journal of Management Studies* 50: 128–52.

Alvesson, M. and Thompson, P. 2005. Post-bureaucracy? In S. Ackroyd, R. Batt, P. Thompson, and P. Tolbert, eds., *A Handbook of Work and Organization,* pp. 485–507. Oxford: Oxford University Press.

Alvesson, M. and Willmott, H. 1992. *Critical Management Studies.* London: SAGE.

Alvesson, M. and Wilmott, H. 2002. Identity regulation as organizational control: producing the appropriate individual. *Journal of Management Studies* 39(5): 619–44.

Andrews, K. R. 1968. Introduction. In C. Barnard, *The Functions of the Executive,* 30th anniversary edn, pp. vii–xxiii. Cambridge, MA: Harvard University Press.

Argyris, C. 1992. *On Organizational Learning.* Oxford: Blackwell.

Argyris, C. and Schön, D. A. 1978. *Organizational Learning: A Theory of Action Perspective.* Reading, MA: Addison-Wesley.

Argyris, C, and Schön, D. A. 1996. *Organizational Learning II: Theory, Method, and Practice.* Reading, MA: Addison-Wesley.

Armenakis, A. A., Harris, S. G., and Mossholder, K. W. 1993. Creating readiness for organizational change. *Human Relations* 46(6): 681–703.

Bailey, J. 2013. The political context: why we went to war and the mismatch of ends, ways, and means. In J. Bailey, R. Iron, and H. Strachan, eds., *British Generals in Blair's Wars,* pp. 5–25. Farnham: Ashgate.

Barnard, C. I. [1938] 1968. *The Functions of the Executive.* Cambridge, MA: Harvard University Press.

Barrett, F. J. 1998. Coda: creativity and improvisation in jazz and organizations: implications for organizational learning. *Organization Science* 9(5): 605–22.

Bartlett, C. and Ghoshal, S. 2002. *Managing across Borders.* Boston, MA: Harvard Business School Press.

Bartunek, J. 1988. The dynamics of personal and organizational reframing. In R. E. Quinn and K. S. Cameron, eds., *Paradox and Transformation: Toward a Theory of Change in Organization and Management*, pp. 137–62. Cambridge, MA: Ballinger.

Beck, U. 2005. *Individualization*. London: SAGE.

Beck, U. and Beck-Gernsheim, E. 2002. *Individualization: Institutionalized Individualism and Its Social and Political Consequences*. London: SAGE.

Becker, H. 2014. *What About Mozart? What About Murder? Reasoning from Cases*. Chicago: University of Chicago Press.

Beckhard, R. D. 1969. *Organization Development: Strategies and Models*. Reading, MA: Addison-Wesley.

Beer, M. and Nohria, N. eds. 2000. *Breaking the Code of Change*. Harvard, MA: Harvard Business School Press.

Bejerot, E. and Hasselbladh, H. 2013. Forms of intervention in public sector organizations: generic traits in public sector reforms. *Organization Studies* 34(9): 1357–80.

Bennis, W. G. 1969. *Organization Development: Its Nature, Origins and Prospects*. Reading, MA: Addison-Wesley.

Bennis, W.G. 1989. *On Becoming a Leader*. New York: Addison-Wesley.

Berger, P. L. and Luckmann, T. 1966. *The Social Construction of Reality: A Treatise in the Sociology of Knowledge*. Garden City, NY: Anchor Books.

Betts, R. K. 2007. *Enemies of Intelligence*. New York: Columbia University Press.

Bion, W. R. [1961] 2006. *Experiences in Groups*. Hove: Routledge.

Black's Law Dictionary. 1968. St. Paul, MN: West Group.

Black's Law Dictionary. 1999. 7th edn. St. Paul, MN: West Group.

Blau, P. M. 1968. Organizations. In D. L. Sills, ed., *International Encyclopedia of the Social Sciences*, vol. 11. New York: The Macmillan Company.

Blau, P. M. and Scott, R. W. 1963, *Formal Organizations: A Comparative Approach*. London: Routledge & Kegan Paul.

Boltanski, L. and Chiapello, E. 2007. *The New Spirit of Capitalism*. London: Verso.

Bourke, R. 2009. Theory and practice: the revolution in political judgement. In R. Bourke and R. Geuss, eds., *Political Judgement*, pp. 73–109. Cambridge: Cambridge University Press.

Braverman, H. 1974. *Labor and Monopoly*. New York: Monthly Review Press.

Brighouse, T. and Tomlinson, J. R. G. 1991. *Successful Schools*. London: Institute for Public Policy Research.

Brooks, D. 2015. *The Road to Character*. London: Allen Lane.

Brooks, R. 2014. A call to rally: 'The Fourth Revolution', by John Micklethwait and Adrian Wooldridge. *New York Times*, 26 June.

Brown, S. L. and Eisenhardt, K. M. 1997. The art of continuous change: linking complexity theory and time-paced evolution in relentlessly shifting organizations. *Administrative Science Quarterly* 42(1): 1–34.

Brown, W. 1963. A critique of some current ideas about organization. *California Management Review* 6(1): 3–12.

Brown, W. 1965a. Informal organization? In W. Brown and E. Jaques, *Glacier Project Papers*, pp. 144–62. London: Heinemann Educational Books.

Brown, W. 1965b. *Exploration in Management*. Harmondsworth: Penguin Books.

Brown, W. 1971. *Organization*. Heinemann: London.

Brown, W. 1974. *Organization*. Harmondsworth: Penguin.

Brown, W. 1976. A critique of some current ideas about organisation. In J. Gray, ed., *The Glacier Project: Concepts and Critiques*, pp. 287–301. London: Heinemann.

Brown, W. 1977. *The Grammar of Organization* 'Concepts Book', The Papers of Lord Brown, Churchill Archive Centre, University of Cambridge, BRWN 4/1/2.

Brown, W. 1979. February–September, The Papers of Lord Brown, Churchill Archive Centre, University of Cambridge, BRWN 4/3/3/3–4.

Brown, W. and Jaques, E. 1965. *Glacier Project Papers*. London: Heinemann.

Brunsson, N. 1982. The irrationality of action and action rationality: decisions, ideologies and organizational actions. *Journal of Management Studies* 19(1): 29–44.

Bryson, N. 1986. *Vision and Painting: The Logic of the Gaze*. London: Yale University Press.

Burawoy, M. 1979. *Manufacturing Consent*. Chicago: University of Chicago Press.

Burke, W. W. 1982. *Organization Development: Principles and Practice*. Boston, MA: Little, Brown & Co.

Burns, T. and Stalker, G. M. [1961] 1966. *The Management of Innovation*. London: Tavistock Publications.

Burrell, G. 1997. *Pandemonium*. London: SAGE.

Burrell, G. and Morgan, G. 1979. *Sociological Paradigms and Organizational Analysis: Elements of the Sociology of Corporate Life*. London: Heinemann.

Calás, M. B. and Smircich, L. 2006. From the 'woman's point of view' ten years later: towards a feminist organization studies. In S. Clegg, W. Hardy, C, Nord, and W. T. Lawrence, eds., *Handbook of Organization Studies*, 2nd edn, pp. 284–346. London: SAGE.

Callon, M. ed. 1998. *The Laws of the Markets*. London: Blackwell.

Cao, Q., Gedajlovic, E., and Zhang, H. 2009. Unpacking organizational ambidexterity: dimensions, contingencies, and synergistic effects. *Organization Science* 20(4): 781–96.

Caplan, J. 1988. *Government without Administration: State and Civil Service in Weimar and Nazi Germany*. Oxford: Clarendon Press.

Casile, M. and Davis-Blake, A. 2002. When accreditation standards change: factors affecting differential responsiveness of public and private organizations. *Academy of Management Journal* 45(1): 180–95.

Castells, M. 1996. *The Rise of the Network Society*. Oxford: Blackwell.

Caulkin, S. 2008. When it came to the crunch, MBAs didn't help. *The Observer*, 26 October.

Champy, J. 1995. *Reengineering Management: The Mandate for New Leadership*. London: HarperCollins.

Chapman, R. A. 1992. The End of the Civil Service? *Teaching Public Administration*, xii, 2, 1–5.

Chapman, R. A. 2000. Ethics in public service for the new millennium. In R. A Chapman, ed., *Ethics in Public Service for the New Millennium*, pp. 217–31. Aldershot: Ashgate.

Chapman, R. A. 2006. The Hutton report: judgment, leadership and open government. In R. A. Chapman and M. Hunt, eds., *Open Government in a Theoretical and Practical Context*, pp. 55–68. Aldershot: Ashgate.

Chia, R. 1999. A 'rhizomic' model of organizational change and transformation: perspectives from a metaphysics of change. *British Journal of Management* 10: 209–27.

Child, J. 1969. *British Management Thought*. London: Allen & Unwin.

References

Child, J. 2013. Mary Parker Follett. In M. Witzel and M. Warner, eds., *The Oxford Handbook of Management Theorists*, pp. 74–93. Oxford: Oxford University Press.

Christensen, C. 2011. *The Innovator's Dilemma*. London: Harper Business.

Christensen, T., Lægreid, P., Roness, P. G., and Røvik, K. A. 2007. *Organization Theory and the Public Sector: Instrument, Culture and Myth*. Abingdon: Routledge.

Clarke, J. and Newman, J. 1997. *The Managerial State*. London: SAGE.

Clausewitz, C. von. 1975. *On War*, ed. and tr. M. Howard and P. Paret. New York: Princeton University Press.

Clegg, S., Courpasson, D., and Phillips, N. 2006. *Power and Organizations*. London: SAGE.

Clegg, S., Hardy, C., and Nord, W. R. eds. 1996. *Handbook of Organization Studies*. London: SAGE.

Cohen, M. D., March, J. G., and Olsen, J. P. 1972. A garbage can model of organizational choice. *Administrative Science Quarterly* 17(1): 1–25.

Collini, S. 2009. Impact on humanities: researchers must take a stand now or be judged and rewarded as salesmen. *Times Literary Supplement*, 13 November.

Collini, S. 2012. *What are Universities For?* London: Penguin.

Collins, H. M. 1992. *Changing Order: Replication and Induction in Scientific Practice*. Chicago: University of Chicago Press.

Condren, C. 2002. Between social constraint and the public sphere: methodological problems in reading early-modern political satire. *Contemporary Political Theory* 1(1): 79–101.

Condren, C. 2006. *Argument and Authority in Early Modern England: The Presupposition of Oaths and Offices*. Cambridge: Cambridge University Press.

Contu, A., Grey, C., and Örtenbald, A. 2003. Against learning. *Human Relations* 56(8): 931–52.

Cousins, M. 1980. Men's Rea: a note on sexual difference, criminology, and the law. In P. Carlen and M. Collison, eds., *Radical Issues in Criminology*, pp. 109–22. Oxford: Martin Robertson.

Crozier, M. 1964. *The Bureaucratic Phenomenon*. Chicago: University of Chicago Press.

Crozier, M. and Friedberg, E. 1980. *Actors and Systems: The Politics of Collective Action*. Chicago: University of Chicago Press.

Cyert, R. and March, J. G. 1963. *Behavioral Theory of the Firm*. Englewood Cliffs, NJ: Prentice-Hall.

Czarniawska, B. 2013. Organizations as obstacles to organizing. In D. Robichaud and F. Corren, eds., *Organizations and Organizing: Materiality, Agency and Discourse*, pp. 3–22. New York: Routledge.

Dale, E. 1969. *Management Theory and Practice*. New York: McGraw-Hill.

Dale, H. E. 1943. The personnel and problems of the higher civil service: Sidney Ball lecture, February 26, 1943. Barnett House Papers 26, Oxford University Press.

Dalin, P. 1998. *School Development: Theories and Strategies*. London: Continuum Books.

Dartington, T. 1998. From altruism to action: primary task and the not-for-profit organization. *Human Relations* 51(12): 1477–93.

Davidson, A. 1995. Introduction: Pierre Hadot and the spiritual phenomenon of ancient philosophy. In P. Hadot, *Philosophy as a Way of Life*, pp. 1–45. Oxford: Blackwell.

Davidson, A. 2009. Preface: Éloge: Pierre Hadot. In P. Hadot, *The Present Alone is Our Happiness*, pp. ix–xiv. Stanford, CA: Stanford University Press.

Davis, G. F. 2010. Do theories of organizations progress? *Organizational Research Methods* 13: 690–709.

Davis, G. F. 2011. The twilight of the Berle and Means corporation. *Seattle University Law Review* 34(4): 1121–38.

Davis, G. F. 2015. Celebrating organization theory: the after-party. *Journal of Management Studies* 52(2): 309–19.

Denning, S. 2013. The origin of 'the world's dumbest idea': Milton Friedman. *Forbes Magazine*, 26 June.

Denvir, D. 2011. Cathie Black and the privatisation of education. *The Guardian*, 7 April.

Dewey, J. 1938. *Logic – The Theory of Inquiry*. New York: Henry Holt Company Inc.

Dimaggio, P. and Powell, W. 1983. The iron cage revisited: institutional isomorphism and collective rationality in organizational fields. *American Sociological Review* 48(2): 147–60.

Dobbin, F. and Jung, J. 2010. The misapplication of Mr. Michael Jensen: how agency theory brought down the economy and why it might again. *Research in the Sociology of Organizations* 30(B): 29–64. Emerald Group Publishing Limited.

Du Gay, P. 2000. *In Praise of Bureaucracy*. London: SAGE.

Du Gay, P. 2005. Bureaucracy and liberty: state, authority and freedom. In P. Du Gay., ed., *The Values of Bureaucracy*, pp. 41–62. Oxford: Oxford University Press.

Du Gay, P. 2006. Machinery of government and standards in public service: teaching new dogs old tricks. *Economy and Society* 35(1): 148–67.

Du Gay, P. 2007. *Organizing Identity: Persons and Organizations 'After Theory'*. London: SAGE.

Du Gay, P. 2008. Max Weber and the moral economy of office. *Journal of Cultural Economy* 1(2): 129–44.

Du Gay, P. 2009. Max Weber and the ethics of office. In P. Adler, ed., *Oxford Handbook of Sociology and Organizational Studies: Classical Foundations*, pp. 146–73. Oxford: Oxford University Press.

Du Gay, P. 2015. Organization (theory) as a way of life. *Journal of Cultural Economy* 8(4): 399–417.

Du Gay, P. and Vikkelsø, S. 2012. Reflections: on the lost specification of 'change'. *Journal of Change Management*, 12(2), 121–43.

Du Gay, P. and Vikkelsø, S. 2013. Exploitation, exploration and exaltation: notes on a metaphysical (re)turn to 'one best way of organizing'. *Research in the Sociology of Organizations* 37: 249–79.

Du Gay, P. and Vikkelsø, S. 2014. What makes organization? Organizational theory as a 'practical science'. In P. S. Adler, P. Du Gay, G. Morgan, and M. Reed eds., *Oxford Handbook of Sociology, Social Theory and Organization Studies: Contemporary Currents*, pp. 736–58. Oxford: Oxford University Press.

Duncan, P. 1968. Book review: Miller, E. J. and Rice, A. K. Systems of Organization. *Sociological Review* 16: 261–2.

Dyer, J. H. and Singh, H. 1998. The relational view: cooperative strategy and sources of interorganizational competitive advantage. *Academy of Management Review* 23(40): 660–79.

Efficiency Unit. 1988. *Improving Management in Government: The Next Steps*. London: HMSO.

Eisenhardt, K. M. and Westcott, R. J. 1988. Paradoxical demands and the creation of excellence: the case of just-in-time manufacturing. In R. E. Quinn and K. S. Cameron, eds., *Paradox and Transformation: Toward a Theory of Change in Organization and Management*, pp. 169–94. Cambridge, MA: Ballinger.

Elmore, R. D. 2000. *Building a New Structure for School Leadership*. Washington, DC: Albert Shanker Institute.

Fama, E. 1980. Agency problems and the theory of the firm. *Journal of Political Economy* 88(2): 288–307.

Fama, E. and Jensen, M. 1983. Separation of ownership and control. *Journal of Law and Economics* 26(2): 301–25.

Fayol, H. [1949] 1955. *General and Industrial Management*. London: Sir Isaac Pitman & Sons Ltd.

Fayol, K. [1937] 1977. The administrative theory in the state. In L. Gulick and L. Urwick, eds., *Papers on the Science of Administration*, pp. 99–114. Fairfield: Augustus M. Kelley Publishers.

Feldman, E. and Montgomery, C. 2015. Are incentives without expertise sufficient? Evidence from Fortune 500 firms. *Strategic Management Journal* 36(1): 113–22.

Financial Times. 2009. The future of capitalism – a *Financial Times* series of articles, commentaries and opinion pieces. For an overview of the series, see the editorial introduction: 'The Future of Capitalism', 23 March 2009.

Fineman, S. 2008. *The Emotional Organization: Passions and Power*. Oxford: Blackwell.

Fish, S. 1994. *There's No Such Thing as Free Speech and It's a Good Thing Too*. Oxford: Oxford University Press.

Fish, S. 1995. *Professional Correctness*. Oxford: Oxford University Press.

Fleming, P. 2005. Workers' playtime: boundaries and cynicism in a 'culture of fun' program. *Journal of Applied Behavioural Science* 41(3): 285–303.

Fleming, P. and Sturdy, A. 2009. Just be yourself: towards neo-normative control in organizations. *Employee Relations* 31(6): 569–83.

Follett, M. P. 1940 [2013]. *Dynamic Administration: The Collected Papers of Mary Parker Follett*. Mansfield Centre, CT: Martino Publishing.

Foster Wallace, D. 2012. *The Pale King*. Harmondsworth: Penguin.

Fox, A. 1971. *A Sociology of Work in Industry*. Basingstoke: Collier-Macmillan.

Frankfurt, H. 2005. *On Bullshit*. Princeton, NJ: Princeton University Press.

Freeman, R. E. 2010. *Strategic Management: A Stakeholder Approach*. Cambridge: Cambridge University Press.

Friedman, M. 1970. The social responsibility of business is to increase its profits. *New York Times Magazine*, 13 September.

Galbraith, J. R. 1977. *Organization Design*. Reading, MA: Addison-Wesley.

Ganesh, S. R. 1978. Organizational consultants: a comparison of styles. *Human Relations* 31(1): 1–28.

Garud, R., Jain, S., and Kumaraswamy, A. 2002. Institutional entrepreneurship in the sponsorship of common technological standards: the case of Sun Microsystems and Java. *Academy of Management Journal* 45(1): 196–214.

Gennep, A. van. 1967. *The Semi-Scholars*. London: Routledge & Kegan Paul.

Ghoshal, S. 2005. Bad management theories are destroying good management practices. *Academy of Management Learning and Education* 4(1): 75–91.

Goodsell, C. T. 2005. The bureau as a unit of governance. In P. Du Gay, ed., *The Values of Bureaucracy*, pp. 17–40. Oxford: Oxford University Press.

Goodsell, C. T. 2014. *The New Case for Bureaucracy*. Washington, DC: CQ Press.

Gouldner, A. W. 1957. Cosmopolitans and locals: towards an analysis of latent social roles: I. *Administrative Science Quarterly* 2(3): 281–306.

Granovetter, M. 1985. Economic action and social structure: the problem of embeddedness. *American Journal of Sociology* 91: 481–510.

Grant, R. M. 1991. The resource-based theory of competitive advantage: implications for strategy formulation. *California Management Review* 33(3): 114–35.

Gray, J. ed. 1976. *The Glacier Project: Concepts and Critiques*. London: Heinemann.

Greenberg, J. and Baron, R. A. 2008. *Behavior in Organisations: Understanding and Managing the Human Side of Work*. Upper Saddle River, NJ: Prentice Hall.

Greenwood, R. and Miller, D. 2010. Tackling design anew: getting back to the heart of organizational theory, *Academy of Management Perspectives* 24(4): 78–88.

Greenwood, R., Oliver, C., Suddaby, R., and Sahlin-Andersson, K. 2013. *The SAGE Handbook of Organizational Institutionalism*. London: SAGE.

Grieves, J. 2000. Introduction: the origins of organizational development. *Journal of Management Development* 19(5): 345–447.

Gulick, L. [1937] 1977. Notes on the theory of organization. In L. Gulick and L. Urwick, eds., *Papers on the Science of Administration*, pp. 1–45. Fairfield, NJ: Augustus M. Kelley Publishers.

Hacking, I. 1983. *Representing and Intervening: Introductory Topics in the Philosophy of Natural Science*. Cambridge: Cambridge University Press.

Hadot, P. 1995. *Philosophy as a Way of Life: Spiritual Exercise from Socrates to Foucault*. Oxford: Blackwell.

Hadot, P. 2002. *What is Ancient Philosophy?* Cambridge, MA: The Belknap Press of Harvard University Press.

Hadot, P. 2009. *The Present Alone is Our Happiness*. Stanford, CA: Stanford University Press.

Hadot, P. 2011. *The Present Alone is Our Happiness: Conversations with Jeannie Carlier and Arnold I. Davidson*, tr. M. Djaballah and M. Chase. Stanford, CA: Stanford University Press.

Hambrick, D. C. 2005. Venturing outside the monastery. *Academy of Management Journal* 48(6): 961–2.

Hamel, G. 2009. Management 2.0, *Leadership Excellence* 26(11): 5–15.

Hammer, M. and Champy, J. 1993. *Reengineering the Corporation: A Manifesto for Business Revolution*. London: Nicholas Brealey.

Handy, C. B. 1976. *Understanding Organizations*. Harmondsworth: Penguin Books.

Hannan, M. T. and Freeman, J. 1993. *Organizational Ecology*. Cambridge, MA: Harvard University Press.

Hanushek, E. A. 2010. Total student load: maybe worth a longer book, but hardly an evolution. Book review, *Education Next* 10(2): 84–5.

References

Hassard, J., Holliday, R., and Willmott, H. 2000. *Body and Organization*. London: SAGE.

Heckscher, C. C. and Donnellon, A. 1994. *The Post-Bureaucratic Organization: New Perspectives on Organizational Change*. Thousand Oaks, CA: SAGE.

Helin, J., Hernes, T., Hjorth, D., and Holt, R. eds. 2014. *The Oxford Handbook of Process Philosophy and Organization Studies*. Oxford: Oxford University Press.

Henderson, J. C. and Venkatraman, N. 1993. Strategic alignment: leveraging information technology for transforming organizations. *IBM Systems Journal* 32(1): 4–16.

Hennessy, P. 2004. The lightning flash on the road to Baghdad: issues of evidence. In W. G. Runciman ed., *Hutton and Butler: Lifting the Lid on the Workings of Power*, pp. 61–81. Oxford: Oxford University Press.

Hennis, W. 1988. *Max Weber: Essays in Reconstruction*. London: Allen & Unwin.

Hennis, W. 2000. *Max Weber's Science of Man*, tr. K. Tribe. Newbury: Threshold Press.

Hennis, W. 2009. *Politics as a Practical Science*. Basingstoke: Palgrave Macmillan.

Hernes, T. 2008. *Understanding Organization as Process: Theory for a Tangled World*. London: Routledge.

Hirschhorn, L. 1999. The primary risk. *Human Relations* 52(1): 5–23.

Hirschman, A. 1977. *The Passions and the Interests*. Princeton, NJ: Princeton University Press.

Hobbes, T. 1969. *The Elements of Law, Natural and Political*, 2nd edn, ed. F. Tonnies, intro. M. M. Goldsmith. London: London University Press.

Hobbes, T. 1996. *Leviathan*. Cambridge: Cambridge University Press.

Hoggett, P. 2006. Conflict, ambivalence, and the contested purpose of public organizations. *Human Relations* 59(2): 175–94.

Hoopes, J. 2003. *False Prophets: The Gurus who Created Modern Management and Why their Ideas are Bad for Business*. New York: Basic Books.

Hunt, R. 1976. On the work itself: observations concerning relations between tasks and organizational processes. In E. Miller, ed., *Task and Organization*, pp. 99–119. London: John Wiley & Sons.

Hunter, I. 2006. The history of theory. *Critical Inquiry* 3: 78–112.

Hunter, I. 2007. The time of theory. *Postcolonial Studies* 10(1): 5–22.

Hunter, I. 2008. The desire for deconstruction: Derrida's metaphysics of law. *Communication, Politics and Culture* 41: 6–29.

Hunter, I. 2009a. Postmodernist histories. *Intellectual History Review* 19(2): 265–79.

Hunter, I. 2009b. Theory time: on the history of poststructuralism, keynote address, 40th Annual Symposium of the Australian Academy of Humanities, November.

Hutton, J. B. E. 2004. *Return to an Address of the Honourable the House of Commons dated 28th January 2004 for the Report of the Inquiry into the Circumstances Surrounding the Death of Dr. David Kelly*, C.M.G. HC 247. London: HMSO.

Iedema, R. 2003. *Discourses of Post-Bureaucratic Organization*. Philadelphia, PA: John Benjamins Publishing Company.

Illouz, E. 2007. *Cold Intimacies: The Making of Emotional Capitalism*. Cambridge: Polity Press.

Jaques, E. 1951. *The Changing Culture of a Factory*. London: Tavistock.

Jaques, E. 1953. On the dynamics of social structure. *Human Relations* 6: 3–24.

Jaques, E. 1956. *The Measurement of Responsibility*. London: Tavistock.

Jaques, E. 1961. *Equitable Payment: A General Theory of Work, Differential Payment, and Individual Progress*. London: Heinemann.

Jaques, E. 1965a. Death and the midlife crisis. *International Journal of Psychoanalysis* 46(4): 502–14.

Jaques, E. 1965b. *Glacier Project Papers*. London: Heinemann Educational.

Jaques, E. 1967. *Equitable Payment*. Harmondsworth: Penguin.

Jaques, E. 1976. *A General Theory of Bureaucracy*. London: Heinemann.

Jaques, E. 1990. In praise of hierarchy. *Harvard Business Review*, January–February: 127–33.

Jensen, M. C. and Meckling, W. H. 1976. Theory of the firm: managerial behavior, agency costs and ownership structure. *Journal of Financial Economics* 3(4): 305–60.

Jonsen, A. and Toulmin, S. 1988. *The Abuse of Casuistry*. Los Angeles, CA: University of California Press.

Juelskjær, M., Knudsen, H., Pors, J. G., and Staunæs, D. 2011. *Ledelse af uddannelse: At lede det potentielle*. Frederiksberg: Samfundslitteratur.

Kanter, R. M. 1983. *Change Masters: Corporate Entrepreneurs at Work*. London: Allen & Unwin.

Kanter, R. M. 1989. *When Giants Learn to Dance*. New York: Simon & Schuster.

Kanter, R. M. 1995. *World Class: Thriving Locally in the Global Economy*. New York: Simon & Schuster.

Kanter, R. M., Stein, B. A., and Jick, T. D. 1992. *The Challenge of Organizational Change: How Companies Experience It and Leaders Guide It*. New York: The Free Press.

Kaufman, H. 1977. *Red Tape: Its Origins, Uses and Abuses*. Washington, DC: The Brookings Institution.

Kaufman, H. 1995. *The Limits of Organizational Change*. Piscataway, NJ: Transaction Publishers.

Kaufman, H. 2007. Administrative management: does its strong executive thesis still merit our attention? *Public Administration Review* 67(6): 1041–8.

Keller, S. and Price, C. 2011. *Beyond Performance: How Great Organizations Build Ultimate Competitive Advantage*. London: John Wiley.

Kelly, J. 1968. *Is Scientific Management Possible? Critical Examination of Glacier's Theory of Organization*. London: Faber & Faber.

Khurana, R. 2010. *From Higher Aims to Hired Hands: The Social Transformation of American Business Schools and the Unfulfilled Promise of Management as a Profession*. Princeton, NJ, and Oxford: Princeton University Press.

King, B. G., Clemens, E. S., and Konty, M. F. 2011. Identity realization and organizational forms: differentiation and consolidation of identities among Arizona's charter schools. *Organization Science* 22: 554–72.

King, B. G., Felin, T., and Whetten, D. 2010. Finding the organization in organizational theory: a meta-theory of the organization as a social actor. *Organization Science* 21(1): 290–305.

Kleiner, A. 2001. Elliott Jaques levels with you. *Strategy & Business* 1st Quarter: 1–9.

Kofman, F. and Senge, P. 1993. Communities of commitment: the heart of learning organizations. *Organizational Dynamics* 22: 5–23.

Kotter, J. P. 1996. *Leading Change*. Boston, MA: Harvard Business Press.

Kraatz, M. S. 2009. Leadership as institutional work: a bridge to the other side. In T. B. Lawrence, R. Suddaby, and B. Leca, eds., *Institutional Work: Actors and Agency in Institutional Studies of Organizations*, pp. 59–91. New York: Cambridge University Press.

Kraatz, M., Ventresca, M., and Deng, L. 2010. Precarious values and mundane innovations: the diffusion of enrollment management in U.S. higher education 1970–2005. *Academy of Management Journal* 53(6): 1521–45.

Krackhardt, D. 1992. The strength of strong ties: the importance of philos in organizations. In N. Nohria and R. Eccles, eds., *Networks and Organizations: Structure, Form, and Action*, pp. 216–39. Boston, MA: Harvard Business School Press.

Kronman, A. 1993. *The Lost Lawyer*. Cambridge, MA: Harvard University Press.

Laclau, E. 1990. *New Reflections on the Revolution of Our Time*. London: Verso.

Larmore, C. 1987. *Patterns of Moral Complexity*. Cambridge: Cambridge University Press.

Latour, B. 2005. *Re-assembling the Social*. Oxford: Oxford University Press.

Latour, B. 2011. 'What's the story?' Organizing as a mode of existence. In J. H. Passoth, B. Peuker, and M. Schillmeier, eds., *Agency without Actors? New Approaches to Collective Action*, pp. 163–77. London: Routledge.

Lawler, P. A., Schaefer, R. M., and Schaefer, D. L. 1998. *Active Duty: Public Administration as Democratic Statesmanship*. Lanham, MD: Rowman & Littlefield.

Lawrence, P. R. and Lorsch, J. W. 1967 [1986]. *Organization and Environment*. Boston, MA: Harvard Business School Press.

Lawrence, P. R. and Lorsch, J. W. 1969. *Developing Organizations: Diagnosis and Action*. Reading, MA: Addison-Wesley Publishing Company.

Lawrence, W. G. 1986. A psycho-analytical perspective for understanding organizational life. In G. Chattopadhyay, Z. H. Gangjee, M. L. Hunt, and W. G. Lawrence, eds., *When the Twain Meet: Western Theory and Eastern Insights in Exploring Indian Organizations*, pp. 49–65. Allahabad: A.H. Wheeler & Co.

Leavitt, H. J. 1965. Applied organizational change in industry: structural, technological and humanistic approaches. In J. March, ed., *Handbook of Organizations*, pp. 1144–70. Chicago: Rand McNally.

Lepore, J. 2014. The disruption machine. *The New Yorker*, 23 June.

Levinthal, D. A. and March, J. 1993. The myopia of learning. *Strategic Management Journal* 14(S2): 95–112.

Levitt, B. and March, J. 1988. Organizational learning. *Annual Review of Sociology* 14: 319–40.

Lichtenstein, B. M. 1997. Grace, magic and miracles: a 'chaotic logic' of organizational transformation. *Journal of Organizational Change Management* 10(5): 393–411.

Lilla, M. 1981. Ethos, 'ethics', and the public service. *Public Interest* 63 (winter): 3–17.

Linkner, J. 2014. *Road to Reinvention: How to Drive Disruption and Accelerate Transformation*. San Francisco, CA: Wiley.

Linstead, S. and Höpfl, H. 2000. *The Aesthetics of Organization*. London: SAGE.

Lopdrup-Hjorth, T. 2013. *"Let's Go Outside": The Value of Co-Creation*. Doctoral School of Organization and Management Studies, Ph.D Series: CBS.

Lopdrup-Hjorth, T. 2015. Object and objective lost? Organization-phobia in organization theory. *Journal of Cultural Economy* 8(4): 439–61.

Lounsbury, M. and Beckman, C. 2014. Celebrating organization theory. *Journal of Management Studies* 52(2): 288–308.

MacDonald, I., Burke, C., and Stewart, K. 2006. *Systems Leadership*. Aldershot: Gower.

Maguire, S., Hardy, C., and Lawrence, T. B. 2004. Institutional entrepreneurship in emerging fields: HIV/AIDS treatment advocacy in Canada. *Academy of Management Journal* 47(5): 657–79.

Mant, A. n.d. Draft introduction to 'The German Book', The Papers of Lord Brown, Churchill Archive Centre, University of Cambridge, BRWN 4/1/1/3.

Mant, A. 2007. Wilfred Brown and Elliott Jaques: an appreciation of a remarkable partnership. In K. Shepard, J. L. Gray, J. G. Hunt, and S. McArthur, eds., *Organization Design, Levels of Work and Human Capability: Executive Guide*, pp. 417–27. Ontario, CA: Global Organization Design Society.

Maravelias, C. 2003. Post-bureaucracy: control through professional freedom. *Journal of Organizational Change Management* 16(5): 547–66.

March, J. G. 1991. Exploration and exploitation in organizational learning. *Organization Science* 2(1): 71–87.

March, J. G. 1965. Introduction. In J. G. March, ed., *Handbook of Organizations*, pp. ix–xvi. Chicago: Rand McNally & Company.

March, J. G. and Simon, H. 1958. *Organizations*. New York: John Wiley & Sons.

March, J. G. and Simon, H. 1993. *Organizations*, 2nd edn. Cambridge, MA: Blackwell.

Martin, A., Lopez, S., Roscigno, V., and Hodson, R. 2013. Against the rules: synthesizing types and processes of bureaucratic rulebreaking. *Academy of Management Review* 38(4): 550–74.

Mauss, M. 1979. *Sociology and Psychology*, tr. B. Brewster. London: Routledge & Kegan Paul.

Menzies, I. E. P. [1979] 1988. Containing anxiety in institutions. In I. E. P. Menzies, *Containing Anxiety in Institutions*, pp. 222–35. London: Free Association Books.

Merton, R. K. 1940. Bureaucratic structure and personality. *Social Forces* 18(4): 560–8.

Metcalf, H. C. and Urwick, L. eds. [1940] 2013. *Dynamic Administration: The Collected Papers of Mary Parker Follett*. Mansfield Centre, CT: Martino Publishing.

Miller, E. J. 1976. *Task and Organization*. Chichester: John Wiley & Sons.

Miller, E. J. and Rice, A. K. 1967. *Systems of Organization*. London: Tavistock Publications.

Miller, D., Greenwood, R., and Prakash, R. 2009. What happened to organization theory? *Journal of Management Inquiry* 18(4): 273–9.

Mintzberg, H. 1979. *The Structuring of Organizations: A Synthesis of the Research*. Englewood Cliffs, NJ: Prentice Hall.

Moe, R. 1994. The 're-inventing government' exercise: misinterpreting the problem, misjudging the consequences. *Public Administration Review* 54(2): 111–22.

Mooney, J. D. [1937] 1977. The principles of organization. In L. Gulick and L. Urwick, eds., *Papers on the Science of Administration*, pp. 89–98. Fairfield, NJ: Augustus M. Kelley Publishers.

Moorhouse, F. 1993. *Grand Days*. Chippendale, NSW: Pan Macmillan.

Moos, L. and MacBeath, J. 2000. *Skoleledelse (Pædagogiske linjer)*. Århus: Klim.

Morgan, G. 1980. Paradigms, metaphors, and puzzle solving in organization theory. *Administrative Science Quarterly* 25(4): 605–22.

Morgan, G. 1997. *Images of Organization*. London: Sage.

Morgan, G. 2005. *Images of Organization*. Newbury Park, CA: SAGE.

Morgan, G. and Spicer, A. 2009. Critical approaches to change. In M. Alvesson, T. Bridgman, and H. Willmott, eds., *The Oxford Handbook of Critical Management Studies*, pp. 251–66. Oxford: University of Oxford Press.

Murphy, J. 1994. Transformational change and the evolving role of the principal. In J. Murphy and K. L. Seashore, *Reshaping the Principalship: Insights from Transformational Reform Efforts*, pp. 20–53. Newbury Park, CA: Corwin Press.

Naim, M. 2014. *The End of Power: From Boardrooms to Battlefields and Churches to States, Why Being in Charge Isn't What It Used to Be*. New York: Basic Books.

Newman, A. D. & Rowbottom, R. 1968. Organization Analysis. London: Heinemann Educational Books.

Nohria, N. 1995. *Note on Organization Structure*. Boston, MA: Harvard Business School.

Nohria, N. and Eccles, R. 1992. *Networks and Organizations: Structure, Form, and Action*. Boston, MA: Harvard Business School Press.

Nonaka, I. 1991. The knowledge-creating company. *Harvard Business Review*, November–December: 96–104.

NPR (National Performance Review). 1993. *From Red Tape to Results: Creating a Government that Works Better and Costs Less*. Washington, DC: US Government Printing Office.

Oakeshott, M. 1962. *Rationalism in Politics*. London: Methuen.

Oakeshott, M. 1975. *Hobbes and Civil Association*. Indianapolis, IN: Liberty Fund.

Obholzer, A. and Zagier Roberts, V. eds. 1994. *The Unconscious at Work: Individual and Organizational Stress in the Human Services*. London: Routledge.

O'Connor, E. S. 2012. *Creating New Knowledge in Management: Appropriating the Field's Lost Foundations*. Stanford, CA: Stanford University Press.

O'Connor, E. S. 2013. Initiating for life: Chester I. Barnard and the inculcation of habits of thought. Unpublished paper.

Orlikowski, W. J. and Hofman, J. D. 1997. An improvisational model of change management: the case of groupware technologies. *Sloan Management Review* winter: 11–21.

Osborne, D. and Gaebler, T. 1992. *Re-inventing Government*. Reading, MA: Addison-Wesley.

O'Toole, B. J. & Jordan, G. (eds.). 1995. *Next Steps: Improving Management in Government?* Aldershot: Dartmouth Publishing Company.

Ouchi, W. 2003. *Making Schools Work: A Revolutionary Plan to Get Your Children the Education They Need*. New York: Simon & Schuster.

Ouchi, W. 2006. Power to the principals: decentralization in three large school districts. *Organization Science* 17(2): 298–307.

Ouchi, William G. 2009. *The Secret of TSL: The Revolutionary Discovery That Raises School Performance*. New York: Simon and Schuster.

Ouchi, W., Riordan, R., Lingle, L., and Porter, L. 2005. Making public schools work: management reform as the key. *Academy of Management Journal* 48(6): 929–40.

Parker, M. 2002. *Against Management: Organization in the Age of Managerialism*. Oxford: Blackwell.

Parker Follett, M. 1940. *Dynamic Administration: The Collected Papers of Mary Parker Follett*, ed. H. C. Metcalf and L. Urwick. New York and London: Harper & Brothers.

Parker Follett, M. 1982. *Dynamic Administration*, ed. E. M. Fox and L. Urwick. New York: Hippocrene Books.

Parker Follett, M. and Graham, P. 1995. *Mary Parker Follett—Prophet of Management: A Celebration of Writings from the 1920s*. Boston, MA: Harvard Business School Press.

Parliamentary Report on Banking Standards—Fourth Report. 2013. '*An Accident Waiting to Happen': The Failure of HBOS*, HL Paper 144, HC 705, by authority of the House of Commons. London: The Stationery Office Limited.

Pedersen, O. K. 2008. Folkeskolens formål og nyeste udfordringer. Folkeskolens fremtid. Fremtidens folkeskole. *Jubilæumsudgave af Fagbladet Folkeskolen*: 22–45.

Perrow, C. 1970. *Organizational Analysis: A Sociological View*. London: Tavistock Publications.

Perrow, C. 1972. *Complex Organizations: A Critical Essay*. New York: McGraw-Hill.

Perrow, C. 1979. *Complex Organizations: A Critical Essay*, 2nd edition. Glenview, IL: Scott, Foresman and Company.

Perrow, C. 1986. *Complex Organizations: A Critical Essay*, 3rd edn. New York: McGraw-Hill.

Perrow, C. 1991. A society of organizations. *Theory and Society* 20: 725–62.

Peters, T. 1987. *Thriving on Chaos: Handbook for a Management Revolution*. Basingstoke: Macmillan.

Peters, T. 1992. *Liberation Management*. Basingstoke: Macmillan.

Pfeffer, J. 1981. *Power in Organizations*. Grand Rapids, MI: Pitman.

Pfeffer, J. 1997. *New Directions for Organization Theory*. Oxford: Oxford University Press.

Phelps, E. 2009. Uncertainty bedevils the best system. *Financial Times*, 14 April.

Pil, F. K. and Leana, C. 2009. Applying organizational research to public school reform: the effect of teacher human and social capital on student performance. *Academy of Management Journal* 52(6): 1101–24.

Pocock, J. G. A. 2004. Quentin Skinner: the history of politics and the politics of history. *Common Knowledge* 10(3): 532–50.

Popper, K. [1944] 1985. Piecemeal social engineering. In D. Miller, ed., *Popper Selections*. Princeton, NJ: Princeton University Press.

Porter, M. E. 1985. *Competitive Advantage*. New York: Free Press.

Powell, W. W. 1990. Neither market nor hierarchy: network forms of organization. *Research in Organizational Behavior* 12: 295–336.

Powell, W. 2007. The new institutionalism. In *The International Encyclopedia of Organization Studies*. Thousand Oaks, CA: SAGE.

Powell, W. W. and DiMaggio, P. J. 1991. *The New Institutionalism in Organizational Analysis*. Chicago: University of Chicago Press.

Pozen, R. C. 2010. The big idea: the case for professional boards. *Harvard Business Review*, December: n.p.

Prichard, C. and Mir, R. 2010. Editorial: organizing value. *Organization* 17(5): 507–15.

Quinlan, M. 2004. Lessons for governmental process. In W. G. Runciman, ed., *Hutton and Butler: Lifting the Lid on the Workings of Power*, pp. 115–30. Oxford: British Academy and Oxford University Press.

Quirke, L. 2013. Rogue resistance: sidestepping isomorphic pressures in a patchy institutional field. *Organization Studies* 34(11): 1675–99.

Raisch, S., Birkinshaw, J., Probst, G., and Tushman, M. 2009. Organizational ambidexterity: balancing exploitation and exploration for sustained performance. *Organization Science* 20(4): 685–95.

Reynolds, M. 1999. Grasping the nettle: possibilities and pitfalls of a critical management pedagogy. *British Journal of Management* 9: 171–84.

Rice, A. K. 1958. *Productivity and Social Organization: The Ahmedabad Experiment*. London: Tavistock Publications.

Rice, A. K. 1963. *The Enterprise and Its Environment*. London: Tavistock Publications.

Rice, A. K. 1965. *Learning for Leadership*. London: Tavistock Publications.

Ritzer, G. 2004. *The McDonaldization of Society*. Thousand Oaks, CA: Pine Forge Press.

Robbins, S. P., Bergman, R., Stagg, I., and Coulter, M. 2006. *Management*. Sydney: Pearson Education Australia.

Robé, J. P. 2011. The legal structure of the firm. *Accounting, Economics and Law* 1(1): 1–86.

Roethlisberger, F. J. and Dickson, W. J. [1939] 2000. *Management and the Worker*. Bristol: Thoemmes Press.

Rohr, J. A. 1998. *Public Service, Ethics, and Constitutional Practice*. Lawrence, KA: University Press of Kansas.

Rorty, A. O. 1988. *Mind in Action*. Boston, MA: Beacon Press.

Rynes, S. L. and Shapiro, D. L. 2005. Public policy and the public interest: what if it mattered more? *Academy of Management Journal* 48(6): 925–7.

Salancik, G. R. 1995. WANTED: a good network theory of organization. *Administrative Science Quarterly* 40: 345–9.

Sayles, L. 1960. Report on Brown: exploration in management, May, The Papers of Lord Brown, Churchill Archive Centre, University of Cambridge, BRWN 4/3/1.

Scaff, L. 2014. *Weber and the Weberians*. Basingstoke: Palgrave Macmillan.

Schaefer, D. and Schaefer, R. 1992. Editors' introduction: Sir Henry Taylor and the study of public administration. In D. Schaefer and R. Schaefer, eds., *The Statesman by Sir Henry Taylor*, pp. 3–57. Westport, CT: Praeger.

Schein, E. [1985] 2004. *Organizational Culture and Leadership*. San Francisco, CA: Jossey-Bass.

Schmitt, C. 1986. *Political Romanticism*, tr. G. Schwab. New Brunswick, NJ: Rutgers University Press.

Scott, R. W. 1981. *Organizations: Rational, Natural and Open Systems*. Englewood Cliffs, NJ: Prentice Hall.

Scott, R. W. 1992. *Organizations: Rational, Natural, and Open Systems*, 3rd edn. Englewood Cliffs, NJ: Prentice Hall.

Scott, W. 2014. *Institutions and Organizations*. London: Sage 4th Edition.

Scott, W. and Davis, G. F. 2007. *Organizations and Organizing: Rational, Natural, and Open System Perspectives*. New York: Pearson Education.

Segal, L. G. and Lehrer, M. 2012. The institutionalization of stewardship: theory, propositions, and insights from change in the Edmonton public schools. *Organization Studies* 33(2): 169–201.

Selznick, P. 1948. Foundations of the theory of organization. *American Sociological Review* 13: 25–35.

Selznick, P. 1949. *TVA and the Grass Roots: A Study of Politics and Organization*. Los Angeles, CA: University of California Press.

Senge, P. M. 1990. *The Fifth Discipline*. New York: Currency Doubleday.

Shafritz, J. M. and Ott, J. S. 2001. *Classics of Organization Theory*. Orlando, FL: Harcourt College Publishers.

Shirky, C. 2008. *Here Comes Everybody: The Power of Organizing without Organizations*. New York: Penguin Press.

Silverman, D. 1970. *The Theory of Organizations*. London: Heinemann.

Simon, H. 1946. The proverbs of administration. *Public Administration Review* 6(1): 53–67.

Simon, H. A. 1947. *Administrative Behaviour: A Study of Decision-Making Processes in Administrative Organization*. New York: Macmillan.

Simpson, A. W. B. 1990. Legal Iconoclasts and Legal Ideals. 58 *University of Cincinnati Law Review* 819.

Singer, D. L., Astrachan, B. N., Gould, L. J., and Klein, E. B. [1979] 1999. Boundary management in psychological work with groups. In W. G. Lawrence, ed., *Exploring Individual and Organizational Boundaries*, pp. 21–52. London: Karnac Books.

Skinner, Q. 2002. *Visions of Politics*, vol. 3: *Hobbes and Civil Science*. Cambridge: Cambridge University Press.

Slim, Field Marshall Viscount W. [1956] 2009. *Defeat into Victory*. London: Pan.

Smircich, L. and Stubbart, C. 1985. Strategic management in an enacted world. *Academy of Management Review* 10(4): 724–36.

Smith, W. and Tushman, M. 2005. Managing strategic contradictions: a top management model for managing innovation streams. *Organization Science* 16(5): 522–36.

Stacey, R. D. 1993. *Strategic Management and Organizational Dynamics*. Englewood Cliffs, NJ: Prentice Hall.

Starbuck, W. H. 1982. Congealing oil: inventing ideologies to justify acting ideologies out. *Journal of Management Studies* 19(1): 3–27.

Starbuck, W. H. 2003. The origins of organization theory. In H. Tsoukas and C. Knudsen, eds., *The Oxford Handbook of Organization Theory: Meta-theoretical Perspectives*, pp. 143–82. Oxford: Oxford University Press.

Stark, D. 2010. *A Sense of Dissonance: Accounts of Worth in Economic Life*. New York: Princeton University Press.

Stinchcombe, A. 2001. *When Formality Works: Authority and Abstraction in Law and Organizations*. Chicago and London: University of Chicago Press.

Storing, H. 1998. American statesmanship: old and new. In J. M. Bessette, ed., *Toward a More Perfect Union: Writings of Herbert J. Storing*, pp. 403–28. Washington, DC: The AEI Press.

Stout, L. 2012. *The Shareholder Value Myth: How Putting Shareholders First Harms Investors, Corporations, And The Public*. San-Francisco: Berrett-Kochler Publishers.

Strachan, H. 2013a. British generals in Blair's wars: conclusion. In J. Bailey, R. Iron, and H. Strachan, eds., *British Generals in Blair's Wars*, pp. 327–46. Farnham: Ashgate.

Strachan, H. 2013b. *The Direction of War: Contemporary Strategy in Historical Perspective*. New York: Cambridge University Press.

Suddaby, R., Hardy, C., and Huy, Q. N. 2011. Introduction to special topic forum: where are the new theories of organization? *Academy of Management Review* 36: 236–46.

Suleiman, E. 2001. *Dismantling Democratic States*. New York: Princeton.

Tadajewski, M., Maclaren, P., Parsons, E., and Parker, M. eds. 2011. *Key Concepts in Critical Management Studies*. London: SAGE.

Tapscott, D. 1997. *The Digital Economy: Promise and Peril in the Age of Networked Intelligence*. New York: McGraw-Hill.

Taylor, F. W. 1911 [1998]. *The Principles of Scientific Management*. New York: Dover Publications.

Taylor, Sir H. [1836] 1992. *The Statesman*, ed. D. L. Schaefer and R. R. Schaefer. Westport, CT: Praeger.

Teece, D. J. 2009. *Dynamic Capabilities and Strategic Management*. Oxford: Oxford University Press.

Teece, D. J., Pisano, G., and Shuen, A. 1997. Dynamic capabilities and strategic management. *Strategic Management Journal* 18(7): 509–33.

The Economist. 2009. The pedagogy of the privileged, 26 September: 82.

Thomas, D. and Seely Brown, J. 2011. *A New Culture of Learning: Cultivating the Imagination for a World of Constant Change*. Palo Alto, CA: CreateSpace.

Thompson, G. 2014. *Globalization Revisited*. London: Routledge.

Thompson, G. 2012. *The Constitualization of the Global Corporate Sphere?* Oxford: Oxford University Press.

Thompson, J. D. 1967. *Organizations in Action*. New York: McGraw-Hill.

Thompson, P. and Alvesson, M. 2005. Bureaucracy at work: misunderstandings and mixed blessings. In P. Du Gay, ed., *The Values of Bureaucracy*, pp. 89–114. Oxford: Oxford University Press.

Thornton, P., Ocasio, W., and Lounsbury, M. 2012. *The Institutional Logics Perspective: A New Approach to Culture, Structure, and Process*. Oxford: Oxford University Press.

Tolbert, P. S., David, R. J., and Sine, W. D. 2011. Studying choice and change: the intersection of institutional theory and entrepreneurship research. *Organization Science* 22(5): 1332–44.

Trist, E. 1965. Foreword. In W. Brown ed., *Exploration in Management*, pp. 15–23. Harmondsworth: Penguin.

Trist, E. L. and Bamforth, K. W. 1951. Some social and psychological consequences of the longwall method of coal-getting. *Human Relations* 4: 3–38.

Trist, E. L., Higgin, G. W., Murray, H., and Pollock, A. B. 1963. *Organizational Choice: Capabilities of Groups at the Coal Face Under Changing Technologies*. London: Tavistock.

Tsoukas, H. 2003. New times, fresh challenges. In H. Tsoukas and C. Knudsen, eds., *The Oxford Handbook of Organization Theory: Meta-theoretical Perspectives*, pp. 607–19. Oxford: Oxford University Press.

Tsoukas, H. and Chia, R. 2002. On organizational becoming: rethinking organizational change. *Organization Science* 13(5): 567–82.

Turner, C. 1992. *Modernity and Politics in the Work of Max Weber*. London: Routledge.

Tushman, M. and O'Reilly, C. 1996. Ambidextrous organizations: managing evolutionary and revolutionary change. *California Management Review* 38: 8–30.

Uhr, J. 1993. Administrative responsibility and responsible administrators: an introduction. In R. S. Parker, *The Administrative Vocation: Selected Essays*, pp. xiii–xxiii. Sydney: Hale & Ironmonger.

Umstot, D. D., Mitchell, T. R., and Bell, C. H. 1978. Goal setting and job enrichment: an integrated approach to job design. *Academy of Management Review*, October: 867–79.

Urwick, L. [1937] 1977. Organization as a technical problem. In L. Gulick and L. Urwick, eds., *Papers on the Science of Administration*, pp. 49–88. Fairfield: Augustus M. Kelley Publishers.

Urwick, L. 1943. *The Elements of Administration*. London: Sir Isaac Pitman & Sons, Ltd.

Van Fraassen, B. 2002. *The Empirical Stance*. London: Yale University Press.

Vasgar, J. 2011. Top of the tops: has England really tumbled down school league tables? *The Guardian*, 7 December.

Vera, D. and Crossan, M. 2004. Strategic leadership and organizational learning. *Academy of Management Review* 29(2): 222–40.

Vikkelsø, S. 2015. Core task and organizational reality. *Journal of Cultural Economy* 8(4): 418–38.

Weber, M. 1917 [1988]. *Gesammelte Aufsätze zur Wissenschafstlehre*. Edited by Johannes Winckelmann. Tübingen: J. C. B. Mohr.

Weber, M. 1978. *Economy and Society: Vols I and II*. Berkeley, CA: University of California Press.

Weber, M. 1989. Science as a vocation. In P. Lassman and I. Velody, eds., *Max Weber's Science as a Vocation*, pp. 3–32. London: Unwin Hyman.

Weber, M. 1994. *Weber: Political Writings*, ed. P. Lassman and R. Speirs. Cambridge: Cambridge University Press.

Weick, K. E. 1979. *The Social Psychology of Organizing*, 2nd edn. Reading, MA: Addison-Wesley.

Weick, K. E. 1991. The non-traditional quality of organizational learning. *Organization Science* 2(1): 116–24.

Weick, K. E. 1995. *Sensemaking in Organisations*. London: SAGE.

Weick, K. E. 1996. Drop your tools: an allegory for organizational studies. *Administrative Science Quarterly* 41(2): 301–13.

Weick, K. E. 2000. Emergent change as a universal in organizations. In M. Beer and N. Nohria, eds., *Breaking the Code of Change*, pp. 223–41. Harvard, MA: Harvard Business School Press.

Weick, K. E. 2005. The pragmatics of 'really mattering' in policy issues: William Ouchi as an exemplar. *Academy of Management Journal* 48(6): 986–8.

Weick, K. E. and Sutcliffe, K. 2007. *Managing the Unexpected: Resilient Performance in an Age of Uncertainty*. San Francisco, CA: Jossey-Bass.

Weick, K. E. and Westley, F. 1996. Organizational learning: affirming an oxymoron. In S. Clegg, C. Hardy, and W. Nord, eds., *Handbook of Organization Studies*, pp. 440–58. London: SAGE.

Weinrib, E. 1988. Legal formalism: on the immanent rationality of law. *Yale Law Journal* 97(6): 949–1016.

Williams, B. 2002. *Truth and Truthfulness: An Essay in Genealogy*. New York: Princeton University Press.

Willshire, L. 1999. Psychiatric services: organizing impossibility. *Human Relations* 52(6): 775–804.

Wilson, J. Q. 1994. *Bureaucracy: What Government Agencies Do and Why They Do It*. New York: Basic Books.

Wilson, R. 2004. Issues of evidence: discussion. In W. G. Runciman, ed., *Hutton and Butler: Lifting the Lid on the Workings of Power*. Oxford: British Academy and Oxford University Press.

Wittgenstein, L. 1998. *Culture and Value*. Oxford: Blackwell.

Wittgenstein, L. 2005. Extract from 'On Certainty'. In N. Stehr and R. Grundmann, eds., *Knowledge – Critical Concepts*, pp. 283–305. London: Routledge.

Witzel, M. 2012. *A History of Management Thought.* Abingdon: Routledge.

Wolf, W. 1974. *The Basic Barnard.* Ithaca, NY: Cornell University.

Wren, D. A. 1994. *The Evolution of Management Thought,* 4th edn. New York: John Wiley & Sons.

Wren, D. A. 2005. *The History of Management Thought,* 5th edn. Hoboken, NJ: John Wiley & Sons.

Zajac, E. J., Kraatz, M. S., and Bresser, R. 2000. Modeling the dynamics of strategic fit: a normative approach to strategic change. *Strategic Management Journal* 21(4): 429–54.

Zilber, T. 2013. The work of meanings in institutional processes and thinking. In R. Greenwood, C. Oliver, R. Suddaby, and K. Sahlin-Andersson, eds., *The SAGE Handbook of Organizational Institutionalism*, pp. 150–69. London: Sage.

Index